Good Intentions
Gone Awry

D1073464

Good Intentions Gone Awry

No-Fault Divorce and the American Family

Allen M. Parkman

ROWMAN & LITTLEFIELD PUBLISHERS, INC.
Lanham • Boulder • New York • Oxford

ROWMAN & LITTLEFIELD PUBLISHERS, INC.

Published in the United States of America
by Rowman & Littlefield Publishers, Inc.
4720 Boston Way, Lanham, Maryland 20706
http://www.rowmanlittlefield.com

12 Hid's Copse Road
Cumnor Hill, Oxford OX2 9JJ, England

British Library Cataloguing in Publication Information Available

Library of Congress Cataloging-in-Publication Data

Parkman, Allen M.
    Good intentions gone awry : no-fault divorce and the American family / Allen M. Parkman.
        p.   cm.
    Includes bibliographical references and index.
    ISBN 0-8476-9868-8 (cl. : alk. paper) — ISBN 0-8476-9869-6 (pbk. : alk. paper)
    1. No-fault divorce—United States. 2. No-fault divorce—Economic aspects—United
States. 3. Divorce—United States. 4. Family—United States. I. Title.
HQ834.P37   2000
306.89'0973 21—dc 21   99-045669

Printed in the United States of America

∞™ The paper used in this publication meets the minimum requirements of American
National Standard for Information Sciences—Permanence of Paper for Printed Library
Materials, ANSI/NISO Z39.48—1992.

To Amy, Ian, and Andrew.

Contents

Preface

Much has happened in the decade since I wrote *No-Fault Divorce: What Went Wrong?* in 1992. That book was unique because it provided an economic perspective on why no-fault divorce was introduced and why it had been a misfortune—primarily, it appeared—for many divorced women and their children. Between 1969 and 1985, all the states enacted some form of no-fault divorce modifying the traditional fault grounds of adultery, desertion, and cruelty with no-fault grounds, such as incompatibility or irretrievable breakdown. More important than the change in the grounds was the impact that occurred as divorces shifted from being difficult to obtain to being commonly available to either spouse unilaterally. Whereas sociologists, the academics with the longest interest in the family, employ a variety of approaches to analyze the family, economists focus on individuals' decisions that reflect their attempts to improve their welfare subject to the constraints that they face—they respond to their perceived self-interest. However, Adam Smith noted that this focus on individuals' self-interest can have beneficial effects on society—including the individuals' families. Meanwhile, an important influence on those decisions is the legal environment, such as the grounds for divorce.

I have continued to be interested in the effects of no-fault divorce and its reform, and, on further reflection, I now recognize that the adverse effects of no-fault divorce are much broader and more significant than I had initially concluded. Although many people are concerned about the deterioration in family values, I believe that the weaker commitment of many adults to their families can be traced to the incentives created by unilateral, no-fault divorce. Moreover, the reform of the divorce grounds is going to be much more difficult than I had anticipated. The grounds for divorce are determined by either spouse's domicile, even if for only a limited period. Therefore, a spouse who was married and lived in a state in which divorce was difficult can easily be divorced in another state with no-fault grounds, for example.

As I started to revise the earlier book, I concluded that its title no longer reflected its focus. More than just a worsening of the welfare of divorced women and their children, no-fault divorce has been a misfortune for many people and especially for those who aspire to and would benefit from a happy and successful family life based on a creditable, long-term commitment. A reform of the divorce laws requires a thorough review of the relationship between individuals and their governments. In an attempt to improve social welfare, the states have restricted the ability of couples to structure their marriage, especially when it comes to the grounds for divorce. I argue that social welfare would be improved by giving couples greater control over their marriages while making sure that children's interests are protected. The result of these efforts is this book.

This book has benefited from the guidance of Jill Rothenberg and Christine Gatliffe at Rowman & Littlefield during the development phase; the reviewers whom they contacted, including Margaret Brinig; and Judy Cardanha and Pageworks during the production phase. I have also benefited from discussions with Steve Nock, Robert Rowthorn, and Sheryl Wolf. All have been helpful in assisting me in bringing a broader perspective to this book.

Preface to No-Fault Divorce: What Went Wrong?

In this book I address the repercussions of no-fault divorce, first identifying the problems that have been created by no-fault and then offering a program for divorce-law reform. I first became aware of these problems a decade ago when I was asked to appraise the professional goodwill of an orthopedic surgeon for his divorce settlement. The courts in a number of states, including New Mexico, had held that the goodwill of a professional individual was marital property subject to division at divorce. Although I was familiar with business goodwill, an intangible asset of a smoothly functioning business, professional goodwill was something new to me.

The appraisal of professional goodwill presented many difficult questions. What was professional goodwill worth? The usual procedure for estimating the value of goodwill is to compare the income of an ongoing business to that of a similar, but new, business that has not yet had time to acquire goodwill. Applying this concept to professionals is difficult. Because of differences in characteristics such as intelligence, ambition, and willingness to accept risk, it is virtually impossible to identify the proportion of professional income attributable to goodwill.

When was professional goodwill acquired? Because property must be allocated between the separate property that existed at the time of marriage and the marital property created during the marriage, the timing of the acquisition of property can be important at divorce. Although the date a business was established usually can be determined, it is difficult, if not impossible, to establish when a professional career was initiated—a professional's income is the result of investments made throughout his or her life. Efforts during high school and college often make professional school possible. These investments may have been made by the professional, parents, taxpayers, or a spouse. Therefore, even if the value of professional goodwill can be estimated, its allocation between the separate property of the professional and the marital property of the couple may be unclear. I eventually reached the conclusion that the determination and allocation of professional goodwill at divorce was an extremely arbitrary process. So why had the concept developed? As I thought about that question, the answer became clear: no-fault divorce.

The courts were attempting to mitigate the dire financial situations of many divorced women that resulted from the no-fault divorce laws that became common in the 1970s. These laws replaced the fault grounds for divorce, such as adultery, cruelty, and desertion, with the no-fault grounds of "incompatibility" or "irretrievable breakdown." Under fault divorce, the spouse seeking the divorce had to prove that the other spouse was guilty of a prohibited activity. That was usually not easy, so fabricated testimony was common. If one spouse did not want a divorce, the other spouse had to provide compensation to induce him or her to be the plaintiff and to provide the required testimony that established the fault grounds.

The fault grounds for divorce thus afforded the spouse who wanted to continue the marriage with substantial negotiating power. Alternatively, the no-fault grounds often provided for divorce based on the desire of only one spouse, removing the need to negotiate with an uncooperative spouse and shifting the financial arrangements at divorce to the legal standards. These legal standards, which were especially unfair to wives who had accommodated the career of their husbands, had not been subjected to close scrutiny under fault divorce because of the prevalence of negotiated settlements. The courts reacted to this situation by creating ad hoc concepts such as professional goodwill in an attempt to correct for the limited funds provided older women under the new divorce laws.

The case of the surgeon's wife is a common one. She was a middle-aged woman who had committed herself to being a homemaker and a mother. The couple had lived well on the surgeon's comfortable income, but they had accumulated only a limited amount of marital property. Their children had grown and left the home. At divorce, the wife faced a very gloomy future. Her share of the limited community property did not amount to much. There would be no child support. In the spirit of fairness and equality, the courts had moved toward short-term, rehabilitative spousal support instead of long-term alimony. The wife had limited employment prospects, but her husband was leaving the marriage with his income intact. The provision of professional goodwill created an additional source of funds for her.

The more I investigated how society was reacting to the no-fault grounds for divorce, the more I became convinced that no-fault divorce was creating many problems. It sanctioned socially undesirable divorces. It encouraged family members to make decisions that were not in the best interests of the other family members. It impoverished many divorced women and the children of divorced parents. Furthermore, I became convinced that an important reason the literature on no-fault didn't deal adequately with these problems was largely a failure to consider the insights available from an economic perspective. Economics studies the choices that people make in an environment in which wants exceed resources, so they must weigh the benefits and costs of the alternatives.

Although love and sexual attraction are appropriately associated with marriage and divorce, the benefit/cost framework of economics can provide valuable additional insights into how people decide to marry or to end a marriage. The decision to marry is one of the most important decisions that people make. The decision by an individual to marry another precludes—at least temporarily—the person's remaining single or marrying anyone else. From an economic perspective, that individual is presumed to consider the benefits of the marriage to exceed those of any alternate arrangement. The foregone benefits of the alternative arrangements are among the costs of the marriage. So long as the benefits of marriage exceed the costs for both spouses, the couple stays married. When the costs exceed the benefits for one spouse, that spouse may seek a divorce. The divorce laws influence the costs of dissolving a marriage. For example, no-fault reduced the costs of divorce for many spouses who wanted to dissolve their marriage.

It appeared that my background in both economics and law provided me with a perspective on the problems and the reform of no-fault divorce that was unique among the people analyzing that subject. The primary problem with no-fault divorce is its potential for encouraging divorce when the financial and the psychological benefits to all the persons involved do not exceed the costs. Because a divorce can be acquired in most states based on the desire of just one spouse, the gain experienced by the divorcing spouse can be less than the loss experienced by the other members of the family. These divorces reduce social welfare. Furthermore, no-fault laws encourage the members of families to make other social-welfare-reducing decisions, such as working outside the home and pursuing additional education during marriage, not to benefit the family but to protect themselves from the adverse effects of divorce.

A major reform of the no-fault divorce laws would recognize individuals' earning capacities, which economists call human capital, as property. During marriage, some spouses, such as professionals, may acquire human capital, whereas other spouses, such as homemakers, may lose human capital. Recognizing the effect of marriage on the spouses' human capital would more accurately align the legal costs of divorce with the true costs. Even with this reform, no-fault divorce would not force the spouses, especially the divorcing spouse, to recognize all the costs of divorce.

The incapacity of no-fault divorce to force the divorcing spouse to recognize all the costs of divorce is a fundamental flaw that leads me to conclude that social welfare would be improved if the grounds for divorce were changed to require the consent of both spouses for a divorce. Requiring mutual consent as the normal requirement for divorce might appear to be a radical step; but it is, in effect, a return to the conditions under fault divorce—without the hypocritical grounds that prevailed. In fact, negotiated divorces were common under fault divorce, and mutual consent would again require the spouses to consider the benefits and the costs of divorce to all the parties. Given the importance of the family to all its members and to society at large, it is essential that the divorce laws create incentives for people to make social-welfare-enhancing decisions.

1

Introduction

Thirty years ago, California adopted the first unequivocal no-fault divorce statute in the United States.[1] Over the following fifteen years, all the other states and the District of Columbia enacted similar statutes by establishing "irretrievable breakdown" or "incompatibility" as the only grounds for divorce or by adding them to the preexisting fault grounds.[2] The new laws were viewed as a major, and desirable, reform of the statutes in effect throughout most of the history of the United States, under which a divorce, when permitted at all, usually could only be obtained on fault grounds, such as adultery, cruelty, or desertion,[3] with the assumption that one of the spouses was responsible for the failure of the marriage. Many no-fault divorce statutes also removed the consideration of marital fault from the grounds for divorce, the award of spousal support, and the division of property.

THE EFFECTS OF NO-FAULT

The no-fault divorce laws have had significant, but often subtle and unexpected, effects on individuals and families by dismantling a divorce system that had been based essentially on the mutual consent of the spouses and replacing it with a system that permits either spouse to dissolve a marriage unilaterally, subject often to limited compensation to the divorced spouse and any children. The earlier system had provided some protection to parties who had relied on their marriage continuing, but no-fault divorce reduced this protection because it eliminated much of the negotiating power of the spouse who did not want to dissolve the marriage.[4] The loss of negotiating power has unfortunately reduced the incentive for spouses to make the commitment to their marriage that often was accompanied

1

by sacrifices that benefited their family. These sacrifices can take numerous forms—psychological and financial—and can be made potentially by either spouse. A typical sacrifice occurs when one spouse commits to a career that accommodates the other spouse and the children. Whereas married women frequently made this sacrifice in the past as homemakers and mothers, the expansion in the employment opportunities for married women has increased the inducement for some fathers to limit their careers to assume primary responsibility, for example, for childcare.[5] However, because sacrifices like this are seldom the basis for adequate compensation at divorce, both spouses frequently have become reluctant to make them. As a result, people are focusing more on their own narrowly defined self-interest and less on the best interest of their family.

In this book, I argue that no-fault divorce has made many families worse off than they could be with different grounds for divorce. These alternative grounds for divorce—a combination of no-fault, mutual consent, and fault grounds—are also discussed in this book. Although researchers only slowly became aware of the adverse effects of no-fault divorce, they eventually recognized that the new laws resulted in a decline in the welfare of many divorced women and the children of divorced parents.[6] Lenore Weitzman initially reported, for example, that divorced women and their children experience a 73 percent decline in their standard of living during the first year after a divorce.[7] Elizabeth Peters showed that in 1979 women who were divorced in no-fault divorce states received less alimony and child support than in fault divorce states.[8]

Less obvious, but also substantial, has been the effect of no-fault divorce on divorced men and families in which the parents stay married. Most men marry with the expectation that they are going to have a successful marriage rather than a triumphant divorce. Although being divorced unilaterally is not usually the financial misfortune for men that it is for women, it still can be an emotional tragedy. More subtle is the effect of no-fault on families that do not experience a divorce. The fault grounds for divorce had the effect of providing some protection for a spouse who made a commitment to the family that often incorporated sacrifices for the family's benefit. Because much of this protection disappeared with no-fault divorce, both spouses have been forced to consider other forms of protection against the adverse effects of divorce. Many spouses feel compelled to make decisions based on their self-interest rather than on the best interest of their family. For example, there are reduced incentives for either spouse to work in the home and increased incentives for them to work outside the home and to seek additional education to maintain their human capital—their income-earning capacity, which probably has reduced the welfare of many families.[9] With both parents making a substantial commitment to employment, the family may end up with more financial resources; but frequently the children are receiving less parental attention. Meanwhile, the parents might find that their leisure time has become severely restricted. Often, the adults' placing an emphasis on their personal goals results in a lost of intimacy and communication, which were part of the motivation for them to marry.

These are not the results expected by the proponents of no-fault divorce. Fault divorce was attacked by many reformers because of the hypocritical procedures used by many people to obtain a divorce.[10] The fault divorce system was predicated on the belief that unless the breakdown of a marriage could be attributed solely to the wrongdoing of a single, identifiable spouse, divorce was not permitted. In most states, a divorce was not permitted if both spouses were equally at fault. The procedures used under fault divorce encouraged perjury and brought an adversarial process to situations often calling for conciliation. Normally, only the innocent spouse could ask for a divorce, so most spouses who wanted a divorce—but seldom could provide evidence of fault—found it very difficult to obtain a divorce without the cooperation of the other spouse. This cooperation—usually provided reluctantly—frequently required compensation to the cooperating spouse to encourage fabricated testimony that established the necessary fault grounds for the divorce. In addition, some people who had obtained a divorce argued that the result was not the protection of innocent spouses but the requirement that spouses had to buy their way out of marriage.[11] Although fault provided some protection for spouses who did not want a divorce, it made the poor choice of a mate very costly. If one spouse eventually decided that he or she wanted to dissolve the marriage, substantial compensation might be necessary to induce the cooperation of the other spouse. In some cases, the divorcing spouse could not engender the cooperation of the other spouse and was forced to continue a marriage that he or she would have preferred to dissolve. Last, some reformers felt that a reform of the divorce process could reverse the trend toward higher divorce rates that had been observed during most of this century.[12] For these reformers, the solution was obvious: remove the fault grounds from the requirements for a divorce.

The reasons why that solution did not produce desirable results is a focus of this book. My analysis includes an investigation of why no-fault divorce statutes were introduced and why they have had a detrimental effect on many adults and their families. The framework that I use is based on people responding to incentives, a perspective that is associated with economics.

AN ECONOMIC PERSPECTIVE

Marriage and divorce have long been active areas for analysis and discussion by sociologists and lawyers,[13] but I believe the general absence of an economic perspective has obscured some problems. Economics is the study of choices:[14] the choices that people make, or rationally should make, in an environment in which the array of goods and activities that individuals want exceeds their resources of income and time. It is assumed that people, while making these choices, attempt to improve their welfare subject to the constraints that they face. Other disciplines have started to use the economic perspective to assist them in analyzing the topics that they explore. Public choice theory is being used in political science, and rational choice and exchange theories in sociology.[15]

Economic analysis, based on society's preference for efficient outcomes, provides an alternate explanation to the moralistic one given for the decline in the importance of the family in America by recognizing the role that no-fault divorce has played in changing the incentives that people face. We live in a world in which wants—financial and psychological—exceed the available resources. Choices have to be made. Efficient outcomes occur when choices are made for which the benefits exceed the costs, with these outcomes increasing social welfare. As the benefits and costs of activities change, the efficient choices change. Economists view the decision to marry and, sometimes, to divorce as based on the benefits and the costs associated with those choices. Although economists recognize the importance of love and sexual attraction as a basis for marriage, they have also identified pragmatic considerations based on simultaneous consumption of goods, specialization of labor, and insurance. Many of these benefits of marriage result from a desire for children, which in turn encourages a long-term commitment by the parents to their relationship.

Over time, the costs and the benefits of marriage and divorce can change, and then the incentives to marry and to stay married also change. Economists recognize that changes that have occurred since World War II, such as the expanded employment opportunities for women, the availability of improved forms of contraception, and the increase in labor-saving devices for the home, have reduced both the benefit of marriage and the cost of divorce for some people.[16] Particularly important in this process has been a decline in the number and importance of children for some adults. Under those circumstances, we would expect to observe fewer marriages and more divorces.[17] If the legal system conflicts with some people's new preferences, especially for more flexible grounds for divorce, those people will work to change that legal environment.[18] Thus, social change created pressures to modify the fault grounds for divorce because in a changing society the grounds were no longer efficient for some—often vocal—individuals.

Ignored in this process was the fact that the existing divorce laws may still have been efficient for many less vocal people—many of whom still placed an important emphasis on parenthood. Divorce laws that make it difficult to obtain a divorce encourage people to take a longer-term perspective toward their marriage. If it is easy for a spouse to dissolve a marriage, then a minor controversy can result in the end of a marriage. Knowing that this can occur encourages both spouses to take protective measures. They may be tempted to refrain from making decisions—such as a deep emotional commitment or limiting a career—that would benefit their family but might be costly to them if the marriage ends. Most people marry with the expectation that their marriage is a long-term commitment, and they do not want to face an incentive structure that discourages that commitment. They do not want to face incentives that encourage narrowly focused, self-interested choices that limit their opportunities to receive the rewards that come from a successful marriage, such as satisfying parenthood, improved health, higher income, and more contentment with their partner.[19] The welfare of many families probably has been reduced by the incentives that followed from making divorce easier.

The Political Process

Whatever the acknowledged need for change, actual changes that occur are the result of the political process. Many political analysts assign a public interest motive to legislators. Economists and some political scientists, however, taking a more cynical view, see politicians basing their decisions on self-interest. The primary goal of politicians normally is to be elected and then reelected. With that goal, they are particularly sensitive to the preferences of vocal pressure groups who provide verbal and financial support.[20] In California, for example, the divorce reform process was dominated by men, although they had the support of many women's groups.[21] Sometimes the self-interest of politicians can be more narrowly focused. The assemblyman primarily responsible for the passage of no-fault divorce in California was going through a divorce at the time. It did not take a conspiracy for a legislature dominated by men to enact no-fault divorce legislation that seemed appropriate from their perspective and that was based on the information with which they had been provided. This is especially true when few of the proponents of divorce reform, whether men or women, were arguing that no-fault divorce would be a misfortune, frequently for divorced women and their children, but also for many other adults and their children. The California Family Law Act of 1969,[22] which began the no-fault divorce revolution and set the standard for the statutes enacted in the other states, was passed by a legislature dominated by men.[23]

Much was made of the hypocrisy that occurred under the fault divorce laws, but the hypocrisy was evidence of the change in society's preferences, not the cause of those changes. There are many laws on the books, such as highway speed limits, that are hypocritical, and these laws can remain on the books for indefinite periods, especially if they are not enforced. It takes both new circumstances and undesirable enforcement of existing laws to change laws. Certainly, enforcement of the fault divorce laws was hypocritical, but an increase in the demand for simpler procedures for dissolving marriages by some people was an important impetus for no-fault divorce legislation. The male-dominated reform process, together with the absence of a clear understanding of the repercussions of the legislation, resulted in the enactment of the specific no-fault divorce laws now in existence.

Economics can provide insights into why no-fault divorce frequently resulted in the deterioration of the financial situation of divorced women and the children of divorced parents.[24] Many of the reformers appear to have been so preoccupied with reducing the hypocrisy of the fault divorce system that few of them thought about the consequences of the new system—consequences that included a decline in the bargaining power of spouses who did not want a divorce. Particularly vulnerable were women in long-duration marriages whose financial condition frequently deteriorated after divorce.[25] The California Governor's Commission on the Family that initiated the fault divorce debate in that state did not include any economists or financial analysts. When marriage was a more stable institution and the laws determining the grounds for divorce were strictly enforced, there were only a few divorces, and the laws that controlled the financial repercussions at divorce were of secondary importance. As the demand for divorce by some spouses increased, these individuals found that the legal grounds for divorce were more restrictive than they wished. They also found that the financial repercussions of divorce prescribed by the law were unacceptable. The parties could fabricate evidence to establish the grounds for divorce, and then, in theory, the courts would decide on property settlements based on legal standards.[26] In fact, under the fault divorce laws, most divorcing couples with significant wealth chose to negotiate a settlement rather than to rely on the courts' allocation.[27]

Often one party did not want a divorce, and a more generous financial settlement and custody of any children were necessary to induce that party to initiate the lawsuit and to provide the obligatory testimony.[28] The innocent party had to be the plaintiff, so a contested divorce was difficult under the fault divorce laws.[29] Even if both parties wanted a divorce, they had reasons to reject the legal financial arrangements as inequitable. Most women who had pursued the traditional roles as homemakers and mothers knew that short-term alimony, limited child support, and the property allocation provided by law would leave them in a precarious financial position, especially compared to the financial condition of their husbands. The negotiating power of a spouse who did not want a divorce was substantially reduced by no-fault divorce.

Interrelated Laws

Problems developed with no-fault divorce because the reformers did not recognize the interrelationship among laws concerning the grounds for divorce, parental rights, and the financial condition of the spouses. Changing one set of rules without changing the others destroyed a delicate balance. Under the fault divorce statutes, the custodial and financial settlements were commonly based on the negotiations of the parties, with the spouse who did not want to dissolve the marriage having substantial power over the outcome. With no-fault divorce eliminating negotiations to establish the grounds for divorce, the previously disregarded laws that governed the custodial and financial repercussions of divorce became much more important. These laws usually provided for the divorced spouse to receive half of any marital property and limited child and spousal support, if they were appropriate. Not only were these transfers often modest, but support was often difficult to collect. As a result, the financial condition of divorced women and children of divorced parents frequently deteriorated.

In some states, eliminating the fault grounds for divorce was accompanied by the removal of fault as a factor in the other aspects of divorce, such as property settlements and alimony. No-fault divorce eliminated the presumption that couples had an obligation to remain married and removed any reason for the party seeking the divorce to compensate the other spouse. California, for example, required an equal division of marital property. Another problem arose from the legal definitions of *property* failing to conform to basic financial principles, thereby ignoring the effect of the marriage on the spouses' income-earning capacities. This discrepancy had little practical effect when most divorces were settled with only minimal reference to the applicable laws. But that all changed with the introduction of no-fault divorce.[30]

Because marriage consists of two people coming together to participate in a collective action, economists view the financial aspects of the relationship much as a business partnership: If the marriage is dissolved, the parties should share the gains or losses of the partnership; but assets acquired outside marriage are not part of this distribution. Based on this framework, economic analysis would support a strict application of the principles of community property, in which each spouse has a half interest in property created during the marriage by their collective activities. From a statutory perspective, *marital property* is all property that is not defined as the separate property of either spouse, whereas *separate property* is property that the parties brought into the marriage and property that came to them during the marriage by will, bequest, or devise. Strict community property concepts are the basis of property divisions at the dissolution of marriages in only a minority of the states; but there has been a trend in all states to move toward an equal distribution of marital property at divorce.[31] As we will see, the problem with this distribution of property at divorce is not the definitions of separate and marital property, but rather the underlying definition of *property* itself.

What Is Property?

The statutes that defined how property was to be allocated at divorce, under fault and no-fault, did not define the items that are property.[32] That task has been left to the courts, which tend to recognize as property only items for which there is tangible evidence. These items include houses and cars as well as shares of stock or bonds. What the courts have historically called "property" should be just another name for the items that economists and financial analysts have identified as "assets." From a financial perspective, assets exist and have value because they can provide a stream of future income or services; these items include houses and shares of common stock as well as individuals themselves. From a practical perspective, the actual property settlements under fault divorce had been part of the larger issue of financial settlements with the allocation between property and alimony often driven by tax considerations rather than definitions. With no-fault divorce, it became more likely than under fault divorce that statutes determined the allocation of property. Still, because the definition of property has been too restricted, the items considered in the financial allocations at divorce have also tended to be too restricted.

Human Capital

Financial allocations at divorce tend to ignore the most valuable asset of most people—their income-earning capacities, or human capital. Human capital exists because of prior investments, and its value is based on the expected future earnings of the individual. Depending on when critical investments occurred, human capital can be marital property or separate property. Human capital, which has not been recognized by the legal system in a systematic way as property subject to division at divorce,[33] represents a major difference in the assets identified by the legal system and economists.

Shortly after the introduction of no-fault divorce, state legislatures and the courts recognized that something was amiss with the finances of divorced women and the children of divorced parents. They groped for a way to increase financial awards to women. One way was making ad hoc adjustments to the definition of property, based not on the realization that the definition was conceptually wrong, but instead on a desire to expand the funds available to women and children.[34] The definition of property has been expanded in some jurisdictions to include such obvious assets as pensions and business goodwill.[35] Courts and legislatures also have considered whether intangible items such as degrees, licenses, and the goodwill of professionals should be included in the list of property. Still, the definition of property has not been expanded systematically to cover human capital, and I argue that the failure to incorporate the effects of marriage on the human capital of the spouses into the financial arrangements at divorce in any systematic way is a major cause for some divorced women suffering a substantial reduction in their welfare.[36]

The incorporation of an adjustment for the effect of a divorce on the human capital of the parties would compensate a spouse in the often-cited situation in which one spouse has provided financial support while the other spouse was in graduate school. The recognition of human capital is, however, probably even more important in the situation in which the husband and the wife have decided that the family would benefit from one spouse, frequently the wife, pursuing activities that accommodate the career of the other, usually the husband.[37] This decision often reduces the wife's human capital compared to the position in which she would be if either she had never married or the marriage had accommodated her career rather than that of the husband.

Economic analysis of the spouses' human capital also requires an adjustment in child support awards. The cost of child custody is not just the direct outlays to maintain the children but also the reduction of income from the presence of children limiting the custodial parent's employment and remarrying opportunities. Children can be an encumbrance that reduces income and opportunities for those who rear them, translating into a reduced human capital at divorce. Economics can provide a framework for evaluating these effects, producing a more systematic and equitable outcome to divorce and correcting for the deteriorating financial condition of divorced women and the children of divorced parents.

The Subjective Costs of Divorce

The effect of marriage on the spouses' human capital can be estimated with reasonable accuracy, but other costs of divorce are more difficult to measure. These costs, which can be financial as well as psychological, can include the loss of the companionship of his or her spouse and children, the search for a new mate or social situation, and the impact on the children. The spouse being divorced will often still care about the divorcing spouse and their family, and the loss of this companionship due to the dissolution of the marriage imposes a cost on the divorced spouse. To begin with, the marriage resulted from a search process by the parties. At divorce, the divorcing spouse has decided that he or she is willing to incur the costs, if any, of a new search for another living situation, which often will result in a new mate—and also, unilaterally, imposes search costs on the divorced spouse. If the divorced spouse wants a new mate, this cost can be very high, because many divorced people, especially older women, never remarry.[38] Even if the divorced spouse has no desire to remarry, he or she incurs costs in establishing a new social situation. Last, the divorce can impose costs on the children of the couple. Often these costs are ignored by the divorcing spouse; the failure of no-fault divorce to require the parties to consider these costs directly when considering divorce contributes to the unsatisfactory outcomes of present-day divorce.

THE REFORM OF THE DIVORCE LAWS

Although a number of states have discussed divorce reform,[39] the only two that have changed their divorce grounds to make divorce more difficult have been

Louisiana, which passed its covenant marriage act in 1997,[40] and Arizona, which passed its act in 1998.[41] The Louisiana Act, for example, gives couples planning on marrying in that state a choice between two options: a standard marriage with the potential for a no-fault divorce and a covenant marriage, which requires counseling before marriage and then only permits divorce based on fault grounds or on a lengthy separation. It would seem that couples have not found covenant marriage to be an attractive alternative to no-fault, because only one percent of Louisiana newlyweds have chosen it.[42]

It would be unfair to criticize no-fault divorce without providing an alternative, so in chapter 6 I present a detailed reform proposal. It is unfortunate that the current divorce laws are described as no-fault, when the primary reason that they have had an undesirable impact on society is due to their permitting unilateral divorce. If no-fault divorce is unattractive, people might conclude that we should return to fault divorce. However, if the problem is recognized to be the unilateral basis of divorce, then it is more appropriate to consider mutual consent as the normal ground for divorce. Still, marriage is a more vulnerable institution for many adults than it has been in the past, and it requires a new approach to divorce. Therefore, I propose a program in which the grounds for divorce would change based on the conditions in the marriage.[43]

A combination of no-fault, mutual consent, and fault grounds for divorce would be a substantial improvement over the no-fault divorce laws that are common in the United States. At the beginning of a marriage, most couples are still evaluating each other to determine if they really feel comfortable making a long-term commitment. In many cases, neither spouse has made any major sacrifices based on the expectation that the marriage is going to last. The costs that they might incur due to divorce are less than they will be later. During this period, unilateral, no-fault divorce would appear to be a reasonable basis for divorce.

Eventually, in most marriages, at least one spouse makes personal sacrifices based on his or her marriage being a long-term relationship. These sacrifices are an important source of the gains that couples anticipate from marriage. The most obvious of these sacrifices occurs when spouses become parents, which usually requires at least one of them to alter his or her career to assume child care responsibilities; but a career can also be the basis of a concession because some spouses limit their careers to give their mates the flexibility to pursue more attractive career alternatives. Then, the costs of divorce will probably increase significantly. At this point, the grounds for divorce should change to mutual consent. Mutual consent divorce forces the spouses to consider the full benefits and costs of divorce—psychological as well as financial—with a divorce being more likely only when the collective benefits exceed the costs. A divorce is most likely to occur when the benefit of the change to one spouse exceeds the cost to the other, with a compensation from one to the other creating the incentive for their mutual agreement.

Mutual consent can be unacceptably onerous if one spouse is forced out of a marriage due to the behavior of the other spouse. Therefore, fault grounds for divorce can still be appropriate. Fault as a basis for divorce should not be treated lightly with it only being permitted when there is substantial evidence of socially unacceptable behavior, such as spousal or child abuse. This program for divorce reform would recognize the marital stages, while creating incentives for adults to address the best interests of their family in contrast to the emphasis on their own self-interest, which is encouraged by no-fault divorce.

A problem with covenant marriage laws and my proposal is that divorce is governed not by the state in which a couple marries, but by the state in which either spouse is domiciled—even if for a fairly brief period. This occurs because the U.S. Supreme Court has held that marriage is a status that accompanies spouses, thereby giving their state of domicile—even if only recently acquired—jurisdiction over their marriage.[44] A divorce in one state usually has to be honored in all other states under the "Full Faith and Credit Clause" of the U.S. Constitution.[45] Therefore, as long as there are a substantial number of no-fault divorce states, spouses are forced to recognize the potential for a no-fault divorce even though they were married in a state with different grounds for divorce. On the other hand, if marriage was recognized as a contract entered into at the time of the marriage, the grounds for divorce would be those of that state or, if permitted, the state that the parties chose. Then, the provisions of that agreement probably would continue to be enforceable even if either spouse moved to another state. Therefore, the proposal in chapter 6 also recommends that the U.S. Supreme Court or Congress act to confirm that marriage is based on a contract rather than being a status. Of course, any agreement reached by the spouses would be subject to state regulations protecting the interests of any children.

It would be unrealistic to expect a rapid change in the no-fault divorce laws and their perverse incentives, so I also discuss strategies that couples can use to overcome the adverse effects of no-fault divorce. The most important lesson that this book attempts to teach is that no-fault divorce has subtly warped incentives to induce adults often to make decisions that are against their best interest and the best interest of those that they love the most. A recognition of these incentives is the first step toward learning how to live with no-fault divorce. Even then, the outcome of any marriage is uncertain, and it is reasonable for adults to take steps to minimize the adverse effects of a marriage dissolution due to either death or divorce. Some of these steps are more likely to benefit a person's family than others are.

THE BOOK

In this book, I investigate why no-fault divorce has not lived up to the expectations of its proponents. Even though the criticism of no-fault divorce has grown, no one has presented a satisfactory explanation for why it has not fulfilled its expectations and for how it can be reformed to encourage adults to make better decisions about the welfare of their families and themselves. Those are the goals of this book. First, in the next chapter, the evolution of the marriage and divorce laws that ultimately resulted in no-fault divorce will be presented. In chapter 3, I introduce the economic perspective as it applies to marriage, divorce, and property. This material on the economic framework is followed by a chapter that traces the development of the California no-fault divorce statute, with an emphasis on the economic reasons why the statute was introduced. Economic analysis then is used in the next chapter to evaluate the impact of no-fault divorce on individual decisions. It will be observed that the introduction of no-fault divorce has influenced numerous trends, including changes in the divorce rate and the financial situation of the parties as well as in other areas of human behavior, such as when people marry and whether married women work outside the home. A particular concern is the impact of no-fault divorce on the quality of life for all family members. I conclude with a chapter in which economic analysis particularizes the reforms that could lessen the social and the individual costs of no-fault divorce by making mutual consent the divorce ground for established marriages. Because I do not expect a speedy change in the divorce laws, the book concludes with a discussion of steps that couples can take to minimize the adverse effect of no-fault divorce.

NOTES

1.   Family Law Act, ch. 1608, §§ 1-32, 1969 Cal. Stat. 3312. The first "pure" no-fault statute was enacted in California in 1969. The California statute has been described as "pure" because it based divorce exclusively on the factual breakdown of the marriage. See Herma Hill Kay, "Equality and Difference: A Perspective on No-Fault Divorce and Its Aftermath," *University of Cincinnati Law Review* 56 (1987): 1–90. Prior to 1969, some states included no-fault grounds with their fault grounds for divorce. For example, incompatibility as a ground for divorce was introduced into the United States when it acquired the Virgin Islands from Denmark in 1917, with incompatibility subsequently being adopted by a few states. See Graham Kirkpatrick, "Incompatibility as a Ground for Divorce," *Marquette Law Review* 47 (1964): 453–64. Some states had no-fault grounds for divorce, such as voluntary separation for a period of time or incurable insanity, by the mid-1960s, with eighteen states, Puerto Rico, and the District of Columbia permitting a divorce based on the parties living apart. See Glenda Riley, *Divorce: An American Tradition* (New York: Oxford University Press, 1991), 162. By 1985, all the states had some form of no-fault divorce, either exclusively no-fault grounds or with no-fault grounds added to the fault grounds. For data on the current status of divorce laws, see Linda D. Elrod and Robert G. Spector, "A Review of the Year in Family Law: A Search for Definitions and Policy," *Family Law Quarterly* 31, no. 4 (Winter 1998): 613–65.

2.   No-fault divorce statutes were enacted rapidly by the states. Iowa passed its no-fault divorce statute in 1971. By August 1977, only three states retained essentially fault grounds for divorce. See Doris J. Freed and Henry H. Foster, Jr., "Divorce in the Fifty States: An Overview," *Family Law Quarterly* 11, no. 3 (Fall 1977): 297–313. More than changing the divorce grounds, the important characteristic of the new laws was that they permitted one spouse to obtain a divorce even when the other spouse opposed it. Today only four states (Mississippi, New York, Ohio, and Tennessee) require mutual consent for a no-fault divorce. See Ira Mark Ellman and Stephen D. Sugarman, "Spousal Emotional Abuse as a Tort?" *Maryland Law Review* 55 (1996): 1277, n. 24.

3.   Lawrence M. Friedman, *A History of American Law* (New York: Simon & Schuster, 1973), 179–84, 434–40.

4.   Mary Ann Glendon noted, "The fault-oriented divorce law of the recent past furnished opportunities for one spouse (usually the wife) to obtain a settlement more generous than a court might have awarded in exchange for cooperation in obtaining or expediting the divorce or as the price of avoiding the embarrassing publicity of a contested divorce." Mary Ann Glendon, *The New Family and the New Property* (Toronto: Butterworths, 1981), 61.

The spouse who benefited from these negotiations frequently had been viewed as the wife. No-fault divorce statutes reduced the bargaining power of the spouse who did not want to dissolve the marriage. Because women frequently are adversely affected by divorce, it has been commonly accepted that they are reluctant to seek a divorce. However, there is evidence that often that is not the case. Under fault divorce, most negotiated divorce actions were filed by women because the defendant had to be the party who was at fault; so it was not clear who had initiated the divorce. See B. G. Gunter and Doyle Johnson, "Divorce Filing as Role Behavior: Effect of No-Fault Law on Divorce Filing Patterns," *Journal of Marriage and the Family* 40 (August 1978): 571–74. After the introduction of no-fault divorce, it appears that women often were the spouse who wanted a divorce. See Sanford L. Braver, Marnie Whitley, and Christine Ng, "Who Divorced Whom? Methodological and Theoretical Issues," *Journal of Divorce and Remarriage* 20, nos. 1 and 2 (1993): 1–19. In Margaret F. Brinig and Douglas W. Allen, "These Boots Are Made for Walking: Why Wives File for Divorce," which was presented at the 1998 Canadian Law and Economics Association meeting, Toronto, Ontario, September 27–28, 1998, the authors argued that one reason that married women file is to assure themselves of custody of the children and child support. Among the divorced couples interviewed in the National Survey of Families and Households, a majority of divorces were initiated by women. Allen M. Parkman, "Who Wants Out and Why," Anderson Schools of Management working paper, September 1999.

Still, the spouses who were the most in need of bargaining power at divorce frequently were wives in marriages of long duration. See Lenore J. Weitzman, *The Divorce Revolution* (New York: Free Press, 1985). The vulnerability of women after lengthy marriage has been explained by the timing of the contributions of men and women to marriage. The contributions of married women are often front-end loaded relative to married men: Married women have traditionally placed a special emphasis on child rearing that occurs early in a marriage, but the income earning contribution of the husband tends to increase over the duration of the marriage. When the children leave the home, the contribution of the wife to the marriage can fall, although the contribution of the husband continues to grow. Without the protection of a long-term arrangement such as was provided to a certain extent by fault divorce, some husbands may conclude that they are better off divorced. This is especially true when the financial obligations incurred by the husband to the wife due to the divorce are modest. See Lloyd Cohen, "Marriage, Divorce, and Quasi Rents; or 'I Gave Him the Best Years of My Life,'" *Journal of Legal Studies* 16, no. 2 (June 1987): 267–304.

5. In 20 to 25 percent of dual-earner couples, wives earn more than their husbands. See Anne E. Winkler, "Earnings of Husbands and Wives in Dual-Earner Families," *Monthly Labor Review* 121, no. 4 (April 1998): 42–48, and Lynne M. Casper, "My Daddy Takes Care of Me! Fathers as Care Providers," *Current Population Reports,* P70–59, (Washington, DC: U.S. Bureau of the Census, 1997), 1–9. As women have more aggressively pursued a career, the likelihood has increased that the primary caregiver has been the father. In a celebrated case in Florida, an appeals court overruled a trial court that had awarded an attorney mother primary residential custody of a couple's children in lieu of the architect father, who was the primary caregiver. Not only did the court give the father primary residential custody, it also increased the alimony that he had been awarded. *Young v. Hector,* 1998 Fla. App. LEXIS 7517 (1998).

6. This conclusion is documented in Weitzman, *The Divorce Revolution,* and H. Elizabeth Peters, "Marriage and Divorce: Informational Constraints and Private Contracting," *American Economic Review* 76, no. 3 (June 1986): 437–54. The conclusions and methodology of Weitzman have been challenged by a number of authors, including Herbert Jacob, "Faulting No-Fault," in "Review Symposium on Weitzman's *Divorce Revolution,*" ed. Howard S. Erlanger, *American Bar Foundation Research Journal* 1986, no. 4 (Fall 1986): 773–80; Herbert Jacob, *Silent Revolution: The Transformation of Divorce Law in the United States* (Chicago: University of Chicago Press, 1988); Herbert Jacob, "Another Look at No-Fault Divorce and the Post-Divorce Finances of Women," *Law and Society Review* 23, no. 1 (1989): 95–115; Marygold S. Melli, "Constructing a Social Problem: The Post-Divorce Plight of Women and Children," in "Review Symposium on Weitzman's *Divorce Revolution,*" ed. Howard S. Erlanger, 759–72; Richard R. Peterson, "A Re-Evaluation of the Economic Consequences of Divorce," *American Sociological Review* 61 (June 1995): 528–36; Jana B. Singer, "Divorce Reform and Gender Justice," *North Carolina Law Review* 67 (1989): 1103–21; Marsha Garrison, "The Economics of Divorce: Changing Rules, Changing Results," in *Divorce Reform at the Crossroads,* ed. Stephen D. Sugarman and Herma Hill Kay, (New Haven, CT: Yale University Press, 1990), 75–101; and Stephen D. Sugarman, "Dividing Financial Interests in Divorce," in *Divorce Reform at the Crossroads,* ed. Sugarman and Kay, 130–65.

7. Weitzman, *The Divorce Revolution,* 323. Weitzman's results have been questioned by a number of authors (see note 6). Using the same sample and measures of economic well-being, Richard Peterson produced estimates of a 27 percent decline in women's standard of living and a 10 percent increase in men's standard of living after divorce. See Peterson, "Re-Evaluation."

8. Peters, "Marriage and Divorce," 449. Using a sample consisting of younger couples and a slightly later time period, Yoram Weiss and Robert Willis found that the divorce

settlements received by women were more generous in no-fault divorce states. See Yoram Weiss and Robert J. Willis, "Transfers Among Divorced Couples: Evidence and Interpretation," *Journal of Labor Economics* 11, no. 4 (October 1993): 629–79.

9. See Allen M. Parkman, "Unilateral Divorce and the Labor-Force Participation Rate of Married Women, Revisited," *American Economic Review* 82, no. 3 (June 1992): 67–78; and Allen M. Parkman, "Why Are Married Women Working So Hard?," *International Review of Law and Economics* 18, no. 1 (Winter 1998): 41–49.

10. Michael Wheeler, *No-Fault Divorce* (Boston: Beacon, 1974), 8; and Lynne Carol Halem, *Divorce Reform* (New York: Free Press, 1980), 238.

11. Wheeler, *No-Fault Divorce,* 15.

12. Weitzman, *The Divorce Revolution,* 16, cited Judge Roger Pfaff, who pioneered the use of conciliation courts in Los Angeles, arguing that the trend toward higher divorce rates could be reversed by California adopting premarital and predivorce conciliation procedures.

13. For example, see David Popenoe, Jean Bethke Elshtain, and David Blankenhorn, eds., *Promises to Keep: Decline and Renewal of Marriage in America* (Lanham, MD: Rowman & Littlefield, 1996); Andrew J. Cherlin, *Marriage, Divorce, Remarriage* (Cambridge, MA: Harvard University Press, 1992); Kingsley Davis, *Contemporary Marriage: Comparative Perspectives on a Changing Institution* (New York: Russell Sage Foundation, 1985); Mary Ann Glendon, *The Transformation of Family Law* (Chicago: University of Chicago Press, 1989); Halem, *Divorce Reform;* Max Rheinstein, *Marriage Stability, Divorce and the Law* (Chicago: University of Chicago Press, 1972); and Weitzman, *The Divorce Revolution.*

14. Paul A. Samuelson and William D. Nordhaus, *Economics,* 15th ed. (New York: McGraw-Hill, 1995), 4.

15. See Dennis C. Mueller, *Public Choice II* (Cambridge, UK: Cambridge University Press, 1989); and James S. Coleman, *Foundations of Social Theory* (Cambridge, MA: Belknap Press, 1990). Coleman has applied rational choice theory to the family. Coleman, *Foundations,* 579–609.

16. Gary S. Becker, A *Treatise of the Family,* enl. ed. (Cambridge, MA: Harvard University Press, 1991), 350, noted that between 1950 and 1977, the legitimate birth rate declined by about one-third, the divorce rate more than doubled, the labor force participation rate of married women with young children more than tripled, and the percentage of households headed by women with dependent children also almost tripled. Gary S. Becker, William Landes, and Robert Michael, "An Analysis of Marital Instability," *Journal of Political Economy* 85, no. 6 (1977): 1184, concluded that the divorce rate, which accelerated after 1960, can be explained in part by "the decline over time in the number of children, the growth in labor force participation and earnings power of women, the growth in the breadth of the remarriage market as more persons become divorced and perhaps also the growth in legal access to divorce, illegitimacy, and public transfer payments."

17. Between 1970 and 1997, the percentage of men and of women eighteen years old and older who were married fell from 75.3 percent and 61.5 percent to 65.8 percent and

57.9 percent, respectively. Meanwhile, the percentage of men and of women eighteen years old and older who were divorced rose from 2.5 percent and 8.7 percent to 6.1 percent and 11 percent, respectively. U.S. Bureau of the Census, *Statistical Abstract of the United States, 1998* (Washington, DC: U.S. Government Printing Office, 1998), Table 61, 57.

18. Victor R. Fuchs, *Women's Quest for Economic Equality* (Cambridge, MA: Harvard University Press, 1988), 29, noted that it is less likely that legislation alters behavior than that changes in behavior initiate changes in legislation—legislators tend to be attuned to basic socioeconomic forces and to respond to the legislative demands created by the new behavior.

19. Linda J. Waite, "Does Marriage Matter?" *Demography* 32, no. 4 (November 1995): 483–507.

20. Gary S. Becker, "A Theory of Competition Among Pressure Groups for Political Influence," *Quarterly Journal of Economics* 98 (1983): 371–400.

21. The California Governor's Commission on the Family consisted of individuals from professions dominated by men, including two state senators, one assemblyman, five judges, six attorneys, two law school professors, one social worker, four physicians, and one clergyman. See Halem, *Divorce Reform*, 240. Fourteen of the fifteen members of the public who testified before the commission were men, and ten men identified themselves as divorced. The California Commission on the Status of Women supported the removal of fault from divorce. "Report of the Advisory Commission on the Status of Women," *California Women* (1969): 79–80.

22. Family Law Act, ch. 1608, §§ 1-32, 1969 Cal. Stat. 3312.

23. In 1970, the Uniform Marriage and Divorce Act was approved by the National Conference of Commissioners on Uniform State Laws (NCCUSL). The NCCUSL was strongly influenced by the same legal experts who had been influential in the California reform process. See Jacob, *Silent Revolution*, 67. The uniform act adopted as the sole ground for divorce was "that the marriage is irretrievably broken." *Uniform Laws Annotated* 9A (1979): 91. Homer H. Clark, Jr., *The Law of Domestic Relations in the United States,* 2d ed. (St. Paul, MN: West, 1988), 411.

24. Lenore J. Weitzman, "The Economics of Divorce: Social and Economic Consequences of Property, Alimony and Child Support Awards," *UCLA Law Review* 28 (1981): 1181–1268; Weitzman, *The Divorce Revolution*; and Peters, "Marriage and Divorce."

25. Weitzman, *The Divorce Revolution,* 19.

26. Max Rheinstein noted that collusive practices and migratory divorce had been common in the United States under fault divorce. See Max Rheinstein, *Marriage Stability,* 247–60, and "A Survey of Mental Cruelty as a Ground for Divorce," *De Paul Law Review* 15 (1965): 159, 163.

27. Under fault divorce, approximately 90 percent of divorces were uncontested. This figure understates the percentage that probably were uncontested because those divorces in which the defendant filed an answer or offered any evidence in opposition to the divorce were counted as contested; see Rheinstein, *Marriage Stability,* 248. In California, it was estimated that 94 percent of divorce hearings were uncontested and that they were granted with pro forma testimony as to fault; see the "Report of the Governor's Commission on the Family," Sacramento, CA, December 1966, 30–31, and 119, n. 23.

28. This is supported by evidence that there was an increase in the proportion of men filing for divorce after the introduction of no-fault divorce. Gunter and Johnson, "Divorce Filing," 571–74.

29. Harry D. Krause, *Family Law,* 3d ed. (St. Paul, MN: West, 1995), 335.

30. The interpretation here differs from the one provided in Robert H. Mnookin and Lewis Kornhauser, "Bargaining in the Shadow of the Law: The Case of Divorce," *Yale Law Journal* 88 (April 1979): 950–97. They interpret no-fault divorce as permitting a substantial degree of private ordering. However, with no-fault divorce the spouses had little incentive to give up more than was prescribed by law. So although they might not use the court system, it is unlikely that their settlement would differ substantially from the one provided by law. However, under fault divorce the couple had much broader latitude to fashion their own agreement independent of the law. Otherwise, both spouses would have been unlikely to agree to the divorce.

31. Krause, *Family Law,* 122.

32. Clark, *Domestic Relations,* 595.

33. Mary Ann Glendon, "Family Law Reform in the 1980s," *Louisiana Law Review* 44, no. 6 (July 1984): 1559, expresses the commonly accepted view that the only significant property of a young couple was a house and its contents. She does not recognize that the spouses have their individual human capital that can be valuable and that may have been affected by the marriage. See Allen M. Parkman, "Human Capital as Property in Divorce Settlements," *Arkansas Law Review* 40, no. 3 (1987): 439–67, and Allen M. Parkman, "Bringing Consistency to the Financial Arrangements at Divorce," *Kentucky Law Journal* 87, no. 1 (1998–99): 51–93.

34. There are problems associated with a concept called "professional goodwill" that was one of the attempts by the courts to create property to allocate to wives. See Allen M. Parkman, "The Treatment of Professional Goodwill in Divorce Proceedings," *Family Law Quarterly* 18, no. 2 (summer 1984): 213–24.

35. J. Thomas Oldham, *Divorce, Separation and the Distribution of Property* (New York: Law Journal Seminars-Press, 1997), 7-1–7-153.

36. The principles developed here are relevant for both men and women. The situation that normally requires an adjustment in the property settlement to incorporate the effect of the marriage on the human capital of the spouses is one in which one spouse made major sacrifices in his or her employment opportunities to accommodate the other spouse. Generally, wives have been the spouses that make these adjustments; but as the economic opportunities of women increase, we would expect there to be pressure for more husbands making these sacrifices. Casper, "My Daddy."

37. Marriage tends to reduce women's earnings, and the reduction increases with the number of children. See Waite, "Marriage," 496.

38. While the remarriage rates in 1990 were similar for men and women ages twenty-five to twenty-nine, the rate for women compared to men fell as their ages increased. For example, by ages forty-five to forty-nine the remarriage rate was 88 per 1,000 for men, but 43 per 1,000 for women. See Sally C. Clarke, "Advance Report of Final Marriage Statis-

tics, 1989 and 1990," National Center for Health Statistics, *Monthly Vital Statistics Report* 43, no. 12 (July 14, 1995) Table 6, ii.

39.   Laura Bradford, "The Counterrevolution: A Critique of Recent Proposals to Reform No-Fault Divorce Laws," *Stanford Law Review* 49 (February 1997): 607–36.

40.   La. Rev. Stat. Ann. § 9:272(West Supp. 1998).

41.   Ariz. Rev. Stat. § 25-901.

42.   Christine B. Whelan, "No Honeymoon for Covenant Marriage," *Wall Street Journal,* August 17, 1998, A12. During the last six months of 1998, data collected by Steve Nock, a sociologist at the University of Virginia, indicated that the percentage of couples selecting a covenant marriage had increased to approximately 3 percent. He also determined that people in Louisiana were only gradually becoming aware of the covenant marriage alternative. Conversation with Steve Nock on February 22, 1999.

The newer act in Arizona has also gotten off to a slow start as only 16 out of more than 5,000 couples who married in Mariposa County during the first three months chose it. Associated Press, "Covenant Marriage Not Taking Couples by Storm," November 10, 1998.

43.   Allen M. Parkman, "Reform of the Divorce Provisions of the Marriage Contract," *BYU Journal of Public Law* 8, no. 1 (1993): 91–106.

44.   *Williams v. North Carolina*, 317 U.S. 287, 299 (1942).

45.   U.S. Constitution art. IV, § 1.

2

Marriage and Divorce Laws

The laws that govern marriage and divorce have changed over time. From within a given legal environment, it is often difficult to envision the legal rules that applied at other times and places—especially for matters as pervasive and private as marriage. Not long ago, marriage was a very different institution.[1] Society, rather than the involved parties, defined marriage roles. The expectation was that once begun, marriage would continue for the joint lives of the parties. Divorce could be granted only if one party failed in a very fundamental way to live up to the standards expected by society. That party was held to be at fault for the failure of the marriage. In many states, husband and wife were required to live together at a place chosen by the husband if his choice was a safe and reasonable location. The husband, if able, was required to provide for the support of his wife and children. The stability of marriage was important both for the individuals involved and for society.[2] By removing fault and recognizing the preferences of the parties as preeminent to the dictates of society, no-fault divorce caused a revolution in the family law that had existed for most of the history of the United States. To place no-fault divorce in perspective, we will look in this chapter at the evolution of marriage and divorce laws both as they establish the procedures and grounds for marriage and divorce and as they affect the property of the parties.

MARRIAGE LAWS

The topic of this book is divorce, but marriage is a necessary precondition to divorce, and a society's approach to divorce often is reflected in its laws governing marriage. Every society has had its own idea of marriage.[3] Among early civilizations, marriage was considered a social contract to which the state was not a party. These groups often did not have the nuclear family structure that dominates modern U.S. society, because they operated with extended families or clans. Marriage was not so much a transaction between the two people immediately concerned as between their respective parents or chiefs. Under Roman law, it was possible to initiate a marriage without a ceremony or at least without a ceremony prescribed by law. Christianity changed the regulation of marriage: Marriage as we know it today was formalized by the Roman Catholic Church. The canon law of the Catholic Church was the only law governing matrimonial relations between Christians in Western Europe until the Reformation in the sixteenth century, and it retains considerable authority in Roman Catholic countries.

The influence of the church over marriage was asserted gradually, beginning with restrictions regarding the parties who could marry— marriages between near relatives, which had been common until that time, were no longer allowed. Marriage became monogamous and indissoluble.[4] The doctrine of indissolubility was given special significance by its being combined with the dogma of the sacramental nature of marriage: in the eyes of the church, a marriage could only be dissolved by God through death or by the church through annulment.

The introduction of indissolubility created the need to precisely define what it was that could not be dissolved. In other words, what was a marriage? The church desired, and later demanded, that an act of such deep religious significance as marriage could only be performed with the blessing of the church. It thus became customary that parties planning to be married would meet at the door of the church with the parish priest, who would bestow his blessing on them, although the actual creation of the married state remained the private transaction of the parties. When followed by carnal consummation, their expression of desire to be married matured into the sacrament, and the marriage became indissoluble. The church attempted to require that marriages be blessed by a priest, but the violation of this command did not invalidate the marriage. This informal process continued until the time of the Council of Trent in 1563, which formalized marriage rules and established that a valid marriage required a ceremony performed by a priest in the presence of at least two witnesses.

The procedures created by the Council of Trent resulted from more than religious concerns. The recognition of clandestine marriages could enable strangers to marry into wealthy families without prior parental approval. At the Council of Trent, the same bishops who were the chief proponents of compulsory marriage ceremonies also tried to make parental consent an ecclesiastical marriage requirement. A minister's presence at the wedding was made mandatory in some German states at the time of the Reformation, and these states often required couples to obtain the consent of their parents before they could marry.[5]

From the sixteenth to the eighteenth century, in many parts of Western Europe, the Catholic Church lost its jurisdiction over marriage. England, under Henry VIII, broke from the Catholic Church in 1534. In Protestant regions, this separation occurred because of the Reformation; and in France, it accompanied the assertion of national power by the monarchy. As the power of the church waned, the states assumed control over marriage by default, generally continuing the rules that had been generated by the church. The reformers objected to the power of the church, but not to Christianity; and although some rejected the notion that marriage was a sacrament, most assumed that secular marriage regulations should conform to Christian teachings.

With the dual influences of the Reformation and the Enlightenment, the idea of marriage as a contract took a new turn. Voluntary consent between the parties with or without a ceremony had been the essence of marriage under canon law, but the trend toward codification of the law throughout Europe in the eighteenth century resulted in a more formal regulation of marriage. In France, the desire for legislative regulation during this period caused the development of two important modern institutions affecting the family: the compulsory civil marriage ceremony and public registration of marriages. The civil marriage ceremony became mandatory in France in 1792.

England followed a somewhat different path. Replacing the Catholic Church, the Church of England retained control of marriage laws until the middle of the nineteenth century. Informal marriages remained valid in England until 1753, when Lord Hardwicke's reform of the marriage laws made a church ceremony compulsory and required publication of the vows for a legal marriage, but cohabitation rather than marriage was the norm until the Victorian era.[6]

The marriage laws in the United States evolved out of the laws that had developed in Europe. In England, marriage was based on individual decisions and was generally a lifelong commitment. Because of the realities of the frontier life and the shortage of clergymen, Lord Hardwicke's reforms were not implemented in the American colonies, and informal or "common law" marriages remained legal in many states even after 1753.[7] In New England, the Puritans maintained as a religious doctrine the contractual character of marriage in contrast to the church doctrine of its sacramental character. The U.S. Constitution gave jurisdiction over matrimonial matters to the states, which enacted a variety of statutes. By the end of the nineteenth century, many states abolished informal marriages; but even today, common law marriage is possible in many states.[8]

Despite attacks on the marriage laws in the United States by homosexual couples and the religious groups that advocate polygamy, marriage in the United States has been standardized as a monogamous union between two individuals of opposite sex who are not closely related by blood. People often choose a religious ceremony for their marriage; but the key requirements are secular, and most states require compliance with specific formalities to establish a valid marriage.

DIVORCE LAWS

The regulation of divorce has tended to parallel the regulation of marriage: so long as the regulation of marriage remained outside the purview of church authorities or the state, the regulation of divorce was also outside their jurisdiction. The usual result in ancient law was that marriage could easily be dissolved, either by mutual consent or by unilateral repudiation, sometimes with the payment of a penalty. In the case of arranged marriages, the same parties that arranged them could dissolve them. At the time of Jesus, under Hebrew law, a marriage could be dissolved whenever the husband desired, although no corresponding power existed for the wife.

As the legal regulation of divorce developed, it assumed two forms:[9] Divorce *a mensa et thoro*—from bed and board—provided a legal separation with all of the other obligations of marriage continuing; neither party could remarry. Divorce *a vinculo matrimonii*—from the bonds of matrimony—enabled remarriage. Under pressure from early Christians, the sixth-century emperor Justinian enacted a code strictly regulating the dissolution of marriage in Rome, with adultery being the only major ground.

As the Catholic Church asserted control over marriage, it also established rules for divorce, which dominated the legal requirements for the dissolution of marriage in Europe for the next thousand years. The canon law applied two main principles to divorce: First, given a valid marriage, there could be no divorce *a vinculo matrimonii*, which resulted in the parties, after once marrying, being free to remarry. Second, no divorce at all could be obtained at the will of the parties, but only by the decision of an ecclesiastical court. Annulments were used during this period by influential persons to dissolve a marriage—the declaration that the marriage had never existed left the parties free to remarry. For example, the marriage of Eleanor of Aquitaine to Louis VII of France was annulled in 1152 after fourteen years and the birth of two daughters.[10]

At the time of the Reformation, there were thus two legal remedies for persons dissatisfied with their marriage:[11] They could argue that the marriage had never been valid due to some technicality; if this claim was successful, the marriage was annulled and the parties were both free to remarry. Or, they could seek a divorce *a mensa et thoro* based on one spouse's actions. These divorces were based on fault, with the grounds including adultery, serious mistreatment, and desertion. Divorce was only available to the innocent party and did not permit either party to remarry. If both parties were at fault, neither could be released from the marriage.[12]

Divorce became more flexible after the Reformation. Both Martin Luther and John Calvin cast doubt on the sacramental nature of marriage and its indissolubility, and their followers did not feel bound by canon law. Divorce became more common on the Continent as secular laws and courts replaced the canon laws and the ecclesiastical courts. England followed a different course. The Church of England had replaced the Catholic Church in that country in 1534,[13] and ecclesiastical courts continued to exercise jurisdiction over matrimonial matters in England until the passage of the Matrimonial Causes Act of 1857. After 1602, no divorces were granted by those ecclesiastical courts.[14] The only absolute divorces were obtained by the costly procedure of a private act of Parliament; and until the middle of the nineteenth century, when a new and more flexible divorce law was introduced, only 317 divorces were granted by Parliament. The Matrimonial Causes Act of 1857 permitted divorce primarily on the ground of adultery, but additional grounds have been added over the years.

Divorce was more common in the British colonies in North America than in England. The Puritan leaders permitted divorce for excessive marital incompatibility.[15] In the New England and Middle Atlantic colonies, divorce was available on a sporadic basis; in the southern colonies, divorce was as restricted as in England. With the adoption of the U.S. Constitution, the states assumed responsibility for the regulation of divorce. Still, divorce had been extremely rare in the colonial period, and it continued to be rare well into the nineteenth century.[16] In those areas that had been settled by Protestants, there were divorce laws from before statehood; but in areas with a strong Anglican influence, especially in the South, there were often no provisions for divorce. A variety of statutes were enacted with grounds ranging from adultery to separation for a statutory period. Over time, the number of grounds grew in most states. Cruelty, defined in a variety of ways, was a ground in most states, and its use became increasingly common. A critical characteristic of the grounds was the requirement that one party had to be at fault, and, therefore, a divorce could not be obtained easily.

By the middle of the nineteenth century, the migratory divorce was already part of the American scene as the western states took a more liberal approach to divorce. Migrating temporarily to a state with more liberal standards for a divorce and establishing a domicile in that state, people could receive a divorce more easily than in the state in which they normally resided. The possibility of the migratory divorce had existed since the signing of the Constitution, but it did not become an issue of much concern until the twentieth century. In 1942, *in Williams v. North Carolina*,[17] the U.S. Supreme Court upheld the validity of a divorce that had been obtained in Nevada, where only six weeks were required to create domicile and jurisdiction for a divorce decree. The increased use of migratory divorces, which were only available to those who could afford to travel, created pressures for uniform divorce laws throughout the United States.

Gradually, the divorce rate rose in the United States. During the period for which national data is available, the number of divorces rose from 56,000 in 1900 to 1,213,000 in 1981 before declining to 974,000 in 1998.[18] The pressures to change the divorce grounds accelerated after World War II as more and more people were divorcing. The fault grounds for divorce usually required the plaintiff in the divorce suit to be an innocent party, which resulted in pressure for the couple to negotiate a settlement with the party actually requesting the divorce assuming the role of the defendant. Thus, the party who had not initially wanted the divorce was often the person who actually filed the lawsuit. The common ground for divorce was some form of cruelty, and many couples used perjured testimony to establish the cruelty. This hypocrisy increased pressure to change the divorce statutes, and gradually some small states added no-fault grounds to the existing statutes.[19] In 1970, California became the first state to introduce unequivocal no-fault grounds for divorce. Between 1970 and 1985, all the states enacted no-fault divorce statutes or added no-fault grounds to the existing fault grounds. Initially, the courts retained the right to determine if the no-fault grounds had been established by the parties; but as the courts became more familiar with the new grounds for divorce, they came to acknowledge that the parties' views about their marriage had to be taken at face value.[20] From being almost impossible without evidence of fault or the agreement of one's spouse, divorce has become essentially unilateral in many states.

MATRIMONIAL PROPERTY

Marriage in the modern era is based on the attraction between the parties, but it is also a decision with substantial financial consequences—consequences that become particularly apparent if the marriage is dissolved. Laws regulating the effect of marriage and divorce on the property of the parties sometimes can be preempted by premarital and postmarital agreements or by negotiated settlements. Negotiated settlements, in particular, often were important under fault divorce as an inducement for an otherwise unwilling spouse to agree to divorce. The introduction of no-fault divorce reemphasized the preexisting legal standards for property settlement, support, and custody. Understanding the impact of marriage and divorce on property requires a review of those laws.

The effect of marriage on the properties of the parties has a long history, especially among the wealthy. When marriage was primarily a private arrangement, the effect of the marriage on the parties' properties was also private. Marriage contracts could provide for desired effects of marriage and divorce on property. In Europe, it was traditional for these relationships to be arranged, within certain limits, by private agreements. U.S. courts have been less willing to accept private contracts that define the financial effects of divorce on the parties. Outside private agreements, statutes determine the effects of marriage on property brought into the marriage or acquired during the marriage. In much of Europe, such laws were introduced when the secular governments assumed control over marriage after the Reformation. As early as the thirteenth century, however, laws existed, for example, in Spain to maintain estates, which consisted primarily of land.[21] To make sure that estates would remain in a family, they were passed from generation to generation through the male bloodline. The estate remained the separate property of the husband, and a wife never acquired any rights in the property while there was a male heir.

With the spread of wealth after the Reformation, governments assumed more control over the regulation of the effect of marriage on the title to property. By the time of the Industrial Revolution, the regulation of family economic affairs was similar in all the major Western European countries: The husband had the power to manage all the family property, including the property and earnings of the wife. He was also expected to provide for the maintenance of the members of the household. He was limited by a fiduciary responsibility to manage any property brought into the marriage by the wife.

Matrimonial Property in the United States

In the United States, two different legal systems developed that addressed matrimonial property, one based on the common law of England and the other on the civil law of continental Europe as it developed in Mexico. These legal systems define the items that are the separate properties of the individual spouses and those that are their collective marital property, and they specify rules to allocate property between spouses who divorce.

Common Law

In most of the states, marital property law originally derived from the English common law, under which all the wife's real and personal property came under the husband's control upon marriage. Her property was returned to her if she lived longer than her husband, and she had certain limited rights in her husband's property if he predeceased her; but the general conclusion has been that the common law system favored the husband's interests.

To avoid the harsher aspects of the common law, most states passed Married Women's Property Acts during the nineteenth century.[22] These laws ended the husband's assumption of the wife's property at the time of the marriage. She was permitted to own, sell, and otherwise act on her behalf with respect to her property; and she could sue her husband over property-related issues, enter into contracts, and assume full rights over her earnings. On their face, these laws approached equal treatment, entitling husband and wife to their separate properties and to their earnings. But the spouses were equal only in a strict formal sense: The properties of the spouses were often commingled, so the separate properties were treated as joint property; and because the husband was the principal wage earner, the bulk of the assets acquired during the marriage was in his name. These reforms were thus of little value to women who did not come into the marriage with separate property or who did not work outside the home during the marriage.

The rules in most common law states attempted to make a distinction between the separate property of the spouses and their marital property, normally based on title. Following the example of the Uniform Marriage and Divorce Act, as it was amended in 1973,[23] all the common law states have replaced their fixed rules for determining how property is allocated after a divorce with "equitable distribution" statutes.[24] These statutes frequently give judges broad discretion to distribute all property, both separate and marital, in a way that they consider to be fair.[25] Judges have had a difficult time with the fairness concept, resulting in the predictable pattern that courts frequently return the parties' separate properties and divide the martial property equally.

Community Property

Some western states use a property system based on the civil law system of Mexico.[26] In these jurisdictions, each spouse has a one-half interest in all marital, or community, property. As noted earlier, community property is all property that is not the separate property of the spouses. Separate property is, in turn, defined by statute as the property that the parties brought into the marriage or that came to them during the marriage by will, bequest, or devise. The states regard the management of the community property during the marriage in a variety of ways. Some states give the idea of community property broad play, and in other states the spouses control their property and earnings more directly. Some community property states require a strict equal division of marital property; in others the courts are given some discretion. The usual effect at divorce, however, is that each spouse keeps his or her separate property and the community property is divided equally between the spouses.

Recent Reforms

Traditionally the two systems produced different results, but recent reforms have moved the common law states and the community property states closer together with an emphasis on community property principles. The Uniform Marital Property Act was approved by the Commissioners on Uniform State Laws in 1983;[27] but it has only been enacted in one state, Wisconsin, and there it has been amended substantially.[28] If the Property Act was enacted by the common law states, it would effectively create a nationwide system of community property. The act makes the spouses equal owners of property acquired during marriage, except for those items that have traditionally been treated as separate property, such as gifts and inheritance. The act says nothing about how property shall be divided upon divorce or death, however, which is when the issue of ownership becomes critical. The act does provide for premarital and postmarital property agreements, with the courts scrutinizing postmarital agreements more closely than premarital agreements.[29] If the enforcement of an agreement would result in one spouse going on public assistance, the courts may require the other spouse to contribute enough support so that public assistance is avoided. Thus, both common law and community property systems establish rights of spouses in property, but neither provides a clear definition of the items that are property.

Premarital Agreements

Where the laws of a given jurisdiction do not define or allocate property at divorce or death in a way that meets the particular needs of the parties, a private contract has offered an alternative. Such private contracts, often premarital agreements, are coming into wider use because of changes in marital patterns. By 1990, men and women over thirty years of age accounted for 44 percent and 35 percent, respectively, of marriages.[30] Not only are these people older and, therefore, more aware of the potential problems associated with marriage,[31] they also bring more assets to their marriages. The increasing divorce rate also results in ever more people marrying more than once. For example, in 46 percent of marriages, at least one party has been married before.[32]

In most civil law jurisdictions in Europe, the marriage contract was an established institution until the 1970s,[33] but it has not been looked on favorably by the courts in the United States.[34] Concerns include fears that premarital determinations of the consequences of divorce will encourage divorce against public policy and that no contract could adequately deal with all the circumstances that could confront the parties in a marriage of long duration.[35] Nevertheless, many courts now uphold premarital agreements, especially when strict standards of fairness are met or in the case of a second marriage. The courts ask whether there was a fair disclosure of the parties' wealth at the time of the contract, how the provisions of the contract compare with the legal support obligations that they would replace, and whether enforcement of the contract would make one spouse a burden on society.[36]

The Uniform Marriage and Divorce Act, which has been enacted in some states, makes a premarital contract only one factor to be used by the court in determining whether the division of the spouses' property is equitable. The trend of court decisions is more supportive of agreements relating to property settlements than of agreements affecting support obligations, support being deemed more essential to marriage than matters of property are. The difference between support and property at the time of a divorce has been clouded by practical concerns about, for example, taxes. Premarital agreements that seek to define or to waive support obligations and other essential duties of marriage still tend to be declared invalid, as against public policy. One attempt to clarify these issues is the Uniform Premarital Agreement Act of 1983.[37]

In the current legal environment, the enforcement of premarital agreements is sufficiently uncertain that the agreements do not offer a clear alternative to the legally defined allocation of property at divorce. When the no-fault divorce statutes removed most of the negotiating power of the spouse who did not want a divorce, premarital and postmarital agreements did not offer an attractive option. Spouses who were considering marriage or who were married were confronted with an environment in which their marriage often could be dissolved unilaterally without compensation in any significant manner for any sacrifices they had made.

CONCLUSION

Marriage laws have changed over the years, with a shift toward secular control and legal formality, but they have been stable compared to divorce laws. Until the middle of the nineteenth century, a divorce was difficult to obtain in the United States. The parties who committed themselves to the obligations of marriage were protected by the fault grounds for divorce. Gradually, the grounds for divorce were expanded, and the courts became more willing to accept questionable testimony in establishing the legal grounds for divorce. Still, it was difficult for one spouse to divorce without the cooperation of the other spouse. When a spouse could not establish the grounds but wanted a divorce, the usual outcome was negotiations, often resulting in the initially unwilling party–frequently the wife if it was an established marriage—accepting compensation that made her willing to accept the divorce. The solution was a wealth transfer and the fabrication of evidence to establish the necessary grounds. This situation took a dramatic turn in 1970 with the adoption of no-fault divorce statutes. No-fault not only changed the grounds for divorce but also increased the importance of the legal rules that define and allocate property at divorce.

In the next chapter, I offer an economic analysis of marriage, divorce, and property to aid in understanding why people marry, how they select their spouses, why they sometimes decide that they no longer want to be married, and what property is.

NOTES

1. See "Marriage" in *Encyclopaedia Britannica CD* (Chicago: Encyclopaedia Britannica, 1998) and *Collier's Encyclopedia*, vol. 15 (New York: Macmillan, 1989), 440.

2. Margaret F. Brinig and June Carbone, "The Reliance Interest in Marriage and Divorce," *Tulane Law Review* 62, no. 5 (May 1988): 860.

3. The history of marriage law in Europe and the United States is available from numerous sources. For example, see Max Rheinstein, *Marriage Stability, Divorce and the Law* (Chicago: University of Chicago Press, 1972); and Mary Ann Glendon, *The Transformation of Family Law* (Chicago: University of Chicago Press, 1989).

4. Marriage only became indissoluble when the Catholic Church gained jurisdiction over marital matters for its own courts. Rheinstein, *Marriage Stability,* 7–28.

5. Beatrice Gottlieb, *The Family in the Western World from the Black Death to the Industrial Age* (New York: Oxford University Press, 1993), 68–88.

6. Glendon, *Transformation,* 33.

7. Homer H. Clark, Jr., *The Law of Domestic Relations in the United States,* 2d ed. (St. Paul, MN: West, 1988), 23.

8. Harry D. Krause, *Family Law,* 3d Ed., (St. Paul, MN: West, 1995), 60.

9. Brinig and Carbone, "Reliance Interest," 860–61.

10. "Divorce" in *Encyclopaedia Britannica CD* (Chicago: Encyclopaedia Britannica, 1998).

11. Mary E. O'Connell, "Alimony after No-Fault: A Practice in Search of a Theory," *New England Law Review* 23 (1988): 449.

12. Brinig and Carbone, "Reliance Interest," 861.

13. The establishment of the Church of England was in part a response to the Pope's refusal to grant an annulment to Henry VIII for his marriage to Catherine of Aragon. Clark, *Domestic Relations,* 407.

14. "Divorce" in *Encyclopaedia Britannica CD* (Chicago: Encyclopaedia Britannica, 1998).

15. Glenda Riley, *Divorce: An American Tradition* (Oxford, UK: Oxford University Press, 1991), 9.

16. Most divorces during the colonial period were legislative rather than judicial. See Lawrence M. Friedman, "Rights of Passage: Divorce Law in Historical Perspective," *Oregon Law Review* 63 (1986): 651–52.

17. 317 U.S. 287(1942). This case is referred to as *Williams I.* In a subsequent case, *Williams v. North Carolina (Williams II),* 325 U.S. 226 (1945), the U.S. Supreme Court held that states such as North Carolina could make their own determination of whether an individual had taken sufficient steps to establish a domicile in another state that granted a divorce. The North Carolina court had decided that a brief stay in Nevada was not adequate to establish domicile in that state, and any divorce granted there was, therefore, not

valid in North Carolina. Eventually, the passage of no-fault divorce statutes made migratory divorces no longer attractive.

18.   The number then fell to a slightly lower level for the remainder of the decade. The rate per 1,000 married women rose from 8 in 1920 to 22.6 in 1981 before declining to 19.5 in 1996. See *Historical Statistics of the United States* (Washington, DC: U.S. Government Printing Office, 1975), Series B 216-220, 64; National Center for Health Statistics, *Births, Marriages, Divorces and Deaths: Provisional Data for November 1998* (March 16, 1999); and *Statistical Abstract of the United States, 1998* (Washington, DC: U.S. Government Printing Office, 1998), Table 156, 111.

19.   Riley, *Divorce,* 162.

20.   Clark, *Domestic Relations,* 517.

21.   William A. Reppy, Jr., "Major Events in the Evolution of American Community Property Law and Their Import to Equitable Distribution States," *Family Law Quarterly* 23, no. 2 (Summer 1989): 163–92.

22.   Lawrence M. Friedman, *A History of American Law* (New York: Simon & Schuster, 1973), 184–86.

23.   Uniform Marriage and Divorce Act, § 307, alternative A, 9A *Uniform Laws Annotated* (1973): 142–43.

24.   Krause, *Family Law,* 434.

25.   For a discussion of this process and a description of the statutes, see Mary Ann Glendon, *The New Family and the New Property* (Toronto: Butterworths, 1981), 57–68. Glendon argued that the "equitable distribution" statutes have resulted in too much ambiguity. See Mary Ann Glendon, "Family Law Reform in the 1980s," *Louisiana Law Review* 44 (1984): 1553–73.

26.   These states are Arizona, California, Idaho, Louisiana, Nevada, New Mexico, Texas, and Washington.

27.   Uniform Marital Property Act(UMPA), § 10(b), 9A *Uniform Laws Annotated* 35 (Supp. 1983).

28.   Krause, *Family Law,* 128.

29.   UMPA, §§ 3, 10(c)(3)–(4).

30.   Census, *Statistical Abstract,* Table 158, 112.

31.   However, there is empirical evidence that individuals often are unrealistically optimistic about the likelihood that their own marriages will succeed. See Lynn A. Baker and Robert E. Emery, "When Every Relationship Is Above Average: Perceptions and Expectations of Divorce at the Time of Marriage," *Law and Human Behavior* 17 (1993): 439–50.

32.   Census, *Statistical Abstract,* Table 157, 111.

33.   Max Rheinstein and Mary Ann Glendon, "Interspousal Relations," in ed. A. Chloros, *International Encyclopedia of Comparative Law,* 4 (Tubingen, Germany: Mohr, 1980).

34.   Homer H. Clark, Jr., "Antenuptial Contracts," *University of Colorado Law Review* 50, no. 2 (Winter 1979): 141–64. *Dawley v. Dawley,* 551 P.2d 323(Cal. 1976) rejected

the traditional public policy objections and accepted that prenuptial agreements can serve a useful purpose as a planning device when there is recognition of the possibility of dissolution.

35. Krause, *Family Law,* 94.

36. Glendon, *Transformation,* 137.

37. See Uniform Premarital Agreements Act (UPAA), 9B U.L.A. 369 (1987). As of May 1998, twenty-six jurisdictions had adopted the UPAA. See Brian Bix, "Bargaining in the Shadow of Love: The Enforcement of Premarital Agreements and How We Think about Marriage," *William and Mary Law Review* 40 (October 1998): 154.

3

The Economics of Marriage and Divorce

During the past few decades, the use of economic analysis has been expanded to many nonmarket activities, including marriage, divorce, education, and crime.[1] Because marriage and divorce can affect the financial welfare of the parties, it is not difficult to understand that economics has some relevance to the analysis of the effects of marriage and divorce. But I will also show here that economics can provide important insights about marriage and divorce that go far beyond just the financial repercussions.

THE ROLE OF ECONOMIC ANALYSIS

On a general level, economics is the study of the choices individuals make. The economic perspective fundamentally assumes that resources are scarce when compared to human wants, that these resources can be put to alternative uses, and that people have diverse wants, not all of which can be satisfied. It follows that the basic economic problem of every society—and of every individual—is to allocate the available resources in the most efficient manner to satisfy wants. Especially in the United States, where legal marriage is a monogamous relationship, the need for a person to make a choice when selecting a spouse is obvious: Here economic analysis goes far beyond the comparison of alternatives according to prices denominated in dollars.

Ever since Adam Smith published *The Wealth of Nations* in 1776, social scientists have been using the economic framework to gain a better understanding of why people make the choices that they make. Much of the power of economics to explain human behavior is rooted in the following set of assumptions:

1. People are constantly confronted with the necessity of making choices in their roles, for example, as consumers, workers, and lovers. Many alternatives are mutually exclusive.

2. In making these choices, people try to improve— rather than reduce—their welfare. The choices are made by comparing the costs and the benefits of the alternatives in a context of constraints, such as laws, time, abilities, and income.

3. Choices are influenced by the relative sacrifices, or "prices," involved with the different alternatives; these sacrifices can involve money, time, and psychic costs.

4. These "economic" decisions are made in an environment that is influenced by a range of other factors, such as religion, social class, and physical and psychological needs. Economists have traditionally assumed that these environmental factors change slowly.[2]

When we observe systematic changes in human behavior, economists argue that we would be well advised to investigate whether there has been a change in the incentives—constraints or the relative prices—confronting the individuals. People will usually buy less of a good if their incomes fall or if the price of the good rises. Economists assume that values, tastes, and preferences change more slowly than do the prices and the constraints that individuals face. At the same time, different groups can have preferences for different commodities and activities. Irish-Americans might eat more corned beef and cabbage than persons of other ethnic groups, but all consumers—including the Irish—would be expected to buy less corned beef if its price rose. Although it is difficult to determine if values have changed and, equally important, why, substantial empirical work has confirmed the ability of the economic framework to explain and to predict a broad range of human activities.[3]

The economic framework that considers incentives provides a different explanation for the commonly accepted view that the quality of family life has deteriorated because people are responding to a shift in values.[4] The values-based argument holds that people have shifted their preferences from long-term fulfillment within a family to short-term gratification through personal independence.[5] Alternatively, an economic perspective recognizes that people's most fundamental goal of increasing their own welfare is very durable. Often there is confusion between self-interest and being selfish. Self-interest frequently dictates that people consider others and, especially, their responses. For many people, keeping their spouse content with their marriage and having a cordial relationship with their children are major components of their self-interest. Selfishness, on the other hand, implies a disregard for the welfare of others, which frequently would not be in an individual's self-interest.

In the pursuit of their self-interest, people tend to respond to a change in incentives—costs and benefits associated with choices—rather than changes in their fundamental values. Economics suggests that people are making a weaker commitment to their families not because their fundamental values have changed but because the costs or the benefits of that commitment have changed. When a marriage was difficult to dissolve, spouses could make personal sacrifices—such as limiting a career—for the benefit of their family with the expectation that they would be compensated in the future by the earnings and affection their spouse and children. When no-fault divorce made it easier for a marriage to be dissolved unilaterally, the anticipated benefits of these sacrifices were reduced along with the incentive to make them. It is no surprise that the quality of family life deteriorated.

The framework used by economists has also been accepted by other social scientists. For example, some sociologists—the academics with the longest history of studying the family—use exchange or rational choice theories,[6] in which people are viewed as purposeful beings who exchange goods and services in a manner that they anticipate will increase their welfare. These theories place a primary emphasis on people responding to incentives in an environment in which values, especially self-interest, remain stable, but not fixed. At least some sociologists have found rational choice particularly attractive because none of the other theoretical traditions provide a framework for the systematic deductive modeling of "social reality."[7]

Our next step is to apply the economic framework to key decisions affecting relationships. Because people must marry before they can divorce, I initially will analyze why people marry. The decision to marry consists of two steps: (1) the decision by an individual that he or she will be better off married than single and (2) the choice of a particular person for a spouse. These decisions are not necessarily sequential, but they will be addressed sequentially here with first a look at why people marry. The process by which an individual chooses a preferred mate will be discussed in the economic analysis of divorce.

An understanding of why people marry is important because the incentives that induce people to marry can change so that they no longer want to be married. The result is often a divorce. Economics provides a foundation for understanding why people rationally choose to marry and why some of these people, also rationally, choose to dissolve their marriages. As marriage and divorce have effects on the financial condition of the parties, economics can be particularly relevant for analyzing the effect of marriage and divorce on their wealth. Economics also can be used to evaluate whether marriage and divorce decisions have the capacity to improve social welfare. Last, economics can provide insights about other issues concerning divorce: Why do the spouses litigate the divorce instead of negotiating a settlement? Why does the political process produce particular laws affecting divorce? Why is only one step toward the reform of the fault divorce laws potentially worse for society than no reform at all?

THE ECONOMIC APPROACH TO MARRIAGE

One has to wonder why it took economists so long to turn their attention to the analysis of marriage. As the study of choice, economics should be a valuable tool for analyzing one of the most important decisions made by individuals. Economic analysis goes far beyond the financial aspects of marriage such as dowries and bride prices noted by historians. It was not until the 1960s, however, that economists started to develop a concerted interest in decision making outside markets, including marriage.[8] Marriage in the United States has characteristics that are similar to the other transactions that economists observe. First, marriage is voluntary, and therefore it can be assumed that the parties expect that decision to raise their individual welfare above the level that they could attain if they remained single. Second, the parties compete in markets for the best mates.

Gary Becker argued that the economic approach can be used to explain the variety of marriage patterns around the world.[9] Although economics also can provide insights about same-sex unions and heterosexual relationships that do not result in legal marriage, here the primary focus is on why a man and a woman in the United States choose to marry. Fundamentally, people marry when they expect to be better off married than single. Economists recognize the strong bonds created by love and sexual attraction as part of what makes people better off, but they also have identified pragmatic forces that encourage people to marry.

Traditionally, the decision for a couple to live together was synonymous with the decision to get married. That is no longer the case. Before the broad availability of contraceptives, it was uncommon for couples to live together without being married because regular sexual relations usually resulted in their becoming parents. Social mores tended to require marriage as a prerequisite for regular sexual relations because children potentially could be a burden on society if the parents did not marry. Society responded by placing a significant social stigma on premarital sex.[10] With effective contraceptives, living together does not have to lead to children, and, therefore, it has often been separated from the decision to get married.[11]

Incentives to Live Together

A first step toward marriage is the recognition that a couple is better off living together than living on their own. There are advantages for people living together besides love and physical attraction, such as opportunities for economies of scale, specialization, and insurance, that do not necessarily make marriage attractive.

Economies of Scale

Households provide opportunities for economies of scale that are not available to someone living alone. The size of a comfortable house does not normally increase as much as the increase in the number of occupants; thus the cost per occupant falls as the number of occupants increases up to some point. A two-bedroom apartment is usually not twice as expensive as a one-bedroom apartment. In addition, some commodities consumed in a household are public goods, which are a special case of commodities with economies of scale: A *public good* has the characteristics that additional people can consume it at little or no additional cost, and people cannot easily be excluded from the enjoyment of the commodity. A *private good*, by way of contrast, is costly to provide to additional people, and people can be excluded from enjoying it. A television set can be a public good; an apple exemplifies a private good. Most households can reduce the number of these public goods relative to the number that they would have if the members were living on their own.

Gains from Specialization

Economists have also recognized that there are gains from specialization when people live together.[12] Specialization increases the welfare of individuals by expanding the commodities available to them. Economic analysis of consumer behavior traditionally focused on the acquisition of goods and services, but economists have come to recognize that individuals do not necessarily receive enjoyment from just the acquisition of goods and services—enjoyment comes from combining goods and services with time to produce commodities.[13] An individual does not receive enjoyment just from merely *buying* a compact disc, but from buying it, which requires money, and then listening to it, which requires time.[14] Commodities often can be produced using a variety of time-money combinations. A meal, for example, can consist of a dinner at an elegant restaurant and can cost many dollars and several hours of time. Alternatively, a meal can consist of a picnic in the country, which costs less money but more time. The enjoyment does not come just from buying the food, but from combining the food with time. Commodities produced at home can be an important component of individual welfare; these commodities can be time intensive, including home-cooked meals and an attractive lawn.

The production of these commodities benefits from specialization. We often observe that businesses increase their output and profits by specialization. Businesses gain from specialization that reduces the time lost as workers move between activities and that permits employees to develop the unique skills necessary to perform specific tasks faster. The same principle is appropriate for the production of commodities by consumers. When people specialize, they can become more efficient in the production of commodities. When people cook more frequently, they become better cooks.

The activities in which people specialize tend to be based on comparative advantage, which exists when two people have levels of productivity that vary among activities. Some people will have a comparative advantage in earning income; others will be more productive in domestic activities. On the average, men have earned and continue to earn higher incomes than women; in most households, it is still common for men to emphasize income earning, whereas women still handle the majority of domestic work.[15] In economics terms, they increase their specialization in domestic work.

The reason comparative advantage provides an incentive for men and women to increase their specialization within a relationship is illustrated in figure 3.1. Economists assume that, subject to the constraints they face, people attempt to

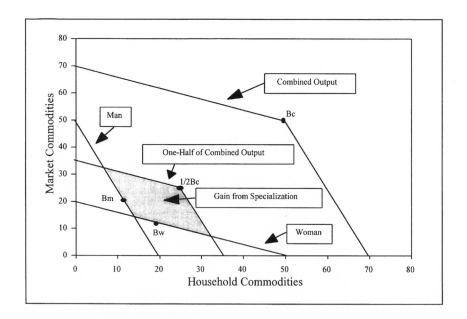

Fig. 3.1 The Advantages of Specialization

obtain the bundle of commodities that provides them with the highest level of welfare.[16] For simplicity, assume that there are only two types of commodities: (1) market commodities, which are income intensive, such as automobiles and houses; and (2) household commodities, which are time intensive, such as meals and gardening. Let us denominate the values of these commodities in dollars. Say the man has the potential by himself to produce either $50 of market commodities, $20 of household commodities, or a combination of the two; the woman has the potential by herself to produce either $20 of market commodities, $50 of household commodities, or a combination of the two. These combinations are called their *production possibility frontiers*. The man has a comparative advantage in the production of market commodities relative to household commodities and the reverse is true for the woman.

By working together and specializing in production, a man and a woman can increase their output beyond the level that is available to each functioning alone. If they specialize, their combined output is illustrated in figure 3.1 by the line labeled "Combined Output." They can produce $70 of market commodities, $70 of household commodities, or a combination of the two commodities. Because of specialization, the combined production possibility frontier is no longer a straight line. It is kinked. If the woman specializes in the production of household commodities and the man specializes in the production of market commodities, they can produce $50 of market commodities and $50 of household commodities, B_c.

So far, this example has illustrated production possibilities. To determine the actual production of the individuals on their own, we need to know their preferences. If it is assumed that both have approximately equal preferences for the two types of commodities, they would choose bundles that lie in approximately the middle of their production possibility frontiers at B_m and B_w. For example, the man's bundle, B_m, could be $20 of market commodities and $12 of household commodities. The woman's bundle, B_w, could be $12 of market commodities and $20 of household commodities. If each lives alone, they are forced to produce the commodities for which they have a comparative advantage as well as the commodities for which they have a comparative disadvantage.

They can both increase their welfare by specializing in production. To show how this occurs, figure 3.1 includes a line that represents one-half their combined output. Between the bundles on their individual production possibility frontiers and the bundles on the line representing one-half the combined output are the bundles of the commodities that are available to each member of a couple that are not available to them as individuals. If the couple has approximately equal preferences for market commodities and household commodities, they might choose to specialize completely and produce $50 of each, B_c. An equal division of that output between the man and the woman results in their each having $25 of each commodity, 1/2 B_c. One-half the combined output is more of both commodities than they each can produce if they live alone. They are both better off if they specialize in production and then exchange their outputs.

The discussion here assumes that men and women specialize in the production of either only market commodities or only household commodities during marriage. Both parties frequently can improve their welfare if they each produce both market and household commodities, so long as they specialize more than they would if they were living alone. As a practical matter, specialization by couples is seldom absolute:[17] men often provide services around the house, and many women work outside the home. Within a relationship, however, men and women have tended to increase their specialization compared with when they were living alone.

Limited Specialization

A couple might limit their specialization either because at least one party prefers flexibility or because both parties have similar capacities. By reducing the extent to which they specialize, they usually reduce the gains from the relationship. For example, if the two people described above considered living together, but expected to continue to produce the same bundles of commodities as before marriage, their combined output would be $32 of market commodities and $32 of household commodities. An equal division of this output would be $16 of each, which is less than the $25 of each that would be available to each of them through specialization. The man would have more household commodities than before, but fewer market commodities; the reverse would be true for the woman, leaving them uncertain about whether they would be better off living together or alone.

Many adults are finding that there are fewer gains from specialization as the opportunities available to men and to women have converged during this century. Higher wages and better employment opportunities have given many women alternatives outside the home that are similar to those of men. Meanwhile, men are capable of replacing some of the services traditionally provided by women through cleaning services and frozen food.

If people find either fewer opportunities or fewer incentives to specialize, then men's and women's production possibility frontiers become more similar. A reduction in the opportunities to specialize occurs as the earnings of men and women converge, for example.[18] Figure 3.2 portrays a man and a woman who have identical production possibility frontiers. Both have similar income-earning capacities and domestic productivities. Pooling their outputs results in double what they could produce by themselves. Half that combined output is the same amount that they could produce alone.

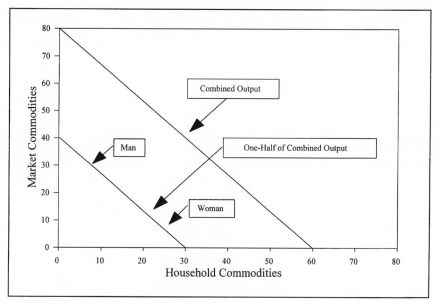

Fig. 3.2 A Relationship without Specialization

Insurance

The last reason that people benefit from living together is insurance. People generally do not like uncertainty, so they frequently buy insurance because they prefer certainty—a fire insurance premium—to uncertainty—having a house that has been destroyed by a fire. Economists call this characteristic of human behavior "risk aversion," concluding that increased certainty can contribute to people's welfare.[19] Because insurance cannot be purchased to cover all uncertain future events, people frequently have to make other arrangements to avoid uncertainty. People can accept a current known situation over an uncertain future. Many interpersonal relationships have that characteristic. A person might currently be having a satisfactory relationship with someone. If this relationship ended, would the next one be better, or would it be worse? How much effort will it take to adapt to a new relationship? If a person has a good job now, what will happen if he or she becomes unemployed or is forced to accept a lower-paying job? The person has excellent health now, but will someone be there to help if his or her health deteriorates? Because people must often face these questions, they can attempt to reduce future uncertainty by maintaining a current relationship.

In summary, people can increase their welfare by living together. These benefits follow from economies of scale, increased specialization, and insurance. So far we have been discussing the reasons why people live together. But why do they go a step further and marry?

Why People Marry

Although we have identified numerous reasons why adults benefit from living together, we have not established a clear reason—other than one based on romance—that would explain why they marry. Economists argue that some of the benefits from living together that we have identified are enhanced by a more formal, long-term arrangement that traditionally has been provided by marriage. Marriage is especially important if a couple decides to have children, but it can be a response to other, often psychological, inducements. Still, many adults want children, and children present substantial opportunities for a couple to enhance its welfare through economies of scale and specialization. In addition, marriage can be viewed as providing more substantial insurance than that available to couples who are living together.

Economies of Scale

From an economic perspective, children are a public good: They can be enjoyed by both parents at no more cost than if only one parent were present; and, if the relationship continues, it is difficult to exclude a parent from that enjoyment. Therefore, there are economies of scale if the parents are living together rather than apart. A more formal arrangement such as marriage increases the likelihood that the couple will continue to live together, thereby being able to take advantage of these important economies of scale.

Gains from Specialization

Often, increased specialization within a relationship can impose long-term costs on a party if the relationship is dissolved.[20] A couple can often avoid this type of specialization until they have children. They can maintain their careers while dividing the responsibilities within their household. Children change this situation by increasing the pressure for a couple to specialize within a relationship. The arrival of children usually results in one party, usually the mother, increasing the emphasis that she places on household activities. Mothers traditionally assumed primary responsibility for caring for children because their earnings usually were less than those of fathers. In addition, some have argued that women tend to develop a closer bond with their children.[21] The importance of the bond between a mother and her child is controversial because it is not clear whether it is biological or socially constructed.[22]

Within marriage in the United States, fathers have tended to specialize in income earning, and mothers have tended to specialize in home-based activities. The parents may be tempted to share the responsibility for child rearing equally. However, on closer inspection, most parents conclude that it is less costly to the couple for just one parent to alter his or her employment than for both to alter their employment. Higher-paying jobs often require unexpected overtime and travel. If both parents reject that type of employment, they may be worse off than if only one parent makes that choice and the other, if he or she is employed, accepts employment that accommodates child care. Lower average wages available to women frequently make the mother the lower-cost provider of child rearing.

The specialization that results from parenthood can have longer-lasting effects than those commonly associated with people living together. Although this specialization is usually in the best interest of the parents and their children while a relationship lasts, it can be revealed as costly if the relationship ends. Skills developed in one household may have little value in another relationship and even less value in the marketplace, leaving a spouse who has emphasized domestic work vulnerable at divorce. This can be a problem in a marriage of short duration, but it is particularly a concern in longer marriages. If a spouse specializes in income earning, that skill will be intact if the relationship ends. If that spouse is the husband, he would lose his share of the household commodities provided by the wife, but these commodities may have decreased in value after any children have grown up and left the home. During the relationship, the wife may have developed skills producing household commodities that do not have substantial value outside the relationship, and her income-earning capacity has deteriorated because of her working primarily at home. She may be worse off if the relationship is dissolved, compared with the situation she would have been in if she had never entered the relationship in the first place. Over the duration of a marriage, the potential contributions of both spouses created the incentive that was the basis for the marriage, but the asymmetry of their contributions can create incentives for men to dissolve their marriage later.[23] Traditionally, women, who emphasized domestic work, were reluctant to specialize unless they had the expectation of the relationship being of a long duration, and marriage was associated with that expectation.

The problems associated with acquiring specialized skills have been recognized by economists in a business setting: when businesses specialize, they often make long-term arrangements to protect themselves from having other firms take advantage of them through opportunistic behavior.[24] For example, a company might build a plant to produce a good that has value to only one buyer. After the construction of the plant, the buyer might be tempted to offer a price for the output of the plant that is only slightly higher than the direct cost of producing the good, a price inadequate to cover all the costs of production. The owner of the plant would be unhappy with that situation, but he would still be better off producing the good and receiving a price greater than the direct cost of production than not producing at all. When producers recognize that opportunistic behavior can occur, they tend to require a long-term contract before the construction of the plant to guarantee a price that covers all its costs. In situations in which these long-term contracts are difficult to draft and enforce, companies have found it attractive to combine all activities within the same firm through vertical integration.

Similar opportunistic behavior can occur within a marriage. Recognizing the potential asymmetry of the timing of the contributions of the parties during a marriage, the marriage laws in the United States historically attempted to create a long-term contract to protect the parties who specialized in household production. Although the fault divorce laws did not define marriage as a long-term contract, the effect of the fault grounds for divorce was to turn marriage into a long-term arrangement in which a spouse who specialized in household production could make that choice with the understanding that compensation would be required as an adjustment for the potential cost that she would incur if the marriage was dissolved.

Because the marriage agreement even under fault divorce was not easy to enforce, men and women have adapted to the problems associated with women specializing in household services in other ways. Lloyd Cohen argued that one way society has dealt with the value of the services provided by women being at an earlier phase of marriage than those provided by men is reflected in the relative ages of spouses.[25] Women tend to marry older men. The effect of this age gap is to make their contributions to marriage more contemporaneous. This increases the period during which women should expect to be widows, but it decreases the likelihood that their marriages will be dissolved. As the comparative advantages of men and women have been reduced and less specialization is found in marriage, the age gap between men and women at the time of their first marriage has fallen.[26] Although there are a variety of reasons why men and women live together, the desire for children—and the resulting incentives for increased specialization within the relationship—is probably the primary reason they marry.

The gains from specialization because of children have decreased as adults have decided that they want fewer children—and in some cases none. As the income available outside the home has increased, especially for women, the cost of children has also risen.[27] Either some income has to be sacrificed so that a parent can remain at home, or arrangements have to be made for child care services. Even professional child care may require at least one parent to accept a less attractive job to have a schedule that accommodates the child care. Higher incomes provide adults with more recreational options that often are restricted by children. Children can bring substantial enjoyment to their parents' lives, but so can a comfortable house, expensive meals, and foreign vacations. A couple may find that they have to make a trade-off between children and things that their earnings permit them to buy. With the lower benefits and higher costs of children, it is no surprise that people are electing to have fewer children, and an increasing number of couples are deciding not to have any.[28] Without children, gains from specialization by couples during marriage exist, but they are more limited and so is the attraction of marriage.[29]

Another trend has been increased specialization by women.[30] Instead of women working in the home to provide a variety of domestic commodities, men and women often purchase these commodities from people outside the family who are specialized in providing them. Some examples are child care and household cleaning services that are often purchased from others, especially other women. Although the ability to purchase these services from specialized women reduces the need for a family member to make a stronger commitment to some types of domestic work, the critical role of the parents in the care of infants places pressure on a parent to alter his or her career to provide those services in the home.[31]

Noncooperative Bargaining

Although a couple can gain from increased specialization by the spouses, the extent to which parties specialize within marriage is often the result of an informal bargaining process.[32] When spouses specialize within marriage, their contributions result in a variety of commodities. Some of these commodities are public goods that can be consumed by more than one person, whereas others are private goods that can only be consumed by one person. Children are a significant public good that can be enjoyed simultaneously by both parents, but there are numerous commodities that have public good characteristics, such as the family home and meals. Some of the family's resources also can be used to acquire private goods, such as clothing and health club memberships, that are enjoyed by only one family member.

Economists have argued that within a family an informal bargaining process occurs that results in the distribution of the household's potential output between public and private goods as well as in the allocation of those goods among the family members. The early literature focused on the spouse who had the better opportunities if there was a divorce—frequently it was perceived to be the man— receiving a disproportional share of the household's output. The more recent literature has focused on this bargaining process resulting in a suboptimal level of output[33] that can occur if one spouse contributes less to the marriage, causing the other to respond by also contributing less. The primary wage earner might reject opportunities for additional income from working overtime, thereby causing the spouse working primarily in the home to respond by reducing the quality of the home-cooked meals. Another trade-off can occur if a spouse attempts to obtain more private goods from a marriage and causes the other spouse to react in a similar manner. Rather than agreeing to remodel the house (a public good), one spouse might buy an expensive set of golf clubs (a private good). This can cause the other spouse to respond by buying other private goods, such as clothing. Often as purchases are shifted from public goods to private ones, overall household welfare is reduced.

Because the spouses may be reluctant to discuss their concerns and motives, this analytical framework is called a noncooperative bargaining model. Spouses are assumed to recognize the reciprocity of their actions during marriage. Positive actions may generate positive responses, whereas negative ones induce negative responses. The dynamics of the relationship will determine the path that is taken. The threat considered by the spouses may be not divorce but less cooperation, which results in fewer commodities for the family. The more durable the marriage is perceived, the more likely spouses are to make sacrifices for which the reciprocal benefits will only occur in the future. These sacrifices can be an important source of the gains from marriage. In extreme cases, this noncooperative bargaining process can deteriorate to the point where there is so little cooperation and specialization that the spouses have reduced the gains from this marriage to the point that dissolution is preferable to a continuation of the marriage. At least one spouse concludes that he or she will be better off single than in this marriage. Therefore, it is important that the legal environment encourages specialization and cooperation.

Insurance

Another anticipated benefit from marriage being a long-term relationship is insurance against an uncertain future.[34] Although specialization and economies of scale are important sources of gains for married couples who want children, insurance can be important both for those couples as well as for those that do not want children.[35] By its most fundamental nature, insurance requires someone who has not incurred a cost to compensate someone else for the cost that he or she has incurred. With fire insurance, it is the insured party's house that burned down, not the insurance company's office. Without a long-term agreement, the insurance company probably would prefer to return its premium and walk away from its obligation. A similar situation can occur with relationships. Two people might informally agree that they will be there for each other in sickness and in health, but when one of them gets severely ill, the other might want to shift that responsibility to someone else if there are no strong emotional or legal ties. Marriage formalizes that emotional and legal obligation, increasing the likelihood that someone will be there if a spouse has unexpected medical, emotional, or financial problems.[36]

Marriage also provides some insurance against the potential costs of spouses altering their career plans for the benefit of their relationship. We have already discussed that parenthood frequently requires at least one parent to alter the career that he or she otherwise would have pursued. A similar adjustment can occur even without children. Seldom does a relationship permit both parties to pursue the careers that they would have pursued without the relationship. Frequently, promotions entail a relocation that requires other parties to make a sacrifice either in their career or in their lifestyle. Another factor can be an income effect. As the incomes of the parties increase, they may decide that they want a more leisurely lifestyle. Just as with parenting responsibilities, it may not make sense for both parties to adjust their careers for increased leisure. One may have a high-paying job that provides tremendous self-fulfillment for that party, whereas the other has a stressful job that no longer is rewarding. It may be in the couple's collective best interest for the party with the less-rewarding job to find more flexible—and potentially lower paying—employment that accommodates the other party's career, thereby increasing their collective welfare. Rather than both spending much of their weekends catching up on domestic activities that could not be accomplished during the week, the party with the more flexible job could accomplish more of those activities during the week, freeing up time for both of them to enjoy their weekends. However, any limiting of a career can have costs later if the relationship is dissolved. Marriage can provide some insurance against those future costs for the person who limits a career.

Last, although it is more psychological in nature, economists have recognized the gains from increased predictability. This predictability is relevant for psychological outcomes as well as for financial outcomes. A strong commitment by spouses to each other has been shown to be an important source of satisfaction in marriage.[37] However, this commitment can be psychologically costly if it is ultimately discovered that one spouse's commitment was not reciprocated. Marriage provides insurance that encourages this commitment by both parties.

Evidence of the Economic Explanation for Marriage

Tests of the economic analysis of marriage conclude that marriage is a rational choice predicated especially on the gains from the specialization of labor. Three factors—the ratio of the sexes, the potential returns to marriage, and the cost of divorce—have been shown to explain the variation in the percentage of married women across different political divisions in the United States.[38] First, based on supply and demand, the proportion of women married is positively related to the men/women ratio. Second, comparative advantage was likely to increase as the ratio of men's wages rose relative to women's wages. For persons over age twenty-five, the percentage of women married in a state was positively related to the men/women wage ratio. This relationship was not statistically significant for people under age twenty-four. In other words, young people are less likely to marry based on a decision to increase the commodities that will be available to them. But people who marry when they are young have higher divorce rates, indicating that they are less likely to make the best long-term decision when they marry. Marriages based on substantial long-term gains from the comparative advantage of the parties can be expected to last. Finally, the marriage rate increases as the difficulty of obtaining a divorce decreases for people under age twenty-four, but not for older people. If the cost of correcting a bad marriage is high, young people will hesitate to marry in the first place.[39]

Gender and the Gains from Marriage

The economists' emphasis on a couple's gaining from increased specialization based on comparative advantage can be interpreted as economists' condoning and encouraging a division of labor based on gender. The present analysis attempts to identify why certain patterns have existed, rather than to place a value judgment on a particular pattern. Marriage is an attractive institution for the spouses if both expect to be better off married than single. When women were confronted with low wages and limited employment opportunities, marriage with increased specialization in household production was a rational choice for essentially all adult women.[40] Because of women's willingness to specialize, marriage was also attractive for most men who often worked long hours at a job. Because the goal of the spouses was to increase their welfare, both forms of work traditionally have been important. Meals required money provided by the husband and time contributed by the wife. Both inputs were essential; so, from an economic perspective, there was no hierarchy of values placed on the spouses' work. Economists would not agree with a common conclusion that time spent earning an income is more valuable than time expended on domestic work. As the incomes of women increase relative to men, we would expect to have more couples in which the woman will have the higher income, and comparative advantage will encourage the man to increase his emphasis on domestic activities during the relationship. However, we have also noted that as the opportunities available to men and women converge, the gains from specialization decrease, as do the incentives for a couple to marry.

In summary, economists note that marriage is not the only choice for adults. Because of economies of scale, specialization, and insurance, people gain from living together but not necessarily marrying. Marriage is usually associated with children, who magnify the gains from economies of scale and specialization.

Insurance also provides an incentive for people to marry. Changes occur. The increase in women's wages and opportunities, the expansion in the availability of labor-saving devices in the home, and the decline in the demand for children have reduced men's and women's comparative advantage and, therefore, the gains from marriage for some adults. Economic analysis concludes that the major reason people marry is the welfare gain that they expect from that state. Not all marriages are successful in fulfilling that expectation. Some end in divorce. As a large percentage of people who divorce remarry, divorce cannot be seen as a rejection of marriage so much as a rejection of a particular mate.[41] In the next section, the search for the best mate will be used to analyze the decision to divorce.

THE ECONOMICS OF DIVORCE

A major influence on the attraction of marriage and a family is the rules governing marriage, especially the conditions under which it can be dissolved. Changing conditions can affect the stability of marriage and the laws that control its dissolution. Marriage has become less stable, as is evidenced by the increase in the divorce rate. Certainly, divorces occur when at least one party to a marriage no longer wants to continue being married to his or her spouse for a variety of reasons that can include a decline in physical attraction and unacceptable behavior. Still, it does not appear that these forces can explain the substantial increase in the divorce rate over past decades. From an economic perspective, a divorce occurs when at least one spouse decides that there is no distribution of the future gains from that marriage that will make him or her better off compared with the opportunities outside that marriage.[42] Two people marry when both anticipate that they will be better off married than single, with the choice of a particular spouse the result of a search process. Sometimes the search that culminates in marriage does not produce the results that were anticipated. The change in the anticipated gains from marriage can be due to various situations, of which economists have focused on two: (1) unanticipated outcomes or (2) the asymmetry of the spouses' contributions.

The Search for a Spouse

The choice by an individual to marry is the result of a search that continues as long as the benefit exceeds the cost. The question is always whether the individual should accept a current candidate or look for a better one. The expected benefit from continuing to search equals the probability of finding a better mate multiplied by the expected increase in welfare from that better mate. The cost of continuing to search for a better mate is the sum of the money, the time, and the emotional effort of searching plus any welfare foregone by remaining single rather than marrying an available mate. The welfare gains from marriage may be available from several potential spouses. Even after marriage, there can remain a question as to whether the current spouse is the best mate. The decision to marry a particular person is made with some uncertainty.

Uncertain Outcomes

A divorce can be caused by the uncertain outcomes that can occur during marriage. People usually marry with the expectation that their marriage is a lifelong commitment, but at least one party can decide at a future date that he or she would be better off outside that marriage. In the seminal work on this topic, Gary Becker, Elizabeth Landes, and Robert Michael concluded that the probability of divorce depends on two factors: (1) the expected gain from marriage and (2) the distribution of the unexpected outcomes.[43] The probability of divorce is smaller the greater the expected gain from marriage and the smaller the variability in the outcomes during marriage. People who do not want to specialize and who do not appreciate the commodities made available by their spouses do not gain very much from marriage. Even if they marry, the marriage is vulnerable. On the other hand, if a couple marries based on certain expectations such as continued good health, a major change in the health of one spouse can increase the likelihood of divorce.

Gains from Marriage

Certain factors have been identified as influencing the amount of the gains from marriage. For example, the increase in specialization during marriage that often accompanies the production of children reduces the probability of dissolution. The more people commit themselves to specialized roles, the more they gain from marriage and the more they lose from divorce. And the more they find that they are compatible with their present spouse, the more likely they are to choose to specialize. Less specialization during marriage increases the probability of divorce.

Variation in Outcomes

Other factors influence the success of the search process. A better search produces a more predictable outcome during marriage. The people who spend more time and energy on their search will be more likely to find the most desirable mate. For example, people who marry when they are younger than average have significantly higher probabilities of divorce. The amount of search also will vary with the cost of search. For example, the costs of search are higher in isolated areas than in urban areas.

A larger deviation between actual and expected outcomes during marriage, such as a significant change in the earnings or the health of the spouses, will raise the probability of dissolution. Another critical outcome for many couples is the quality of their realtionship. If someone enters marriage with the expectation of establishing a close, intimate relationship with his or her spouse and if the quality of the relationship does not meet that expectation, then the marriage becomes vulnerable and the likelihood of divorce increases. These marriage-threatening outcomes are less likely to occur when the spouses are better matched in attributes such as religion and education. A marriage is also less likely to be dissolved the longer it lasts because people tend to discover their mistakes fairly early. But people also tend to repeat their mistakes, so that the probability of dissolution is higher in subsequent marriages.[44]

Asymmetric Contributions

Another potential cause of divorce is the asymmetry of the timing of the contributions of the spouses during marriage, which was discussed earlier. During marriage, it has been common for the man to place more emphasis on earning income and for the woman to shift her emphasis toward the production of household commodities. Initially, both the husband and the wife are better off. But when their children grow up and leave the home, the value to the man of the household commodities provided by this woman may be reduced, even as the value of the market commodities that the man brings to the marriage are likely to have increased. He may decide that he is better off dissolving this marriage. The goal of the man may not be to be single so much as to find a new and more desirable spouse at this point in his life. With a higher income, he may feel that the pool of potential mates is larger than when he married for the first time. Of course, this outcome is also the result of a flawed search. If the search for a spouse by a woman led her to expect this type of behavior from a man, she would have hesitated to marry him in the first place.

Although uncertain outcomes and asymmetrical contributions can lead to a desire for a divorce, the ultimate decision to seek a divorce is influenced by a comparison of the cost and the benefit of dissolving the marriage. The demand for divorce will increase if the cost falls or the benefit rises. One cost of divorce is the loss of the commodities produced by the spouse. An additional cost is the emotional strain and financial transfers required to dissolve the marriage. When a spouse who does not want to dissolve the marriage has legal or social protection, part of the cost will be the incentives, such as additional property or child custody, necessary to convince that spouse not to exercise those rights. The cost shifts over time with changes in laws or social expectations. No-fault divorce significantly lowered the cost of divorce to divorcing spouses by reducing the legal protection of spouses who did not want to dissolve their marriage. The benefits of divorce—being single or marrying a different spouse—also change over time.

The Incentive to Specialize in Household Production

A reduction in the incentives for spouses to increase their specialization during marriage reduces the gains from marriage, thereby, raising the likelihood of divorce. The incentive for people to increase their specialization in household production during marriage is in part based on the expected compensation if the marriage is dissolved. Elizabeth Landes found that in states that prohibit alimony there is a lower rate of marriage and a reduced marital fertility rate than there are in states that do not restrict alimony awards.[45] People marry with certain expectations. A change in the grounds for divorce has a different impact on people already married, under a presumption of the earlier laws, than it does on those people who marry with the expectation that divorces will be governed by the new laws. Historically, spouses, usually wives, increased their specialization in household production during marriage with the expectation that the fault grounds for divorce provided substantial protection against their marriage being dissolved against their will. A change in that contract through a change in the grounds for dissolution came as a surprise to those married women, and they found themselves worse off after divorce than they would have been under fault divorce. Unmarried women contemplating marriage incorporate the new divorce laws in their decision making. They will be less likely to marry and certainly less likely to specialize in household production during marriage.[46]

In summary, people marry when both think that they will be better off married. They divorce when at least one spouse concludes that that premise is not true. The legal grounds for divorce have a strong influence on the decision to dissolve the marriage because they influence the benefit and the cost of divorce.

THE EFFECT OF MARRIAGE ON WEALTH

Decisions during a marriage affect the wealth of the parties. This can be particularly important at divorce. The courts attempt to recognize these effects through the financial arrangements at the dissolution of a marriage, including property settlements, spousal support, and child support; but their decisions are limited by statutory restrictions.[47] The community property system provides an illustration of the factors involved.

The community property system has become increasingly attractive to legal reformers because it treats marriage as a partnership.[48] In an unequivocal community property system, at divorce each spouse recovers his or her separate property, and their community property is divided equally. (As mentioned before, community property is all property that is not statutorily defined as either spouse's separate property; separate property is property that the parties brought into the marriage or that came to them during the marriage by will, bequest, or devise.)

A marriage affects the wealth of the parties in ways that go beyond the property commonly recognized by the courts in practically all jurisdictions. The courts have traditionally recognized physical items such as houses and financial items such as shares of common stock as property; but for a meaningful economic analysis, this definition of property is too narrow.[49] The effect of marriage on the most important property possessed by most people—human capital—has not been recognized by the courts in a systematic way.[50]

The items that courts have defined as property are what economists call assets.[51] An asset has value because it will provide a stream of future returns. No one would pay a positive price for an automobile that was going to be destroyed a moment later, nor would anyone pay a positive price for a share of common stock in a corporation that was never expected to produce any profits or to pay any dividends. An individual's wealth consists of the claims that he or she has on future income flows. That wealth can consist of an automobile providing services that could be converted into a market value, stocks and bonds that will provide dividends and interest, and the earnings based on human capital that he or she can expect in the future. In contrast to a house, a share of common stock, or a bond, the future earnings from human capital cannot be sold. Conceptually, however, these assets are all property.

How and When Do We Acquire Human Capital?

To understand the effect of marriage on human capital, it is important to have an understanding of how and when human capital is acquired. An individual's wealth can be increased through investments. An individual has the innate ability to generate earnings based on natural intelligence and physical strength; but any increase in earnings beyond that level is a result of the investments that are made in the individual. These investments occur in a formal educational environment or on the job; they result in either general or specific skills; and they are financed either by the recipient or by others. This process can be illustrated by formal education, in which different investments that produce human capital are often interconnected. Learning college biology may not result in a substantial increase in an individual's future earnings, but the medical training that it may permit can substantially increase the individual's future earnings. The earnings of a medical doctor, therefore, should be attributed to both his or her medical education and the preceding investments in education that made admission to medical school possible. Investments that result in a professional obtaining, for example, above-average earnings are interrelated and extend over his or her life.

The funding of the investments in human capital can be made by the individual who is the beneficiary of the investments or by others. The cost of an investment in education is the direct expenditures such as tuition and books and the indirect costs due to the individual's sacrificing earnings. The individual will usually personally incur the cost of the sacrificed earnings, but the direct costs are often incurred by others—the direct cost of elementary and secondary education, for example, is usually provided by parents or taxpayers. When the individual reaches an age at which employment is available, the proportion of the cost of the investment incurred by the recipient as sacrificed earnings increases.

At some point, the individual may have to incur both the direct and the indirect costs of the investment in education. This is commonly the case with graduate education, and the question then becomes whether to fund the direct cost through employment or to shift it to the future through borrowing. The amount of borrowing will depend on the cost of the funds and the expected return: the lower the cost or the higher the return, the larger the amount of the loan.[52] The usual criterion for choosing the source of a loan is the one with the lowest cost. Funding by the family or the spouse of the student increases the student's standard of living during the educational period without a corresponding need to make payments later. Usually this form of funding is not essential to obtaining education, but simply reduces the future burden incurred during the educational process. Except for a few high-cost private universities, the greatest impediment to obtaining access to high-quality professional education is probably not the direct cost of the education, but the difficulty of gaining admission. The ability to gain admission is the result of earlier investments; and after admission, the most substantial cost of graduate education is usually the earnings sacrificed by the student.

It is important to recognize that the amount of human capital acquired by an individual is determined by the investments that have been made in the individual. The value of the human capital is based on the future earnings that it will produce. Finally, human capital is accumulated over an extensive period.

The Effect of Marriage on Human Capital

Conceptually, human capital is similar to the assets that the courts traditionally have recognized as property in financial settlements in conjunction with divorce proceedings. At the dissolution of a marriage, the courts have tended to identify property as either separate or marital. Normally, all property acquired by either spouse before marriage or by will, bequest, or devise during marriage is his or her separate property. In contrast, the property acquired by the spouses during the marriage belongs to both of them. From an economic perspective, the critical distinction between separate property and marital property is the timing of the investments that created the property. Separate property is created outside the marriage; marital property is created by the combined activities of the spouses during the marriage.

Human capital can be evaluated within that same framework. At any moment, an individual has a stream of expected future earnings based on the investments that have already taken place in him or her. These earnings are net of any future investments, and the value of this net earnings stream is the individual's human capital. The human capital that individuals possess at their marriage is separate property, just as much as any stocks they owned. If they had not acquired an education, but instead they and their families had taken the cost of the education and invested those funds in stocks and bonds, the courts would have no difficulty treating those financial assets as separate property.

The human capital possessed by an individual at marriage can be illustrated by the example of a medical student. A third-year medical student who marries already has human capital that is based on an anticipated net earnings stream. The value of the human capital has little relation to the medical student's current earnings. Admittedly, some additional investments, such as the completion of medical school, may be required to receive the future earnings. Usually, these additional investments will be small compared with the investments that have already occurred. For a medical doctor, the major increase in his or her anticipated earnings occurred when he or she entered medical school. Medical doctors obtain higher earnings than college graduates who majored in premed courses but who did not go to medical school. The essential investments had already occurred when the student entered medical school, and the probability is high that he or she will finish that education. There remains concern about class work and the financing of medical school expenses, but these are probably a lesser concern than getting admitted in the first place.

Given that the median age of first marriage is in the middle twenties for both men and women, the investments in human capital that usually occur before marriage will be so large and essential compared with the investments after marriage that an individual's human capital is best treated as separate property. When the investments after the marriage are substantial, it may be appropriate to treat the additional human capital as marital property. The courts have used the concept of "professional goodwill" to attempt to describe the increase in the earnings of professionals during marriage.[53] In addition, when the earnings from one spouse's human capital are used to fund an increase in the human capital of the other spouse through education, an adjustment is appropriate at divorce for that funding plus any accrued interest.[54]

Marriage can permit income-earning spouses to increase their specialization in that role, enabling those spouses to acquire human capital that would not have been acquired without their marriage. That is probably not a common situation, because many jobs do not permit greater specialization due to their requiring a set work period, such as forty hours per week. Even when a job is flexible, a single person can often specialize as much as a married person. In most cases, the gain from marriage for the income-earning spouses occurs because of reductions in the time needed to provide household commodities for themselves, rather than a higher income through job specialization. During marriage, income-earning spouses normally receive more household commodities, such as meals and house cleaning, than they provided themselves before marriage. In addition, they can receive additional household commodities, such as children, that were frequently unavailable to them as single individuals.[55]

The same analysis can be used to illustrate the situation in which an individual's human capital decreases in value during marriage. Each individual has an anticipated net earnings stream and, therefore, an amount of human capital when he or she marries. The value of this human capital is based partly on the expectation of future investments, such as those provided by on-the-job training, that complement the prior investments. The future investments may be small compared with the prior investments, but they can have a significant effect on the individual's future earnings and on his or her human capital. If these investments are not made, a person's human capital will decline in value.

Thus human capital can decline in value due to decisions made during marriage. It is common for couples to decide that they will benefit if one of them reduces his or her participation in the labor force to increase his or her specialization in household production. Those individuals sacrifice opportunities for maintaining and increasing their future earnings stream, the loss of which reduces the value of those individuals' human capital.[56] For example, with normal additional training in a chosen field, a married woman might expect to have an annual income of $50,000 at age thirty-five. Instead, she leaves the labor force to work at home and does not receive the additional training. For various reasons, that opportunity may never exist again. If she returns to the labor force after a divorce at age thirty-five, she can then only earn $20,000. The specialization in the production of household commodities has reduced her human capital and her wealth. The reduction in the value of her wealth can be calculated by comparing the stream of net earnings that she can expect after the divorce with the earnings that she could have expected to earn if she had never left the labor force.[57]

In summary, marriage can affect the wealth of the parties in different ways. By saving, the couple can acquire physical and financial assets. The trend has been for the courts to divide these assets equally at the time of a divorce, but courts have tended to ignore the effect of marriage on the human capital of the spouses.

Individuals possess human capital at the time of their marriage based on their anticipated earnings, which is best treated as their separate property. If their anticipated earnings increased during the marriage, additional human capital has been created, which logically should be treated as marital property. Alternatively, if a spouse's anticipated earnings decreased during the marriage, the effect is a reduction in that person's human capital and, therefore, a basis for compensation if the marriage is dissolved.[58] Much of the injustice since the introduction of no-fault divorce is due to the courts' not recognizing the effect of marriage on the spouses' human capital, especially when a spouse limits a career for the benefit of the family.

Overall, no-fault divorce has had detrimental effects of which one has been a deterioration in the financial condition of spouses who emphasized domestic work during marriage. How is it possible that laws were passed that are so adverse to the interests of spouses who work at home? More broadly, why were laws passed that are detrimental to so many people by discouraging spouses' commitment to their family? In the next section, we will look at why the political process created those laws.

THE ECONOMICS OF THE POLITICAL PROCESS

Since 1970, there has been a radical change in the laws establishing the grounds for divorce. Between 1970 and 1985, all the states enacted statutes either making irretrievable breakdown or incompatibility the sole ground for divorce or adding one or both of them to the existing fault grounds. These laws were written and approved by the members of state legislatures.

We often hear elected officials called public servants implying that they base their decisions on a broad vision of the public interest. However, consistent with the basic economic framework is the assumption that if people make decisions in markets based on their self-interest, then it is just as appropriate to analyze the behavior of elected officials from that perspective.

The contrast between the goals of self-interest and the public interest is important for understanding the reasons why no-fault divorce statutes were passed in the United States. The use of economic tools to investigate the issues usually investigated by political scientists, called Public Choice,[59] assumes that the primary goal of elected officials is to be elected and to remain in office. To obtain that goal requires votes, which candidates can attract in two ways: (1) they can vote for specific pieces of legislation voters favor, or (2) they can collect the funds necessary to obtain voter recognition through advertising. Economists have shown that voters do not bother to be very well informed about the people for whom they vote,[60] so name recognition can be particularly important for candidates. The advertising required to generate name recognition costs money and necessitates obtaining financial contributions.

David Friedman uses the Public Choice framework to make three predictions about the behavior of elected officials:[61] First, they will favor concentrated interest groups over dispersed interest groups. Second, they will prefer more efficient to less efficient transfers. Last, they prefer transfers disguised as something else. These predictions can be illustrated with cattle ranchers. It is much easier for concentrated groups—such as cattle ranchers—to organize than it is for dispersed groups—such as beef eaters. The concentrated groups are more likely to vote for candidates for public office based on the candidates' views or record on narrow issues. In addition, these concentrated groups can be more easily organized to provide financial support for the elected officials who support their views. These concentrated groups want to be the beneficiaries of the political process, but they do not want to cause the wealth transfers generated by the political process to elicit an adverse response that would occur if large costs were imposed on other members of society. Therefore, among the alternate ways that they could be benefited by the political process, they have incentives to choose the least expensive. For example, cattle ranchers might receive similar benefits from government programs that restrict the importation of beef or those that provide subsidized grazing on federal land. Public Choice predicts that they would choose the program that imposes the smaller cost on consumers and taxpayers. Last, although the politicians want the ranchers to know that they, the ranchers, have benefited, neither group wants the consumers and the taxpayers to recognize the costs. Often the program chosen to benefit a special interest group will be presented to the voters, who do not have incentives to make a thorough review of the facts, as a reaction to unfair trade practices. The beneficiaries of the program have incentives to understand it better, and they recognize that they have benefited.

In the next chapter, I will use the Public Choice approach to examine the rapid passage of no-fault divorce statutes that turned out to be detrimental to the welfare of many people and especially divorced women and their children. There is no easy answer to why these laws were passed by legislatures so quickly; but as would be predicted by economists, the role of special interest groups, especially divorced men and self-interested politicians, was of particular importance. In addition, we will observe that no-fault was disguised as something different from what it actually was, and it was sold as being desirable for society at large while being fairer to married and divorced women.

Legislatures pass laws that dictate how people should act under different circumstances. When people have disagreements about the law, they can either negotiate a settlement or litigate their dispute before a court. Divorce is no exception: a divorce can be obtained through a negotiated settlement or through litigation. The change in the grounds for divorce from fault to no-fault had a significant change in the incentive for people to either settle or litigate, the most important result being a reduction in the negotiating power of spouses who did not want a divorce, potentially because they had emphasized work in the home during marriage. In the next section, I discuss these issues from an economic perspective.

THE ECONOMICS OF NEGOTIATION AND LITIGATION

Economists conclude that individuals decide either to settle a dispute or to litigate it based on the expected costs and benefits of the alternatives, with the incentive to settle a dispute increasing as the outcome of litigation becomes more predictable.[62] The incentives to settle or to litigate in divorce proceedings have some unique traits because of the role of the state: Because the state was a party to a marriage, it also has to be a party to a divorce. The courts will only grant a divorce when specific procedures and standards have been met. Negotiated settlements were particularly important during the period when the grounds for divorce were based on fault because the outcome of litigation was reasonably predictable. One of the spouses had to be at fault, but spouses opposed to divorce were unlikely to make it easy to prove that they were at fault. Therefore, it was difficult for individuals to dissolve a marriage when their spouse was unwilling to cooperate. Litigation then, was not only expensive, but was unlikely to be successful; and a divorce was usually the result of a negotiated settlement, with evidence being produced to conform to the legal standards.

A desire by both parties to negotiate a settlement is no guarantee that an agreement will be reached. A necessary condition for a settlement is that the result each spouse would receive is better than each expects to receive under any other circumstances. Settlement negotiations will fail when, for example, the minimum offer the wife is willing to accept to cooperate in dissolving the marriage is greater than the maximum offer the husband is willing to pay.

Under fault divorce, the negotiations that resulted in the divorce included the custodial and the financial arrangements that were part of the divorce. The importance of these negotiations changed dramatically with the introduction of no-fault divorce, when the cooperation of the "innocent" party was no longer required. A divorce could be obtained in many jurisdictions by the unilateral action of one spouse. The emphasis in divorce proceedings then shifted from the grounds for the divorce to the custodial and financial arrangements. The range of issues subject to negotiation was reduced. With less negotiating power in the hands of the unwilling party, the minimum compensation acceptable to that party and the maximum compensation offered by the other would be expected to decrease.

Another factor that changed with the shift from fault to no-fault divorce was transaction costs. Influencing whether an agreement could be reached were the costs of settlement incurred by the parties that did not result in a transfer from one to the other. Financial and emotional costs incurred in negotiating a divorce reduced the resources available for transfer and, therefore, the likelihood that an agreement would be reached. With outcomes that were more predictable, no-fault divorce reduced these transaction costs, thereby increasing the likelihood that negotiations would be successful.

The new environment increased the importance of the legal rules that controlled these arrangements. Because under fault divorce the custodial and financial arrangements were usually part of the negotiated settlements, the existing legal standards had not often been the subject of attack as conditions changed. With the introduction of no-fault divorce, there were some changes in the legal rules at dissolution. Fault became much less relevant in determining child custody, and rationale for alimony changed from need to rehabilitation.[63] Differences of opinion about how those new and newly emphasized rules applied in a specific case increased the likelihood of litigation. Similarly, it is common for the frequency of litigation to increase when the legal rules change, as there often is initially some uncertainty about the effect of the law on final outcomes. Thus, more litigation on financial issues could be anticipated after the introduction of no-fault divorce until the legal rules on the financial arrangements became less ambiguous.[64]

Gary Becker argued that the change in the legal grounds for divorce would be expected to change the financial settlements at divorce, but not the divorce rate.[65] If couples contemplating divorce can easily bargain with each other, they may be just as likely to divorce under no-fault divorce as under fault divorce. Becker also argued that although a change in the rules would not change the incentives to reach a negotiated settlement, it would change the bargaining power of the parties, and thus he expected the introduction of no-fault divorce to reduce the financial settlements received by wives.[66]

Some proponents of the reform of the fault divorce laws—especially divorced men—felt that married women had too much negotiating power under fault divorce. They argued that the outcomes of the negotiations were unfair to men and the outcomes under no-fault divorce would be fairer to all parties. The courts' ignoring of some of the other costs of divorce under no-fault divorce would not support those arguments. Because of this loss of negotiating power for women in a divorce under no-fault divorce, fault divorce may have been what economists call a second-best solution to the problems associated with dissolving a marriage.

THE ECONOMICS OF THE SECOND-BEST

Because of the problems with no-fault divorce, fault divorce may have been a second-best solution. Economists are interested in the conditions necessary for efficient outcomes—those with the largest net benefits. If one condition necessary for a desirable outcome cannot be fulfilled, then the best attainable situation—the second-best—can only be achieved by departing from all the other optimal conditions. This principle can be illustrated with competitive markets, which are held in high regard by economists for allocating society's scarce resources efficiently. Efficiency calls for goods to be produced so long as the incremental benefit exceeds the incremental cost. But not all market transactions are efficient. When a production process creates external effects, such as pollution, social welfare will be increased by reducing production below the level chosen by competitive producers. At the competitive level of output, the cost to society, including the cost of the pollution, exceeds the benefit, and social welfare would be improved by reducing output. Often this can be accomplished by forcing the producers to recognize the full cost of their actions—the reduction in output could be accomplished with a tax on pollution. A tax may not be possible, however, and there may be no other way to deal with the pollution. Then society may be better off with a monopolistic producer, who has market power and, therefore, increases prices and reduces output—and pollution—below the level of the competitive producers. The best solution would be competition and a pollution tax; if that is not possible, the second-best solution is a decrease in both pollution and competition.

The divorce laws can be viewed similarly. The most desirable divorce laws might make it easy to obtain a divorce when the marriage relationship has irretrievably broken down, while making arrangements to divide all the costs of the dissolution between the spouses. If it is difficult to identify and to quantify the costs of dissolution that frustrate the second goal, then it might be better to not enact laws that permit the first: if the best outcome is unavailable, the second-best outcome might be to continue the fault grounds for a divorce with the understanding that divorce is available, but only after a negotiated settlement. The preferred long-term solution, however, should force the couple to recognize the full costs of divorce with a divorce only occurring when the net benefits of divorce are positive.

CONCLUSION

In this chapter, I have introduced the economic principles that can be used to more clearly understand the introduction and the effects of no-fault divorce. People can gain from living together without marriage. Marriage occurs when two people go one step further and recognize that they will benefit from a long-term relationship. The gains from marriage flow from economies of scale in consumption, from the parties assuming more specialized roles, and from insurance—all of which can benefit from a long-term arrangement such as marriage. Specialization becomes particularly important if a couple decides to have children, but it can result in an uncompensated cost to the party who specializes in household production if the marriage is dissolved. Divorce, which usually occurs when the parties' expectations about marriage are not realized, as well as marriage, can have substantial effects on the welfare of the parties. The courts have not been able to accurately identify and quantify these effects. Particularly visible has been a narrow definition of the property that is affected by marriage and divorce, partly because under fault divorce most divorces with substantial property were negotiated and the courts were not often asked to address the issue of the appropriate definition of property.

I have argued that the traditional narrow definition of property that has been applied under no-fault divorce has resulted, at divorce, in a deterioration in the welfare of spouses who emphasize domestic work during marriage. Their response to this situation during marriage often has reduced the welfare of many other family members. In the next chapter, I review the development of no-fault divorce in California, using the analysis of Public Choice and the second-best to present new insights into that development.

NOTES

1.   Much of the initial work was done by Gary S. Becker. See *Human Capital,* 3d ed. (Chicago: University of Chicago Press, 1993); *The Economic Approach to Human Behavior* (Chicago: University of Chicago Press, 1976); and *A Treatise of the Family,* enl. ed. (Cambridge, MA: Harvard University Press, 1991). For a discussion of economics as applied to a broad variety of human actions, see Victor R. Fuchs, *How We Live: An Economic Perspective on Americans from Birth to Death* (Cambridge, MA: Harvard, 1983).

2.   Fuchs, *How We Live,* 12.

3.   Fuchs, *How We Live*, provides numerous examples.

4.   Karen Peterson, "Shoring Up Marriage," USA TODAY, July 21, 1998, D1–2.

5.   Both George Bush and Bill Clinton in their presidential acceptance speeches at the 1992 conventions of the Republican and Democratic parties invoked the need for a greater emphasis on the family. George Bush, A New Crusade to Reap the Rewards of Our Global Victory, delivered at the Republican National Convention, Houston, Texas, August 20, 1992; and Bill Clinton, Acceptance Address, delivered at the Democratic National Convention, New York, New York, July 16, 1992.

6.   The social exchange framework was pioneered by the social psychologists John Thibaut and Harold Kelly and the sociologists George Homans and Peter Blau. For example, see John W. Thibaut and Harold H. Kelly, *The Social Psychology of Groups* (New York: John Wiley & Sons, 1959); George C. Homans, *Social Behavior: Its Elementary Forms* (New York: Harcourt, Brace & World, 1961); and Peter M. Blau, *Exchange and Power in Social Life* (New York: John Wiley & Sons, 1964). Although each theorist presents a slightly different perspective, all share common assumptions that would be recognized by economists. F. Ivan Nye, "Choice, Exchange, and the Family," in *Contemporary Theories about the Family,* ed. Wesley R. Burr, Reuben Hill, F. Ivan Nye, and Ira L. Reiss (New York: Free Press, 1979), 6, summarized these assumptions as: (1) Human behavior is rational. Within the limits of available information, people maximize rewards and minimize costs. (2) All behavior involves some costs. No matter how enjoyable something may appear, energy and time are consumed in its enjoyment. (3) Social behavior is more likely to be repeated if it has been rewarded in the past. (4) Social exchanges are governed by principles of reciprocity. Those who receive rewards from others are expected to reciprocate. Similarly, those who give rewards to others expect to be reciprocated. (5) The more of something a person has, the less rewarding are additional amounts of it. More recently,

James S. Coleman, the key figure in rational choice sociology, discusses the family in his treatise *Foundations of Social Theory* (Cambridge, MA: Belknap Press, 1990), 579–609.

Rational choice or exchange theories are commonly used by sociologists to explain decisions within families. For example, Elizabeth Gorman integrates rational choice and ideological and power perspectives to provide insights about how husbands and wives allocate their time between income earning and household roles. See Elizabeth H. Gorman, "Bringing Home the Bacon: Marital Allocation of Income-Earning Responsibilities, Job Shifts, and Men's Wages," *Journal of Marriage and the Family* 61, no. 1 (February 1999): 110–22.

7.   Peter Abell, *Rational Choice Theory*, (Aldershot, UK: Elgar, 1991), ix.

8.   Much of this work, especially as it applies to marriage and divorce, is contained in Becker, *Economic Approach* and *Treatise*.

9.   Becker, *Economic Approach,* 206.

10.   Some have argued that the legalization of abortion and the increased availability of contraception to unmarried women in the United States led to the erosion in the custom of shotgun marriages. See George A. Akerloff, Janet L. Yellen, and Michael L. Katz, "An Analysis of Out-of-Wedlock Childbearing in the United States," *Quarterly Journal of Economics* 111, no. 2 (May 1996): 277–317.

11.   Among the 4.1 million unmarried couples in 1997, more than 2.6 million did not have any children under age 15. See U.S. Bureau of the Census, *Statistical Abstract of the United States, 1998* (Washington, DC: U.S. Government Printing Office, 1998), Table 66, 60.

12.   The standard economic discussion of the gains from specialization within a relationship, assumed to be marriage, is contained in Becker, *Treatise*, 30–53. For a thorough review of the sociological perspective on the division of labor within households, see Sarah Fenstermaker Berk, *The Gender Factory: The Apportionment of Work in American Households* (New York: Plenum Press, 1985).

13.   The idea that individuals do not receive welfare just from goods and services but also from commodities that result from the combining of goods and services with time was developed in Gary S. Becker, "A Theory of the Allocation of Time," *Economic Journal* 75 (September 1965): 493–517; and Kevin Lancaster, "A New Approach to Consumer Theory," *Journal of Political Economy* 74 (April 1966): 132–57.

14.   Shopping, which requires time, can also be viewed as a source of enjoyment for some people.

15.   However, there has been substantial convergence in their earnings over recent decades. Between 1981 and 1989, the ratio of women's wages to men's wages increased from .59 to .68 annual full-time earnings. See June O'Neill, "Women and Wages," *American Enterprise* 1, no. 6 (November-December 1990): 25–33. Among college graduates in 1993, women earn 73 percent as much as men. However, when men and women are in the same major field of study, at the same degree level, and in the same age group, about half of the women earned at least 87 percent as much as the men. See Daniel E. Hecker, "Earnings of College Graduates: Women Compared to Men," *Monthly Labor Review* 121, no. 3 (March 1998): 62–71.

16.   This section benefits from the discussion in Francine D. Blau and Marianne A. Ferber, *The Economics of Women, Men, and Work*, 2d ed. (Englewood Cliffs, NJ: Prentice-Hall, 1992), 58–66.

17.   Blau and Ferber, *Economics*, 9. A central theme in economics is diminishing returns as the incremental gains from consumption and production tend to decline as the quantity increases. Although one person might initially find cooking less tedious, if not more enjoyable, than their partner does, that situation could change with the amount of cooking. As one did more of the cooking, it might become more tedious, thereby, creating an opportunity for the couple to increase their overall welfare by the initially reluctant partner assuming some of the cooking responsibilities. In a similar manner, one person may have a comparative advantage at earning income but finds earning income beyond a certain level extremely unpleasant. The partner who had assumed primary responsibility for domestic activities might be able to earn comparable income on a part-time basis and at a lower opportunity cost to the couple. This is especially true because diminishing returns probably resulted in some of the time spent working in the home having a low value to the couple.

18.   The hourly earnings ratio for white men to white women in the twenty–to–forty-four age group increased from 65.6 percent in 1977 to 71.4 percent in 1987. Standardized for age, region, schooling, industry, occupational skill level, and labor force turnover, the women-to-men hourly earnings ratio for people without children rose to 90.7 percent. For people with children, the ratio was 72 percent. June O'Neill, "Women and Wages," *American Enterprise* 1 (November/December): 30–32. This women-to-men earnings ratio has continued to rise. Between 1969 and 1994, it increased from 60 percent to 72 percent for those in the twenty-five–to–thirty-four age bracket. The trend was particularly impressive for better educated workers as the ratio rose from 66 percent to 83 percent for workers with at least a college education in that age bracket. See Francine D. Blau, "Trends in the Well-Being of American Women, 1970–95," *Journal of Economic Literature* 36, no. 1 (March 1998): 129.

With less specialization by wives in domestic work, one result may be that the wage premium of married men over never married men has decreased. See Jeffrey S. Gray, "The Fall in Men's Return to Marriage: Declining Productivity Effects or Changing Selection?" *Journal of Human Resources* 32, no. 2 (Summer 1997): 481–504.

19.   Paul A. Samuelson and William D. Nordhaus, *Economics*, 15th ed. (New York: McGraw-Hill, 1995), 185.

20.   The idea that marriage is based on the gains from specialization is often ignored. Individuals can usually find members of the opposite sex whom they find attractive and with whom they can acquire the additional commodities available through marriage. In that environment, the focus is usually on the individual mate rather than on the gains from marriage. In other situations, for example, on the American frontier, marriages were arranged without the parties knowing each other because of the gains that the parties expected from a marriage to essentially anyone. See Ray Allen Billington, *America's Frontier Heritage* (Albuquerque: University of New Mexico Press, 1974), 215.

21.   Becker, *Treatise*, 37. Also see Alice S. Rossi, "A Biosocial Perspective on Parenting," *Daedalus* 106, no. 2 (1977): 1–31.

22.   Linda Thompson and Alexis J. Walker, "Gender in Families: Women and Men in

Marriage, Work, and Parenthood," in *Contemporary Families: Looking Forward, Looking Back*, ed. Alan Booth (Minneapolis, MN: National Council on Family Relations, 1991), 76–102.

23.   An excellent discussion of this problem is contained in Lloyd Cohen, "Marriage, Divorce, and Quasi Rents; 'I Gave Him the Best Years of My Life'," *Journal of Legal Studies* 16, no. 2 (June 1987): 267–304.

24.   The seminal article on this subject is Benjamin Klein, Robert G. Crawford, and Armen A. Alchian, "Vertical Integration, Appropriable Rents, and the Competitive Contracting Process," *Journal of Law & Economics* 21, no. 2 (October 1978): 297–326. They discuss the incentives for businesses to vertically integrate to avoid opportunistic behavior, using marriage as illustrating the same problems.

25.   Cohen, "Marriage," 293.

26.   The gap was 2.5 years in 1960, and it fell to 1.9 years in 1990. Census, *Statistical Abstract*, Table 159, 112.

27.   Because domestic work for women was strongly influenced by couples' demand for children, the increased employment and the resulting decline in the demand for children has had a much bigger impact on the roles of women than on those of men. Although some of the domestic activities of women have been assumed by men, many of those activities have been purchased from outside sources. For a discussion of changing gender roles, see Paula England and George Farkas, *Households, Employment, and Gender* (New York: Aldine, 1986), 191–94.

28.   Between 1980 and 1996, the percentage of households consisting of married couples with children under eighteen fell from 31 to 25 percent. Census, *Statistical Abstract*, Table 68, 60.

29.   Paul C. Glick and Graham B. Spanier, "Married and Unmarried Cohabitation in the United States," *Journal of Marriage and the Family* 42 (February 1980): 19–30.

30.   June Carbone and Margaret F. Brinig, "Rethinking Marriage: Feminist Ideology, Economic Change, and Divorce Reform," *Tulane Law Review* 65, no. 5 (May 1991): 990.

31.   Jay Belsky, "Parental and Nonparental Child Care and Children's Socioemotional Development: A Decade in Review," in Booth, *Contemporary Families*, 127.

32.   The seminal contributions to this literature are Marilyn Manser and Murray Brown, "Marriage and Household Decision Making: A Bargaining Analysis," *International Economic Review* 21, no. 1 (February 1980): 31–44; and Marjorie B. McElroy and Mary Jean Horney, "Nash Bargained Household Decisions," *International Economic Review* 22, no. 2 (June 1981): 333–49.

33.   Shelly Lundberg and Robert A. Pollak, "Bargaining and Distribution in Marriage," *Journal of Economic Perspectives* 10, no. 4 (Fall 1996): 139–58. Lundberg and Pollak test their theory using data from a change in the child allowance to wives in the United Kingdom. See Shelly J. Lundberg and Robert A. Pollak, "Do Husbands and Wives Pool Their Resources? Evidence from the United Kingdom Child Benefit," *Journal of Human Resources* 32, no. 3 (Summer 1997): 463–80.

34.   Marriage provides insurance, if one accepts the element of the marriage vow in which the parties agree to fulfill their duty "for richer or for poorer, in sickness and in

66 *Good Intentions Gone Awry*

health." See Cohen, "Marriage, Divorce, and Quasi Rents." Marriage also can provide insurance against risks originating from random events outside the family's control. See Murray Brown, "Optimal Marriage Contracts," *Journal of Human Resources* 27, no. 3 (Summer 1992): 534–50. Some have argued that marriage is a relational contract that includes emotional and financial support in times of need. See Elizabeth S. Scott and Robert E. Scott, "Marriage as Relational Contract," *Virginia Law Review* 84 (October 1998), 1254.

35. Without children, there are usually fewer incentives for a couple to marry. There still can be incentives to take advantage of filing a joint tax return, to receive employer-provided fringe benefits such as health insurance, or to have marriage provide psychological benefits due to the commitment that it represents.

36. Marriage can be viewed as an institution that provides couples with the confidence to make long-term investments in their relationship. See Robert Rowthorn, "Marriage and Trust: Some Lessons From Economics," *Cambridge Journal of Economics* 23, no. 5 (September 1999): 661–91.

37. Robert H. Lauer, Jeanette C. Lauer, and Sarah T. Kerr, "The Long-Term Marriage: Perceptions of Stability and Satisfaction," *International Journal of Aging and Human Development* 31, no. 1 (1990): 189–95.

38. Alan Freiden, "The United States Marriage Market," *Journal of Political Economy* 82, no. 2, Pt. II (March-April 1974): s34–s53. More recently, economists have used data from Hong Kong to lend support to the argument that couples choose each other in a manner that maximizes total marital output. See Wing Suen and Hon-Kwong Lui, "A Direct Test of the Efficient Marriage Market Hypothesis," *Economic Inquiry* 37, no. 1 (January 1999): 29–46.

39. The discussion presented in this book suggests the reverse: I would expect to observe the marriage rate decreasing when the difficulty of divorce is low, but if it is easy to obtain a divorce, women should hesitate to specialize in household production, with the result that there is a smaller gain for her and a man to marry. The variable used in Freiden's study for the cost of divorce was highly subjective and may not have been sufficiently precise enough to pick up that effect. In addition, in 1960, no state had as easily obtainable divorce as became available with no-fault divorce a decade later.

40. Claudia Goldin, *Understanding the Gender Gap* (New York: Oxford University Press, 1990).

41. Approximately one out of every three people who marry have been married at least once before, and almost half of all weddings involve at least one person who has been previously married. See Fuchs, *How We Live*, 151. If their first marriage is dissolved, most women remarry quickly. Nearly 50 percent of women whose first marriage ended in widowhood or divorce remarried within five years. As marriage has become less attractive, the probability of remarriage has declined. See Kathryn A. London, "Cohabitation, Marriage, Marital Dissolution, and Remarriage: United States, 1988," U.S. Department of Health and Human Services, Advanced Data No. 194, January 4, 1991, 5.

42. Becker, *Treatise*, 324–41. Although numerous factors can make a current marriage less attractive, an important factor is the availability of alternative spouses. See Scott J. South and Kim M. Lloyd, "Spousal Alternatives and Marital Dissolution," *American Sociological Review* 60, no. 1 (February 1995): 21–35.

43. Gary S. Becker, Elizabeth M. Landes, and Robert Michael, "An Analysis of Marital Instability," *Journal of Political Economy* 85, no. 6 (1977): 1141–87.

44. People who have little to gain from marriage are likely to have first, as well as subsequent, marriages that are dissolved. The dissolution rate of subsequent marriages might be greater because children and perhaps other specific investments in the first marriage lower the gain from subsequent marriages. See Becker, Landes, and Michael, "Marital Instability," 1157.

45. Elizabeth Landes, "Economics of Alimony," *Journal of Legal Studies* 7 (1978): 35–63.

46. The median age of women at their first marriage rose from 20.6 in 1970 to 24 in 1990, while for men the median age rose from 22.5 to 25.9. Census, *Statistical Abstract,* Table 148, 106. Although there are a number of reasons why fewer women marry, it should be noted that between 1970 and 1996 the percentage of women who were married in the United States fell from 68.5 to 58.8. Table 58, 55. The incentives for married women to shift their emphasis to work outside the home is discussed in H. Elizabeth Peters, "Marriage and Divorce: Informational Constraints and Private Contracting," *American Economic Review* 76, no. 3 (June 1986): 437–54; Allen M. Parkman, "Divorce and the Labor Force Participation Rate of Married Women, Revisited," *American Economic Review* 82, no. 3 (June 1992): 671–78; and Allen M. Parkman, "Why Are Married Women Working So Hard?" *International Review of Law and Economics* 18, no. 1 (Winter 1998): 41–49.

47. Homer H. Clark, Jr., *The Law of Domestic Relations in the United States,* 2d ed. (St. Paul, MN: West, 1988), 589.

48. See Allen M. Parkman, "Dividing Human Capital with an Eye to Future Earnings," *Family Advocate* 12, no. 2 (Fall 1989): 34–37; and Allen M. Parkman, "Bringing Consistency to the Financial Arrangements at Divorce," *Kentucky Law Journal* 87, no. 1 (1998–99): 51–93.

49. *The MIT Dictionary of Modern Economics,* 3d ed. (Cambridge, MA: MIT Press, 1986), 452, defines *wealth* as anything that has a market value and can be exchanged for money or goods. It can include physical goods, financial assets, and personal skills that can generate an income.

50. The concept of human capital is developed in Becker, *Human Capital.*

51. This section is adapted from Parkman, "Consistency." An *asset* is defined in Alan C. Shapiro, *Modern Corporate Finance* (New York: Macmillan, 1989), G-2, as "property that has value, as measured by the asset's ability to generate future cash."

52. Most loans require some security from the borrower. Until the borrower puts some of his or her own effort and money into a project, he or she will find it very difficult to borrow additional funds. The borrower's own resources are called equity; the borrowed funds are called debt. The equity funds are essential and their sources are very limited, usually coming from the individual or from a close associate. The initial investment in human capital that occurred in elementary and secondary school was usually made by members of the individual's family or taxpayers. The sources of debt financing on the contrary can be numerous. Most colleges offer loan programs in addition to the government loans available through lending institutions. In general, someone with an equity in-

terest has a claim to a share of the returns to an investment, those with a debt interest only have a claim to the contracted rate of return.

53.   See Allen M. Parkman, "The Treatment of Professional Goodwill in Divorce Proceedings," *Family Law Quarterly* 18, no. 2 (Summer 1984): 213–24; and Allen M. Parkman, "A Systematic Approach to Valuing the Goodwill of Professional Practices," in *Valuing Professional Practices and Licenses,* 3d ed., ed. Ronald L. Brown (Gaithersburg, NY: Aspen Law & Business, 1998), 6-1–6-18.

54.   The best method for handling an investment made by a working spouse is for the student spouse to pay back the loan with interest if the marriage is dissolved before the working spouse has received a fair return on the investment. See Allen M. Parkman, "An Investment Approach to Valuing Spousal Support of Education," in *Valuing Professional Practices,* ed. Brown, 32-1–32-25.

55.   In 1976, the average woman in a household spent 25 hours a week on meal preparation and cleanup, cleaning, laundry, and child care, while the average man in a household spent 6.9 hours on those activities. The average woman spent 33.6 hours per week on all household services, the average man only 15.1 hours. See Janice Peskin, "Measuring Household Production for the GNP," *Family Economics Review* 20, no. 3 (1982): 22.

56.   The value of an individual's human capital depreciates by approximately 1.5 percent per year during the period that he or she is out of the work force. The depreciation rate increases as the education level of the individual increases. Jacob Mincer and Solomon Polachek, "Family Investments in Human Capital: Earnings of Women," *Journal of Political Economy* 82, no. 2, Pt. II (March-April 1974): s76–s108. More recent work by Jacobsen and Levin showed that when women reenter the labor market after interrupting their career to emphasize domestic work, their earnings are much lower than those of a comparable group of women who did not leave the labor market. Over time, the difference diminishes, but never disappears, even after as long as 20 years. See Joyce P. Jacobsen and Laurence M. Levin, "Effects of Intermittent Labor Force Attachment on Women's Earnings," *Monthly Labor Review* 118, no. 9 (September 1995): 14–19.

57.   This loss of human capital due to a spouse specializing in the production of household commodities can be introduced into the traditional legal definition of property by the use of an implied contract of indemnification. The decision by a couple for one spouse, usually the wife, to specialize in household production is in the best interest of both spouses if the marriage lasts, but it can result in a substantial reduction in the wife's human capital if the marriage is dissolved. If the loss is recognized as the basis for indemnification, the loss is a debt of the couple and an asset of the person incurring the loss.

58.   This is only true if the decrease was done for the benefit of the family. Alternatively, if it is due to activities such as alcoholism, then it should not be the basis for compensation.

59.   The renewed interest was created in this area by Duncan Black, *The Theory of Committees and Elections* (Cambridge, UK: Cambridge University Press, 1958). Dennis C. Mueller, *Public Choice II* (Cambridge, UK: Cambridge University Press, 1989) provides a recent survey.

60.   Anthony Downs, *An Economic Analysis of Democracy* (New York: Harper and Row, 1957), 207–78.

61.   David Friedman, *Price Theory,* 2d ed. (Cincinnati, OH: Southwestern, 1990), 548–49. Another discussion of the economic theory of legislation is contained in Richard Posner, *The Economic Analysis of Law,* 4th ed. (Boston: Little, Brown, 1992), 519–38.

62.   See George L. Priest and Benjamin Klein, "The Selection of Disputes for Litigation," *Journal of Legal Studies* 13, no. 1 (January 1984): 1–56; and Ronald Johnson and Allen M. Parkman, "Premerger Notification and the Incentive to Merge and Litigate," *Journal of Law, Economics and Organization* 7, no. 1 (1991): 145–62. This process is also discussed in Posner, *Economic Analysis,* 554–59.

63.   See Lenore J. Weitzman, *The Divorce Revolution: The Unexpected Social and Economic Consequences for Women and Children in America* (New York: Free Press, 1985), 147, and 215.

64.   Substantial litigation has occurred over the appropriate legal definition of property as applied to such intangible items as degrees and licenses. Also, litigation has addressed the issues of separate and marital property. Annual summaries of this litigation are contained in a series of articles in the *Family Law Quarterly*. For example, see Linda D. Elrod and Robert G. Spector, "A Review of the Year in Family Law: A Search for Definitions and Policy," *Family Law Quarterly* 31, no. 4 (Winter 1998): 613–66.

65.   Becker, *Treatise,* 333.

66.   These conclusions are supported by Peters, "Marriage and Divorce."

4

The Introduction of No-Fault Divorce Statutes

Seldom in U.S. history have laws been enacted with higher hopes and poorer results than the no-fault divorce statutes. In this chapter, we will examine why the no-fault divorce laws were passed and why unexpected results occurred; we will focus on the California experience because of its central role.[1] California had that role in this process for a number of reasons. First, it was the first state to eliminate all fault grounds for divorce. Second, a number of the reformers from California were instrumental in promulgating the Uniform Marriage and Divorce Act (UMDA) in 1974,[2] which influenced the statutes passed in many other states. The UMDA uses the same ground for divorce as California: irretrievable breakdown. Last, in contrast to California, a majority of states added the no-fault grounds for divorce to the existing fault grounds.[3] However, the no-fault grounds made the fault grounds redundant because the fault grounds were hard to prove and, therefore, seldom used in a truly adversarial proceedings. Consequently, in the fifteen-year period after 1970, essentially all states enacted unilateral divorce laws similar to those in California. The economic analysis of Public Choice will be used to help understand the specific laws that were passed in California and the notion of "second-best" to analyze why the no-fault divorce laws have produced poorer results than anticipated.

CASE LAW VERSUS STATUTORY LAW

The rules that control marriage and divorce are based on statutes as construed by the courts. By way of contrast, large areas of U.S. law, such as contracts and torts,

71

are still controlled by judicial decisions in the common law tradition.[4] Economists have argued that the judge-made common law rules tend to produce more efficient outcomes than legislatively created statutory laws do.[5] Efficiency is promoted when the benefits of decisions exceed their costs, and common law rules with those characteristics tend to evolve because inefficient rules—ones that result in more costs or fewer benefits than efficient rules—will be challenged until they are overturned. In addition, the common law is based on judicial decisions that evolve in a decentralized process: Judges are confronted not with abstract ideas, but with actual litigants. As changing conditions render existing rules inefficient, litigants press the common law to change to produce more efficient rules.

Statutory laws respond to different pressures. Statutes are introduced or changed in discrete steps based on the political process of majority rule strongly influenced by special interest groups. Legislators are thus confronted with abstract concepts rather than actual parties, and rules established by the political process are more inclined toward wealth distribution than toward efficiency. These pressures acting on the divorce laws can be illustrated by the history of no-fault divorce in California.

NO-FAULT IN CALIFORNIA

The nations's first unequivocal no-fault law became effective in California in 1970.[6] The earlier law in that state based divorce, property division, alimony, child support, and custody on fault grounds. The new law removed consideration of fault from the grounds for divorce, the award of spousal support, and the division of property. Fault was retained as a relevant factor for only two issues: to prove the existence of the no-fault grounds and to determine child custody. This legislation, the result of six years of deliberation, is especially important because the National Conference on Commissioners of Uniform State Laws based the standard for dissolution in the Uniform Marriage and Divorce Act on the California requirement of "irretrievable breakdown."[7] The remainder of the states followed the California lead in enacting similar statutes over the following fifteen years.

An improvement in the welfare of spouses and their children was the initial goal of the new legislation in California. The numerous criticisms of the fault-based divorce statutes made by proponents of no-fault divorce included the charges that the fault system tended to aggravate and to perpetuate bitterness between spouses and that the widespread practice of using perjured testimony in collusive divorce proceedings promoted disrespect of the legal system. The wide gulf existing between the divorce law on the books that declared that marriage was indissoluble except for fault and the legal system that in practice tolerated divorce by mutual consent made extreme mental cruelty the almost universal ground for divorce.[8] In fact, most divorces were already uncontested and granted on cursory testimony of marital fault.[9] The fact that these cases were uncontested did not mean that they were congenial. Spouses who wanted a divorce knew that it would be difficult to obtain based on the fault ground because their spouse had seldom committed the acts necessary to establish the grounds. The uncontested legal action was probably the final result of heated debate and substantial animosity during which a spouse who did not want the divorce had considerable negotiating power.

It is impossible to identify exactly when the reform movement began, but the California legislature took its first steps in that direction in 1963. In that year, a House Resolution was passed that initiated a study of the laws on divorce, and an interim committee began the study apparently without contemplating any radical change. Four major themes emerged from the 1964 hearings in the California Assembly, which set the agenda for the legislative proposals that followed. There were widespread concerns about:

1. the high divorce rate,

2. the adversary process creating hostility, acrimony, and trauma,

3. a need to recognize the inevitability of divorce for some couples and attempt to make the legal process less destructive for them and their children, and

4. charges made by divorced men that the divorce law and its practitioners worked with divorced women to acquire an unfair advantage over former husbands.[10]

The hearings reached no conclusions, nor was any legislation proposed; the interim committee disbanded. In 1966, Governor Edmund G. Brown, who was enthusiastic about divorce law reform, established a twenty-two member Commission on the Family.[11] This commission consisted of one minister, four legislators, six lawyers, four judges, three psychiatrists, two law professors, one medical doctor, and one member of the State Social Welfare Board. Two assemblymen were appointed cochairmen.[12] Noteworthy for their absence were economists and other professionals with backgrounds in financial analysis. Governor Brown gave the commission four primary tasks:

1. to study and suggest revisions, where necessary, of the substantive laws of California relating to the family,

2. to determine the feasibility of developing significant and meaningful courses in family life education to be offered in the public schools,

3. to consider the possibility and desirability of developing uniform nationwide standards of marriage and divorce jurisdiction, and

4. to examine the establishment of family courts on a statewide basis and recommend the procedures by which they might function most effectively.[13]

The commission reviewed the condition of the family and made recommendations in two areas: First, it suggested revisions in the substantive law of divorce. Second, it examined the feasibility of establishing a system of family courts.[14] The commission proposed legislation in the form of a model Family Court Act that would have created a family court, eliminated fault as a ground for divorce, and revised the community property distribution rules. The family court proposal included both the creation of a family court system and the establishment of procedures to encourage the parties to use the court's conciliation and counseling services. The commission also recommended that dissolution of marriage should be granted whenever the court found that the legitimate objectives of the marriage had been destroyed and that there was no reasonable likelihood that the marriage could be saved.[15]

The commission's standard derived from a 1952 case, *DeBurgh v. DeBurgh*, in which the California Supreme Court overturned the long-standing rule that only an innocent party could obtain a divorce.[16] In that case, with both parties arguing that they had fault grounds for divorce, the court granted the divorce on the grounds that the legitimate objectives of the marriage had been destroyed. The commission recommended a shift from fault to need as a basis for financial settlements. Alimony and support were to be awarded based solely on the needs and circumstances of the parties, with no consideration of fault; and the community property was to be divided equally between the spouses.

Although the commission's recommendations were never enacted, they did serve as the main working model for bills introduced in the California assembly and senate during 1969.[17] The major objection raised to these bills was the potentially high cost of the counseling. No definitive action was taken on the bills in 1967, but they were reintroduced in 1968, when the California State Bar also became involved. It proposed alternate legislation with limited counseling and a family court system that was a division of the existing Superior Court. The bar also recommended giving judges more discretion in property decisions. This proposal was rejected by the legislature.

James A. Hayes, a member of the Assembly Judiciary Committee, independently put together another proposal that eliminated the major cost-incurring features—a separate family court system and mandatory counseling structure—but kept the marriage-breakdown theory of divorce, with an emphasis on voluntary counseling for the parties.[18] The Hayes bill, introduced in the 1968 session, also failed to pass.

In 1969, Hayes was appointed chairman of the Assembly Judiciary Committee, and he introduced Assembly Bill (AB) 530, entitled the Domestic Relations Act of 1969, in which the only grounds for divorce were irreconcilable differences and incurable insanity. *Irreconcilable differences* were defined as those grounds that are determined by the court to be substantial reasons for not continuing the marriage and that have caused the irrevocable breakdown of the marriage. Essentially, the new Hayes bill would enact no-fault divorce without the protective setting of a specialized family court.[19] AB 530 did not pass, but a similar bill drafted by a conference committee made up of Assemblyman Hayes, the chairman of the Senate Judiciary Committee, and two additional members from the judiciary committee of each house was enacted as the Family Law Act of 1969.[20]

The new Family Law Act established two grounds for marital dissolution, "irreconcilable differences which have caused the irremediable breakdown of the marriage"[21] and incurable insanity.[22] Other changes emphasized a new orientation in divorce proceedings. The term *divorce* was replaced by *dissolution of marriage*. A neutral petition form, *In re the Marriage of Mrs. Smith and Mr. Smith*, replaced the adversarial form *Smith v. Smith*. The parties were called "petitioner" and "respondent" rather than "plaintiff" and "defendant," and the pleadings were replaced by a standardized form that permitted the petitioner to select the type of proceeding—legal separation, dissolution, or nullity of marriage.

Under the prior law, the property division was unequal when the grounds for divorce were adultery, extreme cruelty, or incurable insanity, with the innocent party allocated a disproportionately large share of the community property. Under the new act, community property usually was to be divided equally, with no regard for fault, unless the division would impair the value of the property, such as a business, or when community funds had been deliberately squandered or misused by one spouse to the extent that an equal division of the remaining assets would no longer be equitable.[23]

Alimony was redefined as "support" and was to be determined by fairness rather than fault.[24] Fairness was based on three factors: (1) the duration of the marriage, (2) the ability of the supported spouse to engage in gainful employment, and (3) the economic condition of the parties. Child custody continued to be governed by the best interests of the child, but evidence could be presented on parental fault.

The act essentially pushed through the California legislature by Hayes was quite different from the 1966 proposals by the Governor's Commission on the Family. The major changes to the old rules were the elimination of the fault grounds for divorce and the requirement of an equal division of the community property; the new act had no provisions for a family court system or counseling. All the same, the legislation was viewed as path breaking. Lenore Weitzman[25] identified six major innovations:

1. No grounds were needed to obtain a divorce.

2. Neither spouse had to prove fault or guilt to obtain a divorce.

3. One spouse could decide unilaterally to get a divorce without the consent or agreement of the other spouse.

4. Financial awards were no longer linked to fault.

5. New standards for alimony and property awards sought to treat men and women "equally," repudiating the traditional sex-based assumptions.[26]

6. The new procedures aimed at undermining the adversarial process and creating a social-psychological climate fostering amicable negotiations.

The initial response was very favorable. Howard Krom wrote, "But above all, the legislators themselves, at least the members who worked toward and supported the development of the Act and its final adoption, deserve recognition for their courage in instituting a most necessary though highly controversial element of social reform."[27] He added, "It can be expected that the California reform will chart the path for the civilization of domestic relations law throughout the United States."[28] Stuart Brody asserted, "To their credit the California Legislature, by enacting the Family Law Act of 1969, has attempted to bring divorce laws more in line with reality and to reduce the hypocrisy of strict divorce laws administered by a lenient process."[29]

Problems developed when the courts attempted to interpret the new law, aided only by a legislative report drafted by Hayes after the act had been adopted.[30] This report suggested a connection between the act's financial provisions and the achievement of equality between women and men. Herma Hill Kay of the University of California, who had been a member of the Governor's Commission on the Family, argued that the theme of equality between men and women was introduced into the legislative history of the act for the first time after the act had been adopted.[31] Lenore Weitzman's research revealed that trial court judges were interpreting the Family Law Act based on Hayes's idea of equality developed in the legislative report.[32]

Throughout the deliberations, no-fault had broad support.[33] Because the governor's commission's goal was viewed as a reform, groups that would normally have been antagonistic, such as the Catholic Church, were supportive: the efforts were viewed as being aimed at preserving the family and minimizing the opportunities for divorce. Throughout the legislative proceedings, the most vocal proponents of a shift to no-fault divorce were groups of divorced men.[34] Initially, no feminist groups existed to participate in the deliberations, but as women became aware of the movement for no-fault divorce, many supported the idea.[35] The California Commission on the Status of Women supported the removal of fault from divorce as a desirable elimination of hypocrisy in the legal system.[36]

The no-fault divorce movement was not unique to California. The Commissioners on Uniform State Laws conducted a study of the fault divorce laws in 1968 and recommended a uniform divorce statute that contained irretrievable breakdown of the marriage as the sole ground for divorce.[37] Reformers both in California and in the nation at large were preoccupied with the question of fault and its role in both obtaining a divorce and securing a financial settlement. Few thought about the consequences of the new system or foresaw how its fault-neutral rules could work to the disadvantage of many people; but as no-fault laws were enacted across the United States, people started to become aware that the idea had fundamental flaws.[38] Observers argued that new financial provisions were needed to accompany the no-fault laws in order to protect divorced women and children of divorced parents.[39]

There was a feeling that the reformers and the legislators had proceeded with the best intentions but that somehow the process had produced less-than-ideal results. An economic analysis of the introduction of no-fault suggests that the parties had less-innocent motives.

THE ECONOMIC PERSPECTIVE ON THE INTRODUCTION OF NO-FAULT DIVORCE

The economic perspective on the introduction of no-fault divorce recognizes that there was a growing demand for easier procedures for obtaining a divorce in the period after World War II. The specific legislative response to those pressures reflected the self-interest of the elected officials that focused on the response that the legislators felt was most likely to ensure their reelection. Moreover, some legislators may have found that they could initiate legislation that would produce direct benefits for themselves.

The Demand for Reform

Without a demand for reform, there would have been no incentive for the legislators to act. Divorce becomes more attractive for a married couple when either the gain from marriage decreases or the uncertainty of expected outcomes during marriage increases. Although the divorce rate was increasing during most of the twentieth century, Victor Fuchs identified some unusual changes that occurred during the period between 1965 and 1975 and that contributed to a rapid increase in the divorce rate:[40] These included economic changes such as the growth of real earnings and the increase in government entitlement programs; technological changes such as the expanded availability of contraception; and social and cultural changes, including feminist ideology and widespread criticism of traditional institutions and norms.

The growth in the wages available to women increased the divorce rate because higher wages tended to reduce the gains from marriage. Higher wages are an inducement for married women to work outside the home, reducing specialization by both spouses. Evidence that the causality runs from wives' working to divorce is the fact that the rise in the labor-force participation of married women with small children preceded the rise in the divorce rate by several years.[41] Enhanced social programs provided married women with still more flexibility: The large increase in Aid to Families with Dependent Children (AFDC) payments, the relaxation of eligibility requirements, and the growth of other economic subsidies during this period increased the options for women who found themselves in unsatisfactory marriages.

Improvements in contraception were identified by Robert Michael as an important source of the increase in the demand for divorce.[42] Contraceptives made it easier to reduce the number of children per couple, and children are both the cause and the effect of a stable marriage. Children can cause a stable marriage not only because of the traditional moral reasons, but also because their arrival increases the need for one of the parents to increase specialization in household production. Because this specialization may not be in that party's best interest if the relationship is dissolved, it creates pressures for that party to seek the protection traditionally provided by marriage. Also, people who feel that they have desirable spouses are more likely to make the commitment reflected in children. A reduction in fertility would be expected to increase the divorce rate, and fertility did fall during this period, with its decline preceding the increase in divorce by several years. Contraceptives also reduced uncertainty about subsequent fertility, thus encouraging women to focus more on their careers and to increase their economic independence, again resulting in less specialization within marriage. Finally, contraceptives decreased inhibitions concerning extramarital sex by reducing the risk of pregnancy; this result reduced the cost of searching for a better spouse even during marriage.

Some authors have found that changes in the economic and social status of women during this period led to more female-headed households, with a resulting increase in both divorce and births to unmarried women.[43] Certainly, any rapid change in social values will tend to be disruptive for marriages and will increase the divorce rate.

Trends during this period tended to reduce the gains from marriage as well as creating more uncertain outcomes during marriage. The result was an increase in the demand for easier procedures for dissolving marriages. The perjury and fabricated testimony observed in the courts were evidence of this shift. In the face of this increased demand for new procedures for divorce, the state of California considered a range of options when it revised its divorce laws. Some of the possibilities discussed were a family court system, counseling, equal division of property, and more relaxed grounds for divorce, but only the last two were enacted into law. Some observers might conclude that the others were lacking in merit—that elected officials considered the options and in their wisdom decided that a more limited divorce reform act would best serve the public interest.

Public Choice

Public Choice presents the alternate explanation of the elected officials operating in their self-interest rather than in the public interest. Certainly, there was not broad support among voters for divorce reform. In no survey before or after the passage of no-fault divorce in California did a majority of respondents have the opinion that the divorce laws should be easier.[44] One aspect of self-interest is a focus on the issues that an individual finds important. Although divorce reform was undoubtedly important to Governor Brown, to many professionals concerned with the issue, and to some legislators, most legislators probably had other issues that they considered much more important. The bill that passed the California legislature hardly reflected the collective wisdom of that body.

A better explanation for the passage of that particular bill is that it contained the provisions for which there was a strong constituency. Matrimonial lawyers felt a desperate need for reform that was not necessarily based on their desire to increase social welfare. Practical considerations were causing them to encourage their clients to present perjured testimony to establish the grounds for divorce. A couple who desired a divorce for a variety of reasons commonly fabricated testimony to establish the cruelty grounds for their divorce. These procedures were tainting matrimonial lawyers in the eyes of their colleagues.[45] So making their lives easier rather than improving social welfare may have been their primary goal.[46] Another group providing strong support for reform were divorced men. The family court system and counseling had great appeal for academics, but only the change in the grounds for divorce and the financial arrangements had a strongly motivated constituency: men.[47] The histories of this legislation identify groups of men, especially divorced men, as attacking the fault-based divorce law and its financial provisions. Although the fault-based divorce laws gave substantial negotiating power to women that would be lost if the grounds were removed, the histories do not suggest that this concern was expressed with much vigor during the deliberations. Some very critical issues were ignored. For example, no one appears to have questioned whether the legal definition of property subject to division at the dissolution of a marriage was accurate.

Every movement needs a leader. Often the question ex post is whether the leader made the revolution or the revolution made the leader. Pressures existed for change. The individual who recognized those pressures and used them to create a revolution was Assemblyman James Hayes. Often ignored in the histories of the development of no-fault divorce in California was the special interest that Hayes brought to his advocacy of no-fault.[48]

James A. Hayes was involved in a bitter divorce action during the evolution of no-fault in the California legislature. His divorce case was initially filed in 1966.[49] James and Janne Hayes had married in 1941 when they were nineteen-year-old college students. Except for a brief Christmas job during the first year of the marriage, Janne Hayes never worked outside the home. They had four children. After twenty-five years of marriage, the last few of which were reported to be stormy, Janne Hayes filed for divorce under the existing fault divorce laws.[50] A final decree, including a negotiated property settlement, was approved by the court in 1969. Janne Hayes was awarded the family home and custody of the two minor children. In addition, she was to receive $650 per month in alimony until her death or remarriage and $175 per month child support until the children became adults. James Hayes was awarded his law practice.

In 1972, Hayes filed a petition to end his financial obligations to his wife and children based on the argument that his financial condition had changed. His financial situation was complicated by his having remarried. Hayes's brief in support of his request included a quotation from the 1969 California Assembly Judiciary Committee Report on the new California Family Law Act, which he helped write. Part of the quotation included:

> When our divorce law was originally drawn, woman's role in society was almost totally that of mother and homemaker. She could not even vote. Today, increasing numbers of married women are employed, even in the professions. In addition, they have long been accorded full civil rights. Their approaching equality with the male should be reflected in the law governing marriage dissolution and in the decisions of courts with respect to matters incident to dissolution.[51]

When the judge's decision was handed down in March 1973, James Hayes prevailed. Child support was ended, and alimony was gradually reduced to $300 per month. A year later, Hayes returned to court. His monthly expenses had increased because of the purchase of a new house. The mortgage on the house in conjunction with the payments on his country home came to over $2,000 per month. He again triumphed in court. The *Los Angeles Times* reported:

> Los Angeles County Supervisor James A. Hayes, 53, who earns $40,322 a year but complains that his expenses are nearly double his net income, was successful Tuesday in his bid to reduce the alimony he pays to his first wife, Mrs. Janne M. Hayes, 53. Superior Judge Julius A. Title lowered the payment from $300 to $200 monthly and told Mrs. Hayes, who complains of asthma and back pains, to get a job.[52]

On October 3, 1975, the Court of Appeals overruled the 1973 decision, holding that the original agreement was not subject to modification. The court noted that even if the agreement had been modifiable, "The reduction in support made by the trial court appears to constitute an abuse of discretion."[53] Hayes then returned to court arguing that the original agreement was a "mutual mistake." In March 1976, Janne Hayes's demurrer was sustained, based on the prior court proceedings; but James Hayes continued to fight the financial obligations to his former wife.

During the deliberations that resulted in the no-fault statute being enacted in California, Hayes was obviously not a casual observer. He was instrumental in enacting no-fault divorce in California; after its passage, in the report that rationalized its passage, he emphasized the equality between men and women. He then used the law and the report to attempt to reduce the financial arrangements to which he had agreed as a condition for his divorce. When Janne Hayes filed for divorce in 1966, she was forty-four years old. She had had one year of college twenty-five years earlier. Compared with the position that she would have been in if she had not specialized in being a homemaker and mother, she was much worse off. The financial arrangements that they negotiated do not appear to have been excessively generous to Janne Hayes.

In most histories of the passage of the law, James Hayes's role is given only passing notice. If anything, he is pictured as a very active public servant. But the passage of no-fault in California bears witness to the process of legislative self-interest. This is not a well-intentioned law that innocent people permitted to go astray. This is a law that was passed by a legislature dominated by men in a process of benign neglect reenforced by the lobbying efforts of men's interest groups and maneuvered through the California legislature by a man who personally had a great deal to gain from a reduction in the negotiating power of married women.

Public Choice predicts that special interest groups will attempt to sell their proposals as benefiting the groups that are eventually adversely affected. Many proponents of reform argued, and undoubtedly many believed, that "equality" would be beneficial for divorced women. The problem with the passage of no-fault was not so much the new grounds as the lack of recognition of the critical relationship between the grounds for divorce and the financial arrangements after divorce. James Hayes and the male advocates of no-fault were able to pass it because this link was not recognized. As is so often the case, the political process was oriented toward a vague notion of equity with little concern for efficiency.

The proponents of no-fault objected to the hypocrisy of the fault-based divorces without understanding that the fault grounds themselves were not particularly relevant: Their importance lay in their forcing the parties to negotiate a dissolution. Divorce, in effect, was based on mutual consent; and because most divorces involving substantial property under the fault grounds were negotiated, the legal definition of property had not been closely scrutinized.

The fault divorce laws were not perfect, but the no-fault divorce laws enacted in California and the other states have not been an obvious improvement. The problems with no-fault occur because the interrelationship among laws was not recognized. This is especially true of the connection between the grounds for divorce and the financial arrangements at divorce. Under fault divorce, the legally defined financial arrangements served a minor role compared with the agreements worked out by the parties privately; relaxing the grounds for divorce shifted the emphasis in dissolution cases in California to the financial arrangements based on the legal requirements of an equal division of community property.

Negotiations continued after the introduction of no-fault divorce, but the "rules of the game" changed dramatically. Under fault divorce, normally—when fault could not be proved by the spouse wanting a divorce—the only essential "rule" was the agreement of the other spouse. Because that spouse initially probably did not want a divorce, there was a broad range of potential outcomes from these negotiations. For example, in a community property state that provided for an equal division of community assets, a resisting spouse might ask for a much larger share than the one provided by law. With unilateral no-fault divorce, there were fairly clear default rules that the courts would impose on the parties if they did not reach their own agreement. Now, spouses do not have a big incentive to deviate from an equal division of property, for example, unless they do not want to be constrained by the court's determination in other areas, such as child custody. A father who could live with the default rules has no incentive to negotiate, whereas one who had a strong preference for primary custody of any children, in the face of a perception that the court would award it to the mother, may be willing to trade off more property to obtain that custody.[54] A second-best situation deteriorated into a third-best situation.

Second-Best

The concept of *second-best* states that if one of the conditions necessary for a preferred outcome cannot be fulfilled, then the best attainable outcome (the second-best) can, in general, only be achieved by departing from all the other optimal conditions. Within the framework of efficiency, the best divorce law probably should have three components: *First*, the law would contain low-cost procedures for dissolving marriages that are no longer efficient. No-fault would be a reasonable standard for those procedures. *Second*, the law would allocate property based on the effect of marriage on the property. Property unaffected by marriage, separate property, should be returned to its owner, but property created by the joint efforts of the spouses, marital property, should be divided between the spouses. *Third*, a spouse desiring a divorce should be confronted with the true costs of the divorce. No-fault has produced less-than-desirable results because property is not properly defined and divorcing spouses are not confronted with the true costs of divorce.

With hypocritical grounds and inappropriate property awards, especially for the spouse who specialized in household production, fault divorce may have been a second-best solution to the increased demand for easier divorce procedures. The fault divorce laws essentially provided for specific performance of the essential elements of the marital contract, which were the right of a faultless spouse to the continuation of the marriage along with the associated financial obligations. If those contracts had been strictly enforced, as in Great Britain before 1857, the outcomes would have been highly inefficient. But the courts were willing to permit parties to reach negotiated settlements. If the party who wanted to dissolve the marriage wanted the dissolution more than the other party wanted to maintain the marriage, then an agreement was reached that dissolved the marriage. The fault grounds gave the party who did not want the divorce negotiating power. If that person was the wife, she usually was able to extract an acceptable agreement from her spouse. The upper limit on her ability to extract an acceptable agreement was the cost of the alternatives available to the husband for dissolving the marriage.

The fault grounds for divorce gave bargaining power to individuals who did not want to dissolve a marriage, but this power was not absolute. At some cost, a divorce could be obtained in another state with more liberal laws. In Nevada, for example, one of the grounds for divorce was, "When the husband and wife have lived separate and apart for one year without cohabitation, the court may, in its discretion, grant an absolute decree of divorce at the suit of either party."[55] Also, an uncooperative spouse could be harassed or even abandoned. Although the claims of the men's advocacy groups were worthy of concern, it is not clear how many wives under fault divorce received compensation at divorce that exceeded the loss that they were about to experience due to the dissolution of their marriage.

Fault divorce may have been a second-best solution, but no-fault can only be described as third best. The shift from fault to no-fault essentially shifted the remedy in divorce cases from specific performance with the possibility of a negotiated settlement to damages based on reliance.[56] No-fault divorce has resulted in an equal division of marital property, spousal support based on fairness, and child custody based on the best interest of the child. If these rules accurately reflect the reliance costs incurred by the parties who do not want the dissolutions, then people will be encouraged to make welfare-increasing decisions. The parties can increase their specialization during marriage with the knowledge that any sacrifices will be compensated at divorce. In addition, the divorce will tend to occur only when the collective benefits exceed the costs; with an accurate measure of the reliance costs of marriage to the potentially divorced spouse, efficient outcomes are more likely. If the courts understate the reliance costs incurred by the parties, however, the outcomes will tend to be inefficient.

It is difficult to place a monetary value on these decisions, but monetary units can be used here for illustrative purposes. Let us say that the spouse who wants to dissolve the marriage values that alternative at $10,000, and the loss that will be incurred by the other spouse, who relied on the continuation of the marriage, is $20,000; under these circumstances, social welfare is improved by continuing the marriage. This is a situation that can occur later in a marriage because of the timing of the typical contributions of men and women to marriage. If the financial transfer required by law from the divorcing spouse to the divorced spouse is only $5,000, that divorcing spouse will make that payment and dissolve the marriage. The outcome will be inefficient in that the collective benefits do not exceed the collective costs. This may be a common situation, because the financial loss of the divorced spouse who has specialized in household production during the marriage has not been recognized in any systematic way by the courts under the no-fault divorce laws.

Not only is the outcome inefficient and unfair, it has undesirable long-term effects. Men and women marry because they anticipate that they will gain from that arrangement. Some of the benefits of that arrangement flow from their increasing their specialization during marriage. The responsibilities that follow from parenthood contribute to the trend toward additional specialization by spouses, for example, because it is usually difficult or financially unrealistic for the parents to assume equal responsibilities for child rearing. Therefore, one spouse has to increase his or her specialization in that role compared with other potential roles—an increase that leaves that spouse vulnerable later in the marriage.[57] That decision was made by married women during most of the history of the United States based on the assumption that the divorce laws protected them from the opportunistic behavior of their husbands.

No-fault divorce changed that situation. Spouses who committed themselves to specialized roles during marriage often discovered that they had less protection. Women who married with the expectation of this protection were made worse off, incurring a cost in the form of a reduced future income-earning capacity for which there was little compensation if they were divorced. Many men who divorced under no-fault were made better off relative to the negotiated settlements they would have been forced to make under fault-based divorce.

The gains experienced by these men occurred because of the change in the law, not the law itself. Married women specialized in household production, in part, because they felt that it would be difficult for their spouse to dissolve their marriage against their will. While the durability of marriage was due to divorce being restricted to a limited list of causes—none of which the wives had probably violated—the wives were only vaguely familiar with the specific faults grounds. The average married woman was probably unaware that the grounds for divorce had changed. However, it became gradually apparent to many people that a divorce within the new legal environment could be a financial disaster for a woman and her children. When women discovered that the laws would not protect them, many of them changed their behavior. Women started to recognize that the losses that they incurred when they specialized in household production were not the basis of adequate compensation. They rationally reduced their specialization in that activity. More married women chose to work outside the home and maintain their marketable skills. In addition, more married women went back to school during marriage to increase or to maintain their human capital. As women thus adapted to the new legal environment, opportunistic behavior by men became more difficult.[58]

The decisions by married women to increase their labor market participation and education can result in an overall reduction in the welfare of their families, as illustrated in the following example: A married woman recognizes that a decision to specialize in household production during marriage will reduce her human capital by $200,000 at age forty-five due to the lower earnings that she can expect after that age compared with the income that she could earn if she focused on her career. She does not expect to divorce, but she knows that it is a possibility and that the financial arrangements under no-fault divorce provide very little compensation for her sacrifice. The services that she would provide her family by working at home are worth $25,000 a year. The financial and psychic income from her best employment opportunity after adjustment for taxes and job-related expenses come to only $15,000; but she still has an incentive to work outside the home—employment outside the home will assist her in increasing or maintaining her human capital.[59]

Overall, the family would be better off if the wife's loss due to working in the home was protected by the law. Then both spouses could focus on their comparative advantages, which might still involve both working in the home and at a job; but the spouse with the lower earning capacity probably would tend to specialize more in household production.

CONCLUSION

The current no-fault divorce laws can best be described as third-best laws. First-best laws would encourage efficient outcomes at divorce. Because the fault divorce laws were potentially costly and hypocritical, they were a second-best alternative. They did have the advantage of forcing the parties to recognize more of the costs incurred by other family members—especially older married women—at divorce. No-fault divorce laws with inaccurate estimates of the costs of divorce are third-best laws. The change in the laws necessary to arrive at the best outcome will be discussed in the last chapter. In the meantime, no-fault has had numerous effects on individual decisions, which will be the subject of the next chapter.

NOTES

1.   A reform movement was occurring in other jurisdictions. In England, the Archbishop of Canterbury appointed a group in 1964 to investigate the divorce laws in England. It issued a report, *Putting Asunder: A Divorce Law for Contemporary Society* (Lon-

don: SPCK, 1966), that recommended the replacement of fault with no-fault grounds for divorce. New York, which had one of the most restrictive divorce laws in the country, also moved toward reform: In 1966, New York enacted a divorce reform bill that added other fault grounds for divorce to the single existing ground of adultery. The reduction in the waiting period for a divorce based on separation in New York was reduced to one year by legislation enacted in 1968 and 1970. In effect, New York enacted no-fault divorce. See Lynn D. Wardle, "No-Fault Divorce and the Divorce Conundrum," *Brigham Young University Law Review* 1991, no. 1 (1991): 79–142.

2.   Herma Hill Kay from the University of California, who was one of the leaders of the reform movement in California, was co-reporter of the Uniform Marriage and Divorce Act.

3.   For a summary of the grounds for divorce in the various states, see Linda D. Elrod and Robert G. Spector, "A Review of the Year in Family Law: A Search for Definitions and Policy," *Family Law Quarterly* 31, no. 4 (Winter 1998): 663.

4.   The Uniform Commercial Code, which has been adopted in all states but Louisiana, has codified many of principles of the common law of contracts. See Michael B. Metzger, Jane P. Mallor, A. James Barnes, Thomas Bowers, and Michael J. Phillips, *Business Law and the Regulatory Environment* (Homewood, IL: Irwin, 1992), 203. The Restatement (Second) of Contracts, although it does not having statutory authority, also provides a summary of common law contract principles.

5.   Richard Posner, *The Economic Analysis of Law,* 4th ed. (Boston: Little, Brown, 1992), 523.

6.   Some of the sources reviewing the development of California's no-fault divorce laws are contained in Herma Hill Kay, "Equality and Difference: A Perspective on No-Fault Divorce and Its Aftermath," *University of Cincinnati Law Review* 56, no. 1 (1987): 1–90; Herma Hill Kay, "An Appraisal of California's No-Fault Divorce Law," *California Law Review* 75 (1987): 291–319; Howard Krom, "California's Divorce Law Reform: An Historical Analysis," *Pacific Law Journal* 1, no. 1 (1970): 156–81; Lenore J. Weitzman, *The Divorce Revolution* (New York: Free Press, 1985); and Michael Wheeler, *No-Fault Divorce* (Boston: Beacon, 1974).

7.   Uniform Marriage and Divorce Act § 305, 9A U.L.A. 91, 132-3 (1979). The reporter for the Uniform Marriage and Divorce Act presented his reflections on the intentions of the drafters of the uniform act in Robert J. Levy, "A Reminiscence about the Uniform Marriage and Divorce Act—and Some Reflections about Its Critics and Its Politics," *Brigham Young University Law Review* 1991, no. 1 (1991): 43–78.

8.   Lynne Carol Halem, *Divorce Reform* (New York: Free Press, 1980), 250. Although all states now permit divorce on no-fault grounds, some states also permit dissolution by an affidavit procedure when there is mutual consent to the divorce. Mutual consent divorce is also available in some states when the marriage is of short duration and without children, when there is no maintenance request, and when there is an agreement concerning property division. See Doris Jonas Freed and Timothy B. Walker, "Family Law in the Fifty States: An Overview," *Family Law Quarterly* 23 (Winter 1990): 514. Also see Bureau of Vital Statistics, California Department of Public Health, *Divorce in California: Initial Complaints for Divorce, Annulment and Separate Maintenance 1966,* 1967, 14.

9. The "Report of the Governor's Commission on the Family," Sacramento, CA, December 1966, 30–31, found that 94 percent of divorce proceedings in California were uncontested.

10. Wheeler, *No-Fault,* 138.

11. Halem, *Divorce Reform,* 239.

12. "Report of the Governor's Commission," 145–47.

13. "Report of the Governor's Commission," 1.

14. "Report of the Governor's Commission," 60. Herma Hill Kay provides the insights of one of the commission members in "A Family Court: The California Proposal," *California Law Review* 56, no. 5 (October 1968): 1205–48. In contrast to Kay's academic view, John Goddard, Commissioner of the Los Angeles County Superior Court, was concerned about the effect of the commission's proposals on the financial condition of divorced women. See John Leslie Goddard, "The Proposal for Divorce upon Petition and without Fault," *Journal of the State Bar of California* 43 (1968): 90–102.

15. "Report of the Governor's Commission," 91.

16. 39 Cal. 2d 858 (1952).

17. *Journal of the California Assembly,* 8054–55 (Reg. Sess., 1969).

18. Krom, "Divorce Law Reform," 173.

19. Kay, "Equality," 39.

20. Hayes defended the new California law in James A. Hayes, "California Divorce Reform: Parting Is Sweeter Sorrow," *American Bar Association Journal* 56 (July 1970): 660–63. Hayes emphasized that equality between men and women was one of the goals of the legislature in enacting this legislation.

21. Cal. Civ. Code, § 4506(1).

22. Cal. Civ. Code, § 4506(2).

23. This was viewed as a substantial change from the existing law. See William E. MacFaden, "California's New Divorce Legislation," *Journal of the Beverly Hills Bar Association* 3, no. 7 (September 1969): 31–36.

24. Commentators at the time of the passage of the act questioned whether the courts would be willing to award substantial support except in unusual situations. See Stuart A. Brody, "California's Divorce Reform: Its Sociological Implications," *Pacific Law Journal* 1, no. 1 (1970): 223–32.

25. Weitzman, *Divorce Revolution,* 15.

26. Whether the act was intended to create equality between men and women has been hotly contested. Herma Hill Kay, who was active in the development of the divorce law reform, argued that Lenore Weitzman was ill informed and that the idea of equality was introduced in the assembly report by Assemblyman Hayes after the act had been passed. See Kay, "Equality," 3.

27. Krom, "Divorce Law Reform," 181.

28. Krom, "Divorce Law Reform," 181.

Good Intentions Gone Awry

29. Brody, "California's Divorce Reform," 231.

30. Kay, "Equality," 42.

31. Kay, "Equality," 3.

32. Kay, "Equality," 44.

33. Krom, "Divorce Law Reform," 158.

34. Kay, "Equality," 56.

35. Marriage and Family Commission of the National Organization for Women, *Suggested Guidelines in Studying and Comments on the Uniform Marriage and Divorce Act*, April 11, 1971, 3.

36. "Report of the Advisory Commission on the Status of Women," *California Woman* (1969): 79–80.

37. Robert Levy, *Uniform Marriage and Divorce Legislation: A Preliminary Analysis* (Chicago: American Bar Association, 1968).

38. Weitzman, *Divorce Revolution*, 19. Others noted that there was a difference between rule equity under the law and the practical effect on result equity. Although women became legally equal to men under no-fault divorce, the financial impact of divorce was not equal between men and women. See Martha Fineman, "Implementing Equality: Ideology, Contradiction, and Social Change. A Study of Rhetoric and Results in the Regulation of the Consequences of Divorce," *Wisconsin Law Review* 1983 (July-August 1983): 789–886.

39. Kay, "Equality," 57.

40. Victor R. Fuchs, *How We Live* (Cambridge, MA: Harvard University Press, 1983), 150.

41. Fuchs, *How*, 149. However, after the introduction of no- fault divorce, the causation may have shifted in the opposite direction—the labor-force-participation rate of married women continued to rise as the divorce rate leveled off and eventually declined. See Allen M. Parkman, "Unilateral Divorce and the Labor Force Participation Rate of Married Women, Revisited," *American Economic Review* 82, no. 3 (June 1992): 671–78.

42. Robert T. Michael, "The Rise in Divorce Rates, 1960–1974: Age-Specific Components," *Demography* 15, no. 2 (May 1978): 345–47.

43. Heather L. Ross and Isabel V. Sawhill, *Time of Transition: The Growth of Families Headed by Women* (Washington, DC: Urban Institute, 1975).

44. Richard G. Niemi, John Mueller, and Tom W. Smith, *Trends in Public Opinion* (New York: Greenwood Press, 1989), 278.

45. See Herbert Jacob, *Silent Revolution* (Chicago: University of Chicago Press, 1988), 50.

46. Family lawyers continue to be opposed to the rescinding of no-fault divorce laws. In a 1996 survey of the Family Law Section of the American Bar Association, 84 percent of the respondents opposed a change in the current divorce laws; American Bar Association Press release dated October 18, 1996. Unfortunately, the alternative being considered was fault divorce rather than, for example, mutual consent.

47. Although surveys do not show much demand for no-fault divorce, men have generally been more in support of easier divorce laws than women. Niemi, Mueller, and Smith, *Trends.*

48. In the most systematic investigation of the passage of no-fault divorce in the United States by a political scientist, James Hayes's self-interest motivations are ignored. Most of the credit for divorce reform in California was awarded to a small band of self-appointed experts. See Jacob, *Silent Revolution,* 50. Jacob's only reference to Hayes (*Silent Revolution,* 58) is that State Senator Donald Grunsky, the principle sponsor of no-fault legislation in the State Senate, had to win "the cooperation of the chair of the assembly judiciary committee, Los Angeles assemblyman James Hayes, who had not preciously participated in the development of the proposals but presented his own bill as an alternative."

49. *Hayes v. Hayes,* D700 518, Superior Court, Los Angeles, CA, November 6, 1969. For a discussion of *Hayes,* see Riane Tennenhaus Eisler, *Dissolution, No-Fault Divorce, Marriage, and the Future of Women* (New York: McGraw-Hill, 1977), 24–31, and Weitzman, *Divorce Revolution,* 211–12.

50. It was the common practice under fault divorce for the wife to file for divorce even when she was not the party who initially requested the divorce. Because the grounds for divorce required the defendant to be at fault, the normal outcome of the negotiations was for the wife to file the complaint.

51. "Assembly Committee Report on Assembly Bill No.530 and Senate Bill 252 (The Family Law Act)," submitted by Committee on Judiciary, James A. Hayes, Chairman, on August 8, 1969, printed in *Assembly Daily Journal,* August 8, 1969, as quoted in Respondent's Opening Points and Authorities, Order to Show Cause, *Hayes v. Hayes,* D700 518, filed December 13, 1972.

52. "Hayes's Ex-Wife Seeks Welfare, Food Stamps," *Los Angeles Times,* June 6, 1975.

53. *Hayes v. Hayes,* Court of Appeals of the State of California, Second Appellate District, Division Five, 2d Civil No. 45168, October 3, 1975 (unpublished opinion), 27–28.

54. Since the beginning of the nineteenth century, courts have held that custody should be based on the best interest of child. See Carl E. Schneider and Margaret F. Brinig, *An Invitation to Family Law* (St. Paul, MN: West, 1996), 620.

55. Doris J. Freed, "Grounds for Divorce in the American Jurisdictions," *Family Law Quarterly* 6, no. 2 (Summer 1972), 178.

56. For the argument that a central historical theme underlying marriage and divorce has been the protection of the reliance interest in marriage, see Margaret F. Brinig and June Carbone, "The Reliance Interest in Marriage and Divorce," *Tulane Law Review* 62 (1988): 870–82. Damages in a breach-of-contract case can be based on expectations, reliance, restitution, or liquidated damages. The effects of these different standards on whether outcomes are efficient are discussed in A. Mitchell Polinsky, *An Introduction to Law and Economics,* 2d ed. (Boston: Little, Brown, 1989), 27–38 and 59–65. An expectation standard for damages tends to produce more efficient breaches than a reliance standard, but a restitution standard is more likely than a reliance standard to induce an efficient amount of reliance under a contract. The concepts of efficient breach and efficient reliance will be discussed in more detail in Chapter 6.

57.   Some authors have argued that employment is an important source of power during marriage. Male dominance in marriage is stronger when the wife is exclusively a
homemaker than when she is employed outside the home. See Paula England and George
Farkas, *Households, Employment, and Gender* (New York: Aldine De Gruyter, 1986), 54.

58.   See Parkman, "Unilateral Divorce"; and Allen M. Parkman, "Why Are Married
Women Working So Hard?," *International Review of Law and Economics* 18, no. 1 (Winter 1998): 41–49.

59.   Although the increase in the labor-force-participation rate of married women is
often attributed to an increase in financial pressures on families, that contention is not
supported by academic research. Declines in male employment and earnings have been
greatest for low-wage men, but employment and earnings gains have been largest for wives
of middle- and high-wage men. This research casts doubt on the notion that married women
have increased their labor supply in the recent decades to compensate for the disappointing earnings growth of their husbands. See Chinhui Juhn and Kevin M. Murphy, "Wage
Inequality and Family Labor Supply," *Journal of Labor Economics* 15, no. 1 (1997): 72–
97.

Another explanation for the increased labor market activities of married women
has been their new access to rewarding and fulfilling jobs. For some people, the psychic
income from jobs can be important, but it can also be overstated. In many cases people are
paid to work because without the pay they would prefer leisure activities. Higher lifetime
incomes have permitted people to retire earlier—to choose leisure over employment. The
labor-force-participation rate of married men over age sixty-five decreased from 37 percent to 18 percent during the period 1960 to 1997, while the rate for those between ages
forty-five and sixty-four fell from 94 percent to 83 percent; *Statistical Abstract of the United
States, 1998* (Washington, DC: U.S. Government Printing Office, 1998), Table 652, 408.
Obviously, many married men were not receiving substantial psychic rewards from their
jobs because more of them chose leisure over work as retirement benefits rose.

5

The Impact of
No-Fault Divorce

In the period since World War II, U.S. society has undergone dramatic changes. The introduction of no-fault grounds for divorce has played a significant, and often unrecognized, role in those changes. Of particular importance has been the reduction in the stability of marriage. The rising divorce rate and pressure for simpler procedures for dissolving marriages led to no-fault divorce. The introduction of no-fault divorce, in turn, has had feedback effects that have made a major contribution to the changes.

The role of no-fault divorce in the changes that we have observed since World War II is the subject of this chapter. Individuals alter their prior decisions when their tastes and preferences shift or when the costs or the benefits associated with activities change. Tastes and preferences tend to change only slowly, and the following discussion focuses on the more rapid shift in incentives due to changes in the costs and the benefits of activities. Because no-fault divorce reduced the net benefits of making a long-term commitment to a spouse, it influenced many of the trends in U.S. society since 1970. People have done things that they would not have done if the divorce laws had not changed. Many of these effects are subtle. The discussion will include changes in the divorce rate, the condition of divorced spouses and their children, the incentive to marry, the incentive for married women to work outside the home and to continue their education, the quality of life for intact families, and the definition of property subject to division at divorce. We will see that not only did people change their behavior, but often they found themselves worse off than under fault divorce. An inescapable conclusion is that no-fault divorce has reduced the quality of family life for many people relative to the position they would be in if the divorce laws encouraged a long-term commitment to marriage.

THE DIVORCE RATE

The stability of marriage in the United States has declined dramatically since World War II. The annual divorce rate for married women (see table 5.1[1]) rose from 10.3 per 1,000 in 1950 to 19.8 per 1,000 in 1995 after peaking at 22.8 per 1,000 in 1979.[1] The divorce rate doubled between 1965 and 1975. Whether the increase in the divorce rate caused no-fault divorce or whether the causation ran in the opposite direction has been the source of some debate. Certainly, new laws can alter human behavior, but the laws themselves often reflect legislators' attempts to respond to changes in basic socioeconomic forces. Both effects may have been present with no-fault divorce.[2] Because the divorce rate was increasing before the introduction of no-fault divorce, it is difficult to escape the conclusion that some

Table 5.1   Divorce Rates and Related Data

Year	Divorce Rate (per thousand) for Married Women	Average Hourly Earnings[a]	Ratio Women's/ Men's Earnings[b]	Births (per thousand population)
1950	10.3	$5.34		24.1
1955	9.3	6.15	.639	25.0
1960	9.2	6.79	.603	23.7
1965	10.6	7.52	.599	19.4
1970	14.9	8.03	.600	18.4
1975	20.3	8.12	.588	14.6
1980	22.6	7.78	.594	15.9
1985	21.7	7.77	.646	15.8
1990	20.9	7.52	.682	16.7
1995	19.8	7.39	.717	14.9
1998		7.75		14.6

[a]1982 dollars.

[b]Weekly wage ratios, full-time workers.

Sources: Divorce rate, average earnings, and births from *Statistical Abstract of the United States* (Washington, DC: U.S. Government Printing Office, various years), and National Center for Health Statistics, "Births, Marriages, Divorces, and Deaths for November 1998," *National Vital Statistics Report* 47, no. 17 (March 17, 1999). Men's and women's earnings for 1995–1985 are from Claudia Goldin, *Understanding the Gender Gap* (New York: Oxford University Press, 1990), 60–61, and those for 1990 and 1995 are from Francine D. Blau, "Trends in the Well-Being of American Women, 1970–95," *Journal of Economic Literature* 36, no. 1 (March 1998): 129.

causation went from the increase in the divorce rate to the introduction of no-fault divorce laws.[3] That is not to say that the introduction of no-fault divorce laws had no feedback effect.

The increase in the demand for simpler divorce procedures was caused by marriage becoming a less attractive institution for some adults. People marry because they expect to be better off in that state than in the single state. They divorce if this expectation turns out to be false. This can occur when there is either an unexpected reduction in the gains from marriage or an unexpected decline in the predictability of outcomes during marriage—both of which happened after World War II. The effect of these changes on divorce was not broadly recognized at the time.

The Reduction in the Gains from Marriage

Marriage is an attractive institution for both spouses as long as both expect to be better off married than single. A significant share of the benefits of marriage, in contrast to the benefits of dating or living together, flows from an increase in the specialization of labor during marriage that is often associated with children. People become more efficient by focusing their energies on one or on a limited range of activities. This specialization results in people having too much of some goods and too little of others and, therefore, becomes more attractive when there are opportunities for trade. During marriage, the husband traditionally increased his specialization in the production of earnings, whereas the wife increased her specialization in activities in the home. Through an exchange of their outputs during marriage, both spouses were better off.

When women were confronted with low wages and limited employment opportunities, marriage with increased specialization in household production was a rational choice for essentially all adult women. Conditions changed when wages and opportunities available to women increased. After adjustment for inflation, in 1982 dollars, the average hourly real wage rose from $5.34 in 1950 to $8.12 in 1975 and then fell gradually over the next 20 years, before recently recovering slightly[4] (see table 5.1.). The real wage can be used to convert the time spent working at home into purchasing power—the ability to buy a larger house or more restaurant meals. Higher wages therefore create an incentive for families to decide that the value of the goods that the people who would otherwise work at home can generate through outside employment exceeds the value of at least some commodities that these people can produce in the home. In fact, the labor-force-participation rate (LFPR) of white women twenty years and older rose from 32.7 percent in 1954 to 42.2 percent in 1970, when California introduced no-fault divorce.[5] It continued to increase to 60 percent in 1998. This trend is even more dramatic for married women for which the LFPR rose from 24 percent in 1950 to

62 percent in 1997.[6] Particularly noteworthy has been the increase in the labor force participation of married women with young children. The rate for married women with children under six years of age rose from 18.6 percent in 1960 to 62.6 percent in 1997.

When both spouses increase the amount of time during which they work outside the home, the specialization of labor during marriage is usually reduced. Based on data from 1975 and 1976, Janice Peskin reported that women not otherwise employed provided 42.6 hours per week of household services; women who were employed full time outside the home provided 20.1 hours.[7] Women working full time outside the home worked less in the home than women not otherwise employed, but the hours worked outside the home by these women did not result in a corresponding reduction in their work at home. Victor Fuchs observed the work habits of women in 1960 and 1986 and noted a similar pattern over time. He found that women worked less at home as they increased the hours they worked outside the home,[8] but overall they ended up working 7 percent more hours in 1986 than in 1960. Between 1960 and 1986, married women reduced their annual hours of housework by 200 hours, but men only increased their annual hours of housework by 3 hours. Although the specialization between men and women during marriage has decreased, there has been an increase in the specialization among women. Some of the responsibility for household services has shifted to other women, who have increased their specialization by being employed in traditionally domestic activities such as day care or cleaning services.[9]

An unexpected result of this decrease in the specialization between husbands and wives can be a decline in the gains from marriage. This is especially true because higher wages for women reduce the incentive for couples to have children. A rise in the wages available to women increases the cost of children because the mother has to leave the labor force to deliver the child. In addition, at least one parent usually has to limit his or her employment to help in the raising of the child. This has traditionally been the mother because the wages available to women tend to be less than those available to men. For example, during the period before the introduction of no-fault divorce laws, the average wage of women was approximately 60 percent of the average wage of men.[10] Still, as illustrated in table 5.1, as women's wages rose, the fertility rate fell. Between 1950 and 1970, the number of births per thousand population fell from 24.1 to 18.4[11] and continued to fall to 14.6 in 1975, when the maturation of the baby boom generation started to reverse the trend. In the 1990s, the birth rate started to decline again. The desire for children historically has been a primary reason that people marry; as the demand for children fell, so did the gains from marriage.

The higher wages and broader employment opportunities available to women had both a direct and an indirect effect on gains from marriage. The direct effect came from higher wages raising the opportunity cost of either spouse working at home. The upshot was an increase in the percentage of married women working outside the home and a corresponding decrease in their specialization in domestic activities. There is also an indirect effect on the incentive to specialize in domestic production from higher wages decreasing the demand for children. With fewer children, there is less to be gained from either spouse working in the home.

A reduction in the gains from marriage should not necessarily affect the divorce rate. If the reduction is anticipated, it should lead to fewer but equally stable marriages. The divorce rate increases when the change in the gains from marriage is unexpected. Marriage traditionally has been a long-term arrangement, and the higher wages and broader range of employment opportunities that became available to women after World War II were not contemplated at the time of many marriages. As married women entered the labor force in response to the unexpected employment opportunities, they reduced their specialization in household production. Because many couples had not anticipated this change when they married, their marriages became vulnerable, with a resulting increase in the number of married people who wanted a divorce.

The Predictability of Outcomes during Marriage

Rapid changes in society in the postwar period also affected the predictability of the outcomes that people experienced during marriage. Higher wages and the growth of the service sector after World War II led to more women being employed and to wives becoming less financially dependant on their husbands. The increased availability of contraceptives changed sexual habits. At the same time, the fertility rate continued to fall. Few of these changes were anticipated.

People enter marriage with a set of expectations that are the basis of the decision to marry. If the expectations are realized, the marriage is likely to continue; but when actual events during marriage differ from the expectations, the marriage becomes vulnerable. For example, a woman may marry because she feels that her employment possibilities are limited and a marriage proposal has come from an acceptable man. If she later discovers that attractive jobs are available for women, she may decide that she is better off divorced and employed than married to this person. This is especially likely to occur if her husband married with the expectation that his wife would be a homemaker and a mother.

The reduction in the gains from marriage and the predictability of outcomes during marriage made marriage a less-attractive institution for many people—some of whom were already married. In some cases, the reaction to these changes was a desire for a divorce. The fault grounds for divorce made divorce difficult, though not impossible; the increased desire for divorce was accompanied by an increase in the demand for simpler procedures for dissolving marriages.

The Effect of No-Fault Divorce

With no-fault divorce providing less protection for personal sacrifices due to increased specialization during marriage, spouses reduced their specialization during marriage. Less specialization could reduce both the gains as well as the predictability of marriage, thereby, increasing the divorce rate. Furthermore, no-fault divorce also could affect the transaction costs associated with divorce.

If one believes that the legal grounds for divorce under fault divorce controlled whether a marriage was dissolved, then one probably would conclude that simpler grounds such as no-fault divorce would lead to a higher divorce rate. There is evidence, however, that the legal grounds for divorce under fault were not a major impediment to the dissolution of marriages. Mary Ann Glendon found that negotiation was the primary mechanism under fault divorce for settling disputes about property, spousal and child support, and child custody.[12] Settlements were reached when the party wanting a divorce could offer the other party compensation adequate to induce him or her to participate in the dissolution of the marriage. Thus a divorce tended to occur only when both parties expected to be better off divorced than in their current marriage. The divorced spouse might have preferred the continuation of a "happy marriage," but that situation was probably no longer an option. Thus even the spouse unwilling to divorce, if sufficiently compensated, could be better off divorced than continuing with the situation in the current marriage.

Although people continued to negotiate under no-fault divorce, the bargaining power of spouses who did not want to divorce was reduced, with the likelihood increasing that some costs of divorce would be shifted from the divorcing spouses to the divorced spouses. It is not clear, however, if this affected the divorce rate. Observers have argued that when transaction costs are low, the same divorces might occur under no-fault divorce as would have occurred under fault.[13] With low transaction costs, the major difference between the legal environments would be the financial settlement: it would be expected to be smaller under no-fault divorce for the spouse who preferred to continue the marriage.

This process can be illustrated with a numerical example. Although physical attraction is an important factor in people's choice of a particular person for dating, as I have noted earlier, the decision for two people to marry rather than to continue to date or to live together tends to be based on an expected increase in the welfare of both due to marriage. This increase has been presented in the context of the commodities that would be available during marriage, including a house, home-cooked meals, and children. Divorce often occurs when the parties later reject their initial expectations. New information causes them to reevaluate their marriages. For simplicity, let us assume that the commodities produced during marriage are divisible.[14] In the first situation, the husband expects 50 units if he remains in his current marriage sharing his income with his family and 100 units if he divorces and gains sole control over most of his income. The wife expects 50 units if she remains married and 25 units if she divorces. If a divorce requires mutual consent, as was the situation under fault, the husband might offer the wife 30 units if she will consent to the divorce. The husband will then have 70 units if he divorces, which is better than the 50 he expects from marriage, and the wife will have 55 units, which is more than the 50 units that she receives from staying married. They divorce. Furthermore, if divorce is unilateral—which is essentially the situation in many no-fault divorce states—the couple will also divorce. There is no transfer that the wife can make that will make her husband better off in the current marriage than divorced. There is no longer the need for the husband to make a payment to the wife to induce her cooperation. The husband will not have to give up the 30 units to obtain the divorce. He will be better off, and the wife will be worse off. But they divorce under either legal system.

A contrasting situation exists with a couple that does not divorce. A husband might expect 25 units during marriage and 50 units after divorce; his wife expects 50 units during marriage and 10 units after divorce. In a situation requiring mutual consent, the husband's 25-unit gain fails to cover the wife's 40-unit loss, so the marriage continues. With unilateral divorce, the husband might contemplate a divorce. If the output of the marriage is divisible, however, the wife could offer the husband 30 units from her share of the output of the marriage, which would make him better off married.[15] After the transfer, both the husband with 55 units and the wife with 20 units are better off married than divorced and they stay married under both legal systems.

In these situations in which there are no transaction costs, the different laws do not change the divorce rate but only the distribution of the gains and loses. Unilateral divorce, in both cases, increased the resources available to the person who preferred a divorce. This result can change if there are significant transaction costs associated with divorce. Transaction costs are those imposed on the divorcing spouse that are not necessarily gains for the divorced spouse. Under fault divorce, divorce placed a social stigma on the "guilty" spouse that was potentially a cost to that party, especially in small communities. The negotiations and the construction of the evidence required by fault also could be costly. The benefits to the party who wanted to dissolve the marriage are net of these transaction costs as well as of the transfers to the other spouse. Meanwhile, benefits to the divorced spouse consist of only the transfers.

No-fault divorce might reduce the transaction costs of divorce because there no longer is a "guilty" party. Concern about the social stigma associated with that party is reduced or eliminated. In addition, fabricating evidence of fault, such as adultery or mental cruelty, is no longer necessary. The range of issues to be negotiated also has been reduced. Some marriages might have continued under fault divorce that are dissolved under no-fault divorce. This would occur if the parties who wanted to dissolve the marriages realized that after allowance for the costs of the divorce, they would be unwilling to compensate their spouse enough to cover the spouse's costs. The reduction in transaction costs that came with no-fault divorce might make divorce more attractive.

Consider the preceding example in which the couple divorced under both legal systems. If the transaction costs were 30 units under fault divorce and 10 units under no-fault divorce, the couple would stay married under fault but divorce under no-fault divorce. If no-fault divorce reduced the transaction costs, it could induce some divorces that would not have occurred under fault. This shift would only apply to existing marriages, however, so the change in the grounds for divorce would only be expected to cause a short-term increase in the divorce rate.

The long-term effect of no-fault divorce can differ from the short-term effect. No-fault divorce changed the assumptions that people make before marriage. Knowing that it is easier to dissolve a marriage might lead people to enter marriages that they would not have considered when dissolution was more difficult; the result would be an additional number of fragile marriages and eventually an increase in the divorce rate.[16] Alternatively, people might recognize that marriage under no-fault divorce provides less protection for the parties who otherwise would have specialized in household production. Without that protection, the spouses who normally would have assumed that role would be reluctant to specialize and the incentive to marriage would be reduced. Couples might live together but not find it attractive to marry. If the couples who do not have much to gain from marriage under these new circumstances did not marry, the divorce rate might fall.

No-fault divorce can also influence the decisions of people who are already married. People, usually women, who committed themselves to emphasizing domestic activities during marriage now find themselves unexpectedly vulnerable at divorce under no-fault divorce. They can be expected to respond by reducing their commitment to those domestic roles and by taking steps to protect themselves through employment or additional education, which would reduce their specialization during marriage and increase the likelihood of divorce. Because people often entered marriage with different expectations about their marriage, the divorce rate might increase for this group after no-fault divorce was introduced.

Empirical Evidence on the Change in the Divorce Rate

It has been difficult to test for the effect of no-fault divorce on the divorce rate. First, no-fault divorce has taken a variety of forms from "irretrievable breakdown" to "living separate and apart" for a specific period, creating ambiguity about how no-fault divorce should be specified in empirical studies. Second, the effects would be expected to be lagged, and the structure of the lagged effects is unknown. Last, because all states have had some form of no-fault divorce for more than a decade, there are no states with different laws against which the no-fault divorce states can be compared. Any comparison with an earlier period is forced to deal with a broad variety of other changes that have occurred.

These problems have not deterred scholars. Gary Becker found that the change in the grounds for divorce in California in 1970 led only to a short-term increase in the divorce rate in that state, with the rate quickly returning to its old trend.[17] In the first systematic study of the impact of no-fault divorce on the divorce rate, Elizabeth Peters found that residence in a no-fault divorce state in 1979 did not increase the probability that a woman would divorce.[18] Peters's results have been challenged by Doug Allen, who questioned her designation of no-fault divorce states.[19] Allen showed that by removing the influence of the regional variables used by Peters, no-fault divorce had a positive effect on the divorce rate. Using different data than Peters and Allen, Martin Zelder concluded that no-fault divorce caused an increase in the divorce rate.[20] Using still another data set, Jeffrey Gray concluded that unilateral divorce had little effect on the probability that a couple would divorce.[21] Leora Friedberg determined that divorce rates would have been about 6 percent lower if states had not adopted no-fault divorce.[22] Because some states that have no-fault grounds for divorce still consider fault in determining financial settlements, a true no-fault divorce state would be one in which the laws governing both the dissolution and the financial settlement are no-fault. Using that definition for no-fault divorce, Peg Brinig and Frank Buckley found that no-fault divorce was associated with higher divorce levels.[23] In conclusion, the more recent evidence lends some support to the argument that no-fault divorce has increased the divorce rate above the level that it otherwise would have reached.[24]

THE EFFECT ON DIVORCED SPOUSES

Because no-fault divorce commonly permits a spouse to dissolve a marriage unilaterally, subject often to limited compensation, no-fault has frequently had a devastating effect on divorced spouses. Perhaps the most striking consequence of the introduction of no-fault divorce has been the deterioration in the financial condition of divorced women and the children of divorced parents. Another concern, which is more subtle, has been the psychological effect of no-fault divorce on divorced men and women who find that a marriage to which they have made a commitment can be dissolved with their having very little control over the process.

The Financial Effect on Divorced Women

The dissolution of a marriage can include financial arrangements to cover the property settlement, spousal support, and child support, but after the introduction of no-fault divorce, the financial settlements received by divorced women appear to have declined substantially. This was especially the case for women in marriages of long duration. The smaller settlements are due to no-fault divorce reducing the negotiating power of spouses who do not want to dissolve their marriage. The surprising thing is that it took so long for this effect to be recognized.[25] Lenore Weitzman was the first author to present this effect to a large audience with her 1985 book, *The Divorce Revolution*.[26] As she summarized the problem in California, "The reformers were so preoccupied with the question of fault and its role in both obtaining a divorce and securing a financial settlement, that few of them thought sufficiently about the consequences of the new system to foresee how its fault-neutral rules might come to disadvantage the economically weaker party."[27]

When Weitzman initiated her research in the 1970s, she reported that she had "assumed, in the optimistic spirit of the reformers, the 'California experiment' with no-fault divorce could only have positive results,"[28] but her research led her to the conclusion that no-fault divorce eliminated the leverage possessed by the "innocent" parties.[29] This leverage had given those parties power, with the outcome of the parties' negotiations being private agreements. Weitzman, however, emphasized that those financial awards were linked by the courts to fault.[30] Without the fault grounds, she attributed most of the deterioration in the financial condition of divorced women to the courts' decisions. She implied that the courts established the awards under both fault and no-fault divorce.

It appears that it was not common for the courts to decide the actual amounts under fault divorce.[31] The initially unwilling plaintiffs usually would have been unlikely to agree to filing the suit if they did not already know the financial outcome. The negotiations and the settlements were essential for inducing their cooperation. The fault grounds for divorce were important for providing leverage for the initially nonconsenting spouses, not for determining the details of financial arrangements. The courts' role was generally only to certify the parties' agreements.

No-fault divorce reversed the roles of the parties and the courts. With fault divorce, there were incentives for the couple to negotiate their own arrangements, ignoring the applicable statutes. Alternatively, with no-fault divorce the parties who did not want their marriage to be dissolved had significantly less negotiating power, and in many states a divorce could be obtained unilaterally. If the divorce was litigated, the courts based these settlements on the existing laws that dictated how property was to be divided and how alimony and child support were to be awarded. These laws had not been critically analyzed during the fault divorce era because they had seldom been applied in controversial cases. The divorced spouse could then expect to receive half of the limited marital property, short-term rehabilitative spousal support, and child support if there were minor children. The spousal and child support was often difficult to collect. The laws governing property settlements had serious problems because they considered only a narrow set of assets as property. Most important, they ignored the spouses' income-earning capacities, which financial analysts would recognize as just as much an asset as a car, a house, or a share of stock. This omission was particularly egregious when a spouse had reduced his or her future income-earning capacity by limiting a career during marriage. Recognizing the fairly predictable outcome of litigation probably resulted in negotiated settlements that were not substantially different from those expected at trial. Although a couple might trade off the different components of the settlement, a spouse was not likely to receive greater value overall than that provided by law.

The change in the financial settlements in no-fault divorce states can be illustrated by reviewing the situation in California. As the leader in this movement, that state has been subjected to the most scrutiny. Although the divorce statutes vary slightly in other states, the effects should be similar with their being more pronounced the easier it is for just one spouse to obtain a divorce.

For some couples, the financial arrangements at divorce in California changed dramatically after the introduction of no-fault divorce in 1970. The California Family Law Act[32] specified that courts must divide the marital property equally,[33] a rule touted as fair and "protective" of wives, being based on the idea that marriage was an equal partnership in which the financial and nonfinancial contributions of the two spouses were of equal value. Weitzman found that the idea of an equal division of the community property had met with widespread approval by both men and women, including lawyers and judges, whom she interviewed.[34] No one appears to have questioned whether the legal definition of property was accurate or appropriate.

In practice, the average couple had few assets at divorce. This is not surprising because many divorces occur in the early years of marriage.[35] The women who were the most adversely affected by a reduction in negotiating power at divorce, however, were women who had been married for a long time. These women were more likely to be in marriages in which some property had accumulated, and no-fault divorce had a particularly adverse effect on them. Under fault, the wife usually received most of the couple's property at divorce,[36] but the percentage of cases in which the community property was divided equally rose dramatically after the introduction of no-fault divorce.[37]

The percentage of divorced women receiving property settlements has declined during the period after the introduction of the no-fault divorce laws.[38] This trend was similar for old as well as for young women. Under fault divorce, negotiating spouses had incentives to place a special emphasis on the property component of the settlement. The law treated the property settlement, alimony, and child support as serving different purposes and subject to different criteria; but spouses were concerned primarily with the size and predictability of the overall amount. They would have been expected to trade smaller amounts of alimony and child support for larger property settlements because property settlements usually occur in a lump payment, whereas alimony and child support come in smaller, periodic payments that can be difficult to collect. Furthermore, property settlements, in contrast to alimony and child support, are not subject to modification. As the unequal distribution of property under fault tended to benefit unwilling plaintiffs, often women, the shift toward equal divisions of property under no-fault divorce appears to confirm that divorced women were financially worse off under no-fault divorce.

Weitzman found a similar pattern for spousal support after 1970,[39] although the evidence is weaker than for property settlements. First, there was a shift away from permanent awards, based on the idea that the wife was able to become self-sufficient after the marriage. Second, in calculating support, the courts looked at the wife's skills and experience rather than at the issue of fault.[40] Even women with custody of young children, women in need of transitional support, and older homemakers incapable of self-sufficiency were seldom awarded support.[41]

Weitzman's research did not detect any effect of no-fault divorce on child support. In the period after the introduction of no-fault divorce, the amount of child support received was low, reflecting both the low awards and the low probability of collection.[42] Her discussion of child support includes a valuable insight on the process that has been emphasized in this book—she notes that a third of divorced women reported that their husbands had threatened to ask for custody as a ploy in negotiations to reduce the amount of child support.[43] This situation further illustrates the change in position of spouses under no-fault divorce. Under fault divorce, the husband who wanted a divorce had to negotiate with the wife; under no-fault, the wife who wants the children has to negotiate with the husband. In both cases, the party with negotiating power is likely to receive a settlement more in line with his or her preferences.

Overall, husbands have rarely been ordered to part with more than a third of their income to support their ex-wife and children.[44] Based on interviews with divorced men and women in Los Angeles County, California, in 1978, Weitzman concluded that divorced men experienced an average 42 percent increase in their standard of living in the first year after divorce and that divorced women and their children experienced a 73 percent decline.[45]

The 42 percent increase for men and 73 percent decline for women from divorce rapidly became two of the most commonly cited statistics with respect to the effects of no-fault divorce. Other scholars started to question the magnitude of the impact that Weitzman had observed. Saul Hoffman and Greg Duncan also found that the financial condition of divorced women deteriorated after the introduction of no-fault divorce,[46] although they argued that Weitzman's 73 percent decline in economic status for divorced women is probably too large. Using longitudinal data from the *Panel Study of Income Dynamics* collected by the University of Michigan, they found the economic status of divorced women fell an average of approximately 30 percent in the first year after divorce.[47]

Richard Peterson also questioned the magnitude of Weitzman's numbers.[48] He replicated her analysis and demonstrated that the estimates reported in her book are inaccurate. His analysis, which used the same sample and measures of economic well-being as her book, produced estimates of a 27 percent decline in women's standard of living and a 10 percent increase in men's standard of living after divorce.[49] In Weitzman's response to his article, she acknowledged that a subsequent review of her data revealed problems.[50] For example, her sample oversampled people in longer marriages, who were more adversely affected by divorce. Moreover, she noted that she had questioned the 73 percent decline in women's postdivorce standard of living, but she had been reassured by her computer assistant that the number was accurate. Certainly, we now have to conclude that her often-quoted numbers are inaccurate and that the more accurate effects are substantial, but smaller, than she reported.

Elizabeth Peters made a direct test of the effect of no-fault divorce on the financial arrangements at divorce, arguing that the introduction of no-fault divorce should reduce the bargaining power of married women at dissolution so that their financial settlements would be reduced. As the components of the financial settlements are fungible, she investigated the effects of a divorced woman residing in a no-fault divorce state on all the components of the financial arrangements at divorce, including alimony, child support, and property.[51] Using data from the March-April 1979 *Current Population Survey* collected by the U.S. Bureau of Labor Statistics, Peters found that divorced women in no-fault divorce states received $185 less alimony and $462 less child support per year than women in fault divorce states. These average figures are small, but the impact on some women must have been substantial. Because many marriages are of a short duration and only limited alimony and child support would have been appropriate under fault or no-fault divorce, women from marriages of longer duration probably experienced substantial reductions.

Peters found that divorced women in no-fault divorce states received property settlements that were $137 smaller than those in fault divorce states, a difference that is not statistically significant. Peters could not conclude that the property settlements were affected by the grounds for divorce in the states, but the evidence could in part reflect the fact that many divorces involved couples who owned little property. If they owned little property, there was little room for the awards to vary across states. For divorced women from marriages of longer duration, the effect of no-fault divorce on their property settlements may again have been significant.

The financial conditions of divorced women continued to be dire after divorce. Using data from the mid-1980s, Eleanor E. Maccoby and Robert H. Mnookin found that both fathers' and mothers' incomes plus-or-minus any court awards fell after divorce, with the income of the mothers falling substantially more than that of the fathers.[52] After adjustment for family size, Maccoby and Mnookin concluded that the fathers' incomes increased by 15 percent even three years after the divorce, while the mothers' incomes fell by 35 percent.[53] This was frequently due to support payments being a small percentage of the mother's postdivorce income.[54]

The observations of others confirmed that the courts were generally not generous to spouses who had worked primarily at home during marriage. Mary Ann Glendon noted that awards, especially for child support, received by divorced women after no-fault divorce were limited.[55] She cited a former welfare commissioner of New York City, who observed that judges are reluctant to impose any significant burden on the absent father or to reduce the burden on society of Aid to Families with Dependent Children(AFDC) payments. Carol Bruch found judges unaware of or greatly underestimating the actual cost of raising a child.[56] Under fault divorce, the courts' influence on the level of child support would have been much smaller, with divorced women negotiating the child support as part of the financial settlement.

There have not been any studies using more-recent data on the effect of no-fault divorce on the financial condition of divorced spouses. Because no-fault has been in place for so long, scholars are no longer able to compare the situation in which people would have been under fault divorce to their situation under no-fault divorce. Still, it is hard to escape the fact that many of a family's costs, such as housing and utilities, do not vary substantially with household size. Therefore, with a divorce, even if the higher-income ex-spouses live up to their legally imposed financial obligations, the members of both households are frequently going to be worse off than they were before divorce.

Because husbands usually have higher incomes than wives, divorced women and their children are particularly vulnerable if the husbands do not live up to their legal obligations. During the period 1989 to 1991, only 42 percent of divorced or separated mothers received any child support, alimony, or funds from their extended family.[57] Without the limited protection provided by fault divorce, both spouses have been forced to provide themselves with some protection against the potential costs of divorce by increasing their commitment to employment and education. Therefore, with higher incomes, on average, both spouses are less financially vulnerable at divorce.

Women Were Not Worse Off

All scholars do not agree that divorced women became worse off after the introduction of no-fault divorce. The Weitzman and the Peters studies, in particular, were attacked by some authors. Without acknowledging the change in the negotiating power of divorced women that occurred with the introduction of no-fault divorce, Herbert Jacob objected to Weitzman's and Peters's focus on asset division, alimony, and child support.[58] Jacob argued that any changes in property division and child support may be the result of changes in other statutes as much as the impact of no-fault divorce. He did not recognize that laws controlling the financial arrangements at divorce were generally not applied under fault divorce. It is true that the laws that controlled financial arrangements changed slightly with the introduction of no-fault divorce, but their importance has changed far more dramatically. It seems clear to me that the outcomes changed not because the laws changed, but because the laws rather than negotiated settlements began determining the awards in situations in which substantial assets or children existed. These laws were very detrimental to divorced women.

Jacob used data from the *National Longitudinal Surveys of Labor Market Experience* collected by Ohio State University to make three tests of the effects of no-fault divorce on divorced women to attempt to show that women were not worse off under no-fault divorce. His sample consisted of women who were considerably younger than those in the samples used by Weitzman and Peters. He looked first at the change in the salary and the wage income of divorced women who had not remarried at the first contact by the survey after their divorce during the period 1968 to 1983. In all legal environments, fault and no-fault, he found that women's income at divorce and after divorce was substantially lower than before divorce[59] and that the effect of no- fault divorce laws on postdivorce salary and wage income was either weak or nonexistent.[60] His test is ambiguous, however, as salary and wage income at and after divorce reflects the market conditions in the divorced women's state of residence rather than their financial settlements at divorce. The critics of no-fault divorce argue that the deterioration in the financial condition of divorced women and their children is due to the reduction in their negotiating power, not to labor market conditions in no-fault divorce states. The key distinction is whether the financial settlements received by divorced women differed under the two legal systems, and Jacob's test did not address that question.

Using data from 1983, Jacob further concluded that no-fault divorce did not affect whether a woman would receive child support. Again, the relevance of his test is not clear, because the awarding of child support was common under both fault and no-fault divorce. The real issues would seem to be how much was awarded and whether it was collected. Most critics of no-fault divorce have concluded that the amount of child support received decreased under no-fault, and Jacob found no evidence to refute that conclusion. His conclusion that the probability of receiving any child support was not affected by no-fault divorce should not be a surprise, because receipt is a result of the enforcement laws unrelated to the amount of the award or to the grounds for divorce.

Last, Jacob concluded, based on a limited sample, that no-fault divorce lacked a substantial effect on which party received the family house at divorce. Again, this should be no surprise. As Weitzman pointed out, few divorcing couples have substantial property, and Peters determined that the property settlement was not sensitive to the grounds for divorce. For most couples, the property settlement was not important; but it was very important for *some* couples, especially those who had been married for a long time. Jacob did not discuss the effect of no-fault divorce on the property settlements received by women from lengthy marriages.

Marygold S. Melli is another critic of the conclusions of the Weitzman study. She questioned Weitzman's conclusion that the financial condition of divorced women deteriorated after no-fault divorce and pointed out that it just continued at a depressed level.[61] Moreover, Melli was particularly sensitive to the condition of married women who wanted to initiate a divorce, noting that "by emphasizing the bargaining power of innocent spouses under fault divorce, Weitzman ignores the fate of mothers who decide to end a marriage and who therefore would suffer the economic hardship of a guilty spouse."[62] This was clearly a major problem with fault divorce.

Melli also expressed concern that "Weitzman's preoccupation with the contemporary no-fault divorce structure and gender-neutral rules as major causes of straitened economic circumstances of many women and children following divorce leads her to inaccurately credit fault divorce with economic protection for women and children that it in fact never provided."[63] It is not clear how Melli explains how men under fault divorce were able to obtain the agreement of their wives to be plaintiffs in divorce cases. We have to be careful when accepting arguments that have been made before legislatures, but the divorced men who advocated no-fault divorce in California certainly felt that fault was providing protection to married women. In fact, they felt that it was providing too much.

Finally, Melli stated, "By assuming that the disastrous economic consequences of divorce were caused by a change in the law, *The Divorce Revolution* makes the problem appear to be a simple one: a few more changes in the law and the problems will be rectified."[64] When a social concern is not the result of incorrect laws, a change in the laws is probably not the solution to the problem. The difference between the wages of men and women is an example of this situation. But when the problem exists because of the laws, the appropriate solution *is* to change the laws. The problems created by no-fault divorce are due to the existing laws that inaccurately define the property affected by marriage and the costs of divorce to the divorced spouses and their children. This situation can only be corrected by changing these laws. Reform of the current divorce laws is discussed in Chapter 6.

Additional objections to Weitzman's conclusions have come from Jana Singer,[65] who attempted to prove that divorced women were not better off under fault divorce. Failing to acknowledge the critical role of the wives' negotiating power and private settlements in determining outcomes under fault divorce, Singer argued that married women were vulnerable under fault. She found evidence that fault-based divorces were awarded to husbands on such weak grounds of marital misconduct as failure to prepare meals. As a large percentage of divorce cases were filed by women under fault, it is difficult to believe that many men succeeded in obtaining a divorce using those arguments.

The only aspect of the financial arrangements analyzed by Singer is alimony. She reviewed Weitzman's data on alimony and found no significant change between the two legal environments. As discussed earlier, of the elements of the divorce settlement, the least attractive component for the wife would be alimony, which was difficult to collect and was subject to modification in case of changed circumstances of either the husband or the wife. Thus the wife would rationally prefer a large property settlement if the resources were available. Singer made no mention of the decrease in the property settlements of older divorced women documented by Weitzman—the decrease that is probably the strongest evidence of the decline in the welfare of the divorced women who were most worthy of concern: those who were married for a long time.

Alimony was also the subject of an attack by Marsha Garrison,[66] advertised as "an assessment of the currently available evidence on the responsibility of the no-fault divorce revolution for divorcing women's declining fortunes."[67] Her original research analyzed the effect of the introduction of equitable distribution in New York in 1980. Although New York permits no-fault divorce, the no-fault grounds have to be based on mutual consent. Garrison demonstrated that the likelihood and duration of alimony fell during the period from two years before to four years after the equitable distribution law was enacted.[68] This is not, however, a test of the impact of no-fault divorce because the grounds for divorce did not change during this period. More important, she acknowledged that she had comprehensive financial data only for contested divorces and that these were probably based on fault grounds. For mutually consensual no-fault divorces and default divorces, the information was more limited, and it was typically impossible to determine the "spousal income or the value of assets owned and transferred."[69]

Other authors argued that divorce settlements actually increased in no-fault divorce states.[70] However, Weiss and Willis looked at the period ending in 1986, by which time concerns about no-fault divorce were probably well established in all states. In addition, because they were using a sample of people who graduated from high school in 1972, they did not have any long-duration marriages, which would be the ones that I would expect to be particularly adversely affected by no-fault divorce.

Stephen Sugarman, who also reviewed Weitzman's data, was unconvinced that "California women as a group fare importantly worse under no-fault as compared with how they fared under the fault system."[71] The *average* figures provided by Weitzman were not dramatic; Weitzman deliberately focused on the cases in which there was some property to divide and some spousal support was awarded to demonstrate the effect of no-fault divorce. Looking at all divorced women, Sugarman concluded that "overall, things are pretty much the same as always."[72] This argument misses the point. No-fault divorce probably had very little impact on many couples who decided after a few years of marriage and no children to divorce. They had made few changes to accommodate their marriage and acquired little property. The women who were adversely affected by no-fault divorce were the ones identified by Weitzman and ignored by Sugarman: those in marriages of long duration. Divorce was potentially very costly to these women, and no-fault divorce deprived them of leverage to obtain compensation at divorce. Sugarman offered nothing to contradict that conclusion.

The most systematic attack on the proposition that most women are financially worse off after divorce was launched by Sanford Braver.[73] He was involved in a long-term project investigating the effects of divorce—especially on noncustodial parents—using a sample of couples from Phoenix, Arizona. He found a number of flaws in the earlier studies. First, he argued that the U.S. government tables used by other scholars to adjust for the needs of different family configurations are out-of-date and inaccurate; for example, the fixed costs, like housing costs, incurred by households have increased relative to variable expenses, such as food. Second, custodial parents have tax advantages that are usually not considered. Child support is not subjected to income taxation and custodial parents can often get a child care tax credit. Consequently, they usually have a lower tax rate and more disposable income than would be implied by their gross income. Third, noncustodial parents often incur the additional expenses of giving gifts to their children and of providing for them during visitation periods, which often reduce the financial burden of the custodial parent. Applying these adjustments to his sample, Braver concluded that men were only 2 percent better off after divorce and women were only 1 percent worse off after divorce. Even though his sample was random, it did have some interesting characteristics—all the employed fathers reported that they were paying all their child support obligations in the period after the divorce was filed. Clearly, when noncustodial parents are less responsible, the financial condition of the custodial parents deteriorates, and that has to be the case for many women. Still, this research is important in pointing out the additional factors that need to be considered when addressing the effect of divorce on men and women, as well as when recognizing that the consequences of divorce vary among couples and their children.

So Why Do Women File?

An anomaly in the face of the deteriorating financial condition of many divorced women is that a majority of divorces under both fault and no-fault divorce have been filed by women. Because of the negotiated settlements under fault divorce, it was common that the filing spouse—usually the wife—was not necessarily the spouse who initiated the divorce. This was probably due to a combination of the fault standards for alimony and the property settlement requiring the plaintiff to be "innocent" and chivalrous. Although many women may have been dissatisfied with their marriage during the fault divorce era, it probably would have been very costly for them to pursue a divorce. If the women could not prove fault grounds, they would be required to provide compensation to the men as an inducement for their participation in the divorce. This compensation would have to come from the financial settlement that they would otherwise have received, therefore increasing the likelihood that divorce would be a financial disaster for them. Their predicament was compounded by the poor employment opportunities available to women.

With the introduction of no-fault divorce, the party who actually wanted the divorce was more likely to file, and a majority of divorces have continued to be filed by women. Ruth Dixon and Lenore Weitzman found that in Los Angeles the proportion of divorces filed by men rose from 22 percent in 1968 under fault divorce to 36 percent in 1977 under no-fault divorce, but still not a majority.[74] They concluded that the husband was more likely to file when the marriage was longer or when the wife was older.

Evidence is also available on the party initiating the divorce. Eleanor Maccoby and Robert Mnookin in their study of how well children fared after a mid-1980s divorce found that two-thirds of divorces were initiated by the wives.[75] Other researchers have also found that women frequently are the spouses initiating a divorce. According to the Gallup Organization, most divorces were initiated by men a few decades ago, but more recently more than half of divorced women told them that the divorce was their idea.[76] Sanford Braver's research also showed that women are twice as likely as men to initiate a divorce.[77]

So if a divorce can create financial difficulties for some women, why do they prefer to dissolve their marriages? Men may be getting more and women less out of marriage than has normally been assumed. Some researchers argue that men benefit more from marriage than women and, therefore, are reluctant to divorce.[78] Men tend to receive more health, sexual, and financial benefits from marriage than do women. Meanwhile, there may be incentives for women to divorce that have not been commonly recognized. Certainly, a major influence has been the increase in the financial independence of married women which leaves them less vulnerable if they are divorced.[79]

Part of the explanation also may lie with interpersonal dynamics within marriage. William Goode argued that during the fault divorce era, even though it was typically the wife who first mentioned divorce in cases of marital conflict, the husband usually was the first to desire it.[80] His behavior, whether intentional or unconscious, may often have followed a course that would lead the wife to see divorce as the most viable alternative. Others have pointed out that the prevailing expectation in the history of American divorce has been for the man to assume the active role in the provocation for divorce, but for him to take the passive role in the actual initiation of the procedures.[81] This is also in line with how men and women generally respond to marital disputes. Wives are significantly more likely to criticize a given situation, whereas husbands are more likely to stonewall any discussion of change.[82]

Another factor causing women to initiate divorce may be the position in which many men and women find themselves if the quality of a marriage is deteriorating. If a man is the primary income earner and he no longer finds his marriage attractive, he has the option of leaving. Meanwhile, if the wife wants to assure herself of custody of the children and financial support for herself and the children, she has to take legal ac⸱⸱ n. Margaret Brinig and Doug Allen found that being the spouse who receives custody of the children was a major factor influencing who filed for divorce.[83]

My research confirms that women tend to be the spouse who most strongly wants a divorce, and it sheds some light on why they made that choice frequently in the face of a decline in their financial welfare.[84] This analysis used data from the *National Survey of Families and Households*,[85] which consisted of 13,007 households that were interview   in 1988 with a follow-up in 1992 and 1993. I was particularly interested in the couples who were divorced during the intervening period. Each divorced spouse was given five responses to a question about the party who wanted the divorce: (1) I wanted it, but my spouse didn't; (2) I wanted it more than my spouse; (3) we both wanted it equally; (4) my spouse wanted it more than me; and (5) my spouse wanted it, but I did not. Of the women who responded, 36 percent stated that they wanted the divorce and their husband did not. When this number was coupled with the 23 percent of women who said that they wanted the divorce more than their husbands did, the result is a substantial majority of women strongly wanting their divorce. A concern was that the women had an unrealistic view of what was going on at the time of the divorce, with their husbands also responding that they were the ones who more strongly wanted the marriage to end. However, when a comparison was made of the couples' responses, there was substantial agreement between the ex-spouses. Forty percent of their responses were perfectly correlated; for example, if the wife said that she wanted the divorce but her husband did not, the husband responded that he did not want the divorce, but his wife wanted it. When the adjacent responses were included (e.g., if the wife said that she wanted the divorce and her husband did not, and the husband responded that she wanted it more than he wanted it), there was a greater than 80 percent agreement between the responses of the men and women. Clearly, it is much more common that women want to dissolve a marriage than their husbands.

Although marriages fail for a variety of reasons, an analysis of the responses to this survey provided us with some valuable insights about the motives behind the strong feelings of women. One important factor appears to be that women look for different things in marriage than do men. Particularly relevant to women is intimacy and communication with the reality of marriage frequently failing to meet their expectations.[86] The survey asked divorced spouses about their marriage just prior to their divorce. Questions addressed the affection and the understanding that they were getting from their spouses. The women responded that they were much more unhappy with those aspects of their marriage than were the men. To some extent, men may have been oblivious to bad marriages or looking for different things in marriage. Maybe many women have always found marriage to be a frustrating experience, and now it is just easier and less costly for them to dissolve these disappointing marriages. My analysis in this book suggests that no-fault divorce reduced the commitment that couples made to each other and that women have been more sensitive to the changes than men have been.

Another factor influencing women's decision to divorce was their financial condition. The better off the women turned out to be after a divorce, the more likely they were to strongly want to end their marriage. After a divorce, the average household income of the women who indicated that they had wanted the divorce but their husband did not was $39,592; whereas the average household income of the women who indicated that they did not want the divorce at all was $29,073. Probably reflecting the lack of compensation for limiting a career, women felt less strongly about wanting a divorce as the duration of the marriage increased. Whether the women got custody of the children, which was fairly common, did not appear to influence how strongly they wanted the marriage to end. It seems reasonable to assume that divorced women would prefer to be better off—rather than worse off—after divorce, so that focusing only on the financial effects of divorce ignores other important nonmonetary motives for divorce, especially among women.

Women's Earnings

Before concluding this discussion of the effect of no-fault divorce on divorced women, I must make a distinction between the adverse effects on women's earnings due to their working at home and the adverse effects on the earnings of workers

Good Intentions Gone Awry

because they are women. Most women marry and have children. The decision by many married couples for the wife to take primary responsibility for child rearing traditionally has made women less attractive employees than men, with the result that businesses have tended to pay them less and to promote them more slowly.[87] The problem is circular. Women earn less than men, so it is rational for families to decide that the mothers will be the parent with the primary responsibility for rearing the children; but at the same time, one of the reasons why women tend to have lower wages is because they assume that role. Career-oriented women find it difficult to convince employers that they are not the typical woman, and as a result, they often are adversely affected. As women have demonstrated their stronger commitment to the labor force, it has become easier for career-oriented women to convince employers of their dedication to their job.

The loss in human capital experienced by women due to divorce is based on what they can earn after divorce being less than the wages they would be earning if they had pursued more continuous employment; it is *not* based on the average wage or on the wages of men. The wage differential between the average man and the average woman has little to do directly with no-fault divorce.

No-fault divorce probably has had an indirect effect on the women/men wage differential. With less security during marriage, married women have increased their labor force participation. With an increase in women's attachment to the labor force, the ratio of women's wages to those of men has increased (see table 5.1).[88] This trend has been particularly pronounced for younger, better educated women. For women aged twenty-five to thirty-four with a college education or more, the ratio of their wages to those of men increased from .66 to .83 over the period from 1970 to 1995. This is due to a number of reasons. With more attachment to employment, women have been willing to invest in the skills necessary to enter higher-paying fields such as management where on-the-job training is important. Because of their stronger attachment to the labor force, women are more likely to be chosen for important in-house training programs. When their employment was more intermittent, women tended to specialize in jobs such as nursing and teaching where certificates were more important than on-the-job training.

In summary, there remains some disagreement about the effect of no-fault divorce on the financial condition of divorced women. But the fact is that fault divorce required innocent spouses to be the plaintiffs in divorce actions; and in a large number of the cases, the wives were those parties. It is difficult to believe that it was common that these wives were the parties who truly initiated the divorces,[89] and if they were not the initiating parties, their cooperation had to be induced. The primary inducements were financial settlements. No-fault divorce reduced this process to the financial detriment of the divorced spouse. The one group that may have benefited was married women who wanted a divorce and no longer had to make the concessions necessary under fault divorce.

The Effect on Divorced Men

Although less documented, no-fault divorce has probably been a tragedy for numerous divorced men. The deterioration in the financial condition of divorced women that has occurred since the introduction of no-fault divorce often has been viewed as benefiting men, especially divorced men. When no-fault divorce was introduced, there were some men who obviously benefited from the new legal environment—the men who wanted to dissolve their marriage and who found that the cost of divorce had been reduced benefited from the reduced negotiating power of their spouses. Most men, just like most women, marry because they feel that marriage will increase their quality of life.

A divorce is frequently a tragedy for men. As the labor force attachment of married women has risen, the likelihood that the husband has made a career sacrifice for the benefit of his marriage has increased. For these husbands, divorce can have dire financial repercussions. Moreover, husbands—just like wives—develop strong bonds with their spouses and children that are disrupted by a divorce. Because of unilateral divorce, these men can easily have a marriage to which they had committed themselves dissolved against their will. Then, they frequently can be forced to provide financial support for two households instead of one. The financial support may be going to an ex-wife who left him for another man with whom she is then living. In addition, child support can be going to his ex-wife with him essentially having no control over how it is spent. For legal as well as practical reasons, fathers often are given limited access to their children after divorce.[90] Still, research has shown that most fathers are deeply attached to their children and that a divorce frustrates the relationship that they want to have with those children.[91]

In conclusion, no-fault divorce has resulted in numerous injustices for those who are divorced. Without the limited protection provided by fault divorce, spouses have been forced to provide themselves with some protection against the potential costs of divorce by increasing their commitment to employment and education. Therefore, with higher incomes on average, both spouses are less financially vulnerable at divorce.

THE INCENTIVE TO MARRY

So far, we have observed that no-fault divorce often has had a detrimental effect on the divorced women and men and their children. Adults should not be expected to remain passive in this changing environment, and one change could be a new skepticism about marriage. Two people marry because they believe the arrangement will make both better off. It has already been noted that the increase in the labor-force-participation rate of women due to higher wages and better employ-

Good Intentions Gone Awry

ment opportunities reduced the gains from marriage, decreasing the incentive for some women to marry. This is especially true when their prospective mates are low-income men.

No-fault divorce laws also contributed to this trend. The willingness to specialize in household production depends on the protection provided to that spouse if the marriage is dissolved. No-fault divorce removed the requirement of mutual consent for divorce and replaced it with a financial settlement that underestimated the loss experienced by spouses who emphasized domestic activities during marriage. The reduced protection caused a corresponding decline in the willingness of people to specialize in household production during marriage. Without this specialization, both men and women might find marriage less attractive.

The Effect on Women

If more women than men are likely to limit a career if they marry, that makes them more vulnerable under no-fault divorce. Then they also have more to lose from making a premature decision under no-fault divorce. Consequently, they can be expected to require stronger assurances of the durability of a relationship before they are willing to marry after the shift from fault to no-fault divorce. The marriage rate for unmarried women has fallen steadily since World War II. Above 80 per thousand in the 1950s, the rate fell below 60 per thousand after 1980.[92] Particularly noteworthy is the marriage rate among never-married women, which fell from 93 per thousand in 1970 to less than 60 per thousand in 1990 (see table

Table 5.2   Marriage Rates and Related Data

Year	Marriage Rate (per thousand never-married women)	Unmarried Couples (in thousands)	Median Age at First Marriage: Women
1970	93.4	523	20.6
1975	75.9		20.8
1980	66.0	1,589	21.8
1985	61.5	1,983	23.0
1990	57.7	2,856	24.0
1995		3,668	24.5
1997		4,130	
1998			25.0

Sources: U.S. Bureau of the Census, *Statistical Abstracts of the United States, 1998* (Washington, DC: U.S. Government Printing Office,1998), Table 60, 60 and Table 159, 112; and U.S. Bureau of the Census, *Marital Status and Living Arrangements: March 1998*, December 1998.

5.2). In addition, the median age of women when they married for the first time rose from 20.3 in 1950 to 25 in 1998.[93]

The Effect on Men

For the reasons already discussed, no-fault divorce made marriage less attractive, thereby reducing the incentives for men to marry and to stay married. This had potentially destructive results for many men because the responsibilities associated with marriage have traditionally been important for men. George Gilder argued that a crucial process of civilization is the subordination of male impulses and short-term focused psychology to long-term horizons of female biology.[94] Basically, men instinctively have some very unattractive characteristics. They can be violent, with a tendency to take a short-term perspective toward problems. Meanwhile, maternal instincts in mothers force them to take a long-term perspective for the benefit of their children. Traditionally, to obtain regular sexual relations, men were pressed to provide financial support and faithfulness to women. In the process of competing for the attention of women, men were forced to accept many of women's values—such as a longer-term perspective—that were alien to men's fundamental nature. This process benefited women and, in the long run, men by improving the quality of relationships. Marriage—and the socialization of men—was based on this critical exchange.

Men are more likely to revert to their fundamental nature if the attraction of marriage is reduced. The appeal of marriage to men appears to have declined—between 1970 and 1997, the percentage of men eighteen years old and older who were not married rose from 24 percent to 38 percent.[95] Without marriage, some men may develop antisocial characteristics. Unattached men are the chief perpetrators of most crimes.[96] Single men earn substantially less than married men.[97]

The combination of fewer gains from marriage due to no-fault divorce and increased public support for unmarried mothers probably has reduced the commitment that women expect from the fathers of their children.[98] This has produced unfortunate results for the mothers, but also for the fathers. Steven Nock has determined that men who have children out of wedlock experience many of the same consequences as women who have nonmarital births because unwed fathers are less likely to marry and more likely to cohabit than men without children before marriage.[99] Yet the positive consequences of marriage for men have been well documented—married men live longer, drink less, take fewer risks, and are more satisfied with life, and they have higher incomes, educational attainments, and labor force attachments than unmarried men do.[100]

Due to no-fault divorce, men may be more inclined toward antisocial behavior even during marriage. It has also been argued that the removal of the fault grounds has permitted some men to act irresponsibly, with no-fault divorce leading to more abuse and to other undesirable behavior in marriage.[101] This occurs because after one spouse has made a substantial investment in a marriage, such as women do when they limit a career, they will be reluctant to dissolve a marriage even if the behavior of the other spouse becomes objectionable under normal circumstances. Because most men indicate that they prefer being married, a reduction in the incentives for them to commit themselves to their marriage frequently works to their detriment and that of their family.

Cohabitation

With less to gain from marriage, the number of couples living together can be expected to increase and did increase from approximately a half million in 1970 to over 4.1 million in 1997.[102] Paul Glick and Graham Spanier reported that between 1960 and 1975 the number of unmarried couples in households with children present had not varied—the increase in the rate of nonmarital cohabitation was due primarily to young couples without children.[103] After 1975, the number and the proportion of cohabitating households with children increased. Part of this trend can be explained by the increase in the number of people who live together who have already been married; the children in the household are often from prior marriages. The lack of children is still a characteristic of most unmarried couples; in 1997, no children were present in approximately 65 percent of unmarried cohabitating couples.[104]

We would expect cohabitation without marriage in the period after no-fault divorce among couples in which the women had the most to lose from leaving the workforce and working at home. These women would tend to be those with an above-average education who are employed—women who are more likely to receive on-the-job training that would enhance their future productivity and earnings. In both 1975 and 1980, the women in unmarried cohabitating couples tended to be better educated than average with a high employment rate.[105] Probably the central characteristic of cohabitation without marriage is the limited sacrifices of employment or education that the individuals make to the relationship. Steven Nock has noted that whereas cohabiting men plan on having as many children as married men, cohabiting women report lower levels of ideal fertility than their married counterparts.[106] This is as would be expected because parenthood without the limited protection offered by marriage can be potentially much more costly for the person who would be expected to assume primary responsibility for child care—usually the mother—than for the other parent.

Not only are marriage rates decreasing and cohabitation rates increasing, but people's age at first marriage is increasing. As noted earlier, the median age of women when they married for the first time rose from 20.3 in 1950 to 25.0 in 1998.[107] Most of the increase occurred after 1970—the median age at first marriage was 20.6 in that year (see table 5.2). If the cost of a poor choice by a woman has gone up, there is an incentive for her to spend more time searching for an acceptable spouse. A similar pattern occurred for men; their median age at first marriage rose from 22.8 in 1950 to 26.7 in 1998. The median age for men did not increase as rapidly as it did for women, with the result that the gap between the median ages of men and women fell slightly from 2.5 years in 1950 to 1.7 years in 1998. No-fault divorce has made marriage a less attractive institution for many people, thereby contributing to numerous recent trends: fewer people are marrying, more people are living together, and people are waiting longer before marriage.

THE LABOR-FORCE-PARTICIPATION RATE OF MARRIED WOMEN

Not only did no-fault divorce cause women to approach marriage more carefully, it caused them to take steps during marriage to protect themselves from the adverse consequences of divorce. One response to no-fault divorce has been an increase in women working outside the home during marriage. The labor-force-participation rate (LFPR) of women has increased dramatically since World War II, with the rate of married women rising from 23.8 percent in 1950 to 61.6 percent in 1997 (see table 5.3).[108] This increase was particularly evident for the women who traditionally had the strongest attachment to the home, mothers with young children. The LFPR of married women with children under six years of age rose from 11.9 percent in 1950 to 30 percent in 1970, the year in which no-fault divorce was introduced in California. It continued to rise to 63.6 percent in 1997, having accelerated after 1970.

Table 5.3 Labor-Force-Participation Rates for Married Women

Year	All Married Women	Married Women with Children under Six
1950	23.8%	11.9%
1955	27.7	16.2
1960	30.5	18.2
1965	34.7	23.3
1970	40.8	30.0
1975	45.4	36.6
1980	50.1	45.0
1985	54.2	53.4
1990	58.2	58.9
1995	61.1	63.5
1997	61.6	63.6

Source: U.S. Bureau of the Census, *Statistical Abstract of the United States* (Washington, DC: U.S. Government Printing Office, various years).

James Smith and Michael Ward found that the growth in real wages explains a majority of the increase in the LFPR of women between 1950 and 1980.[109] In the period after the introduction of no-fault divorce, however, the growth rate of the LFPR of women rose, whereas the growth rate of real wages slowed. The introduction of no-fault divorce has been identified as contributing to the change from the earlier pattern. Without the protection of fault divorce, married women have had to take steps to protect themselves. Employment that increased, or that at least maintained, the women's human capital during marriage was one of those steps. With the introduction of no-fault divorce, married women would be expected to maintain a stronger attachment to the labor force.

No-Fault Divorce and the Labor Force Participation of Married Women

Elizabeth Peters showed that living in a no-fault divorce state in 1979 increased the probability that a married woman would be in the labor force.[110] She argued that the increase was due to the married women's response to the lack of compensation for marriage-specific investment in being better homemakers and mothers.

I agree that no-fault divorce increases the LFPR of married women, but I argue that incentives follow for a lack of compensation for sacrificing opportunities outside the home that result in a decline in the value of the human capital of wives who do not work outside the home.[111] A lack of compensation for marriage-specific investment implies that women are not being compensated for being good homemakers and mothers, a situation that would not be expected to vary across the demographic characteristics of women. But marriage could affect the human capital of women based on their demographic characteristics. For example, younger married women have more to lose from foregoing opportunities for enhancing or maintaining their human capital through working outside the home, and they have a longer period over which to receive the benefit of that investment. As a consequence, younger women should be more likely to be in the labor force in a no-fault divorce state than in a fault state. The empirical results from my study suggest that married women are sensitive to the effect of no-fault divorce on their human capital and that the married women who are most adversely affected by no-fault divorce have reacted by increasing their labor force attachment.

The Importance of Financial Necessity

Others have argued that the increase in the labor force participation of married women is based on financial necessity.[112] Certainly, it appears that the earnings of some married men have decreased as average hourly earnings for production or nonsupervisory workers in inflation-adjusted 1982 dollars declined from $8.12 in 1975 to $7.39 in 1995 before recovering slightly in recent years (see table 5.1). This argument asserted that married women are working outside the home to make up for the decline in the earnings of their husbands.

Some analysts have questioned whether these earnings figures accurately reflect the change in these workers' purchasing power. The consumer price index (CPI) that is used to deflate the current wages probably overstates the erosion in the purchasing power of money. The Advisory Commission to Study the Consumer Price Index (Boskin Commission) in 1996 estimated that the CPI overstates the reduction in the purchasing power of money by 1.1 percent per year due to quality changes and shifting consumption patterns.[113] If this adjustment is made, the inflation-adjusted hourly wage in 1995 would be over $9 per hour rather than the reported figure of $7.39. The compensation of workers is not only wages. Part of the compensation is fringe benefits such as pensions and health insurance, and many workers have shifted some of their compensation away from earnings to fringe benefits. Fringe benefits have grown from just 20 percent of payroll in 1953 to more than 41 percent in 1995. Over that period, health benefits, for example, grew from 3 percent to 14 percent of compensation, while pensions grew from 5 percent to 13 percent.[114] After recognizing the effect of the inaccurate inflation adjustment and the expanded role of fringe benefits, the situation of these working men certainly improves. Does that mean that all workers—and their families—have comfortable incomes? Of course, not. Some married men have seen the purchasing power of their earnings stagnate or decline over the past decades.

Necessity historically was an important explanation for married women's labor force participation because the highest rates were for those women married to low-income men.[115] It has been a less convincing argument for employment by other married women because it is difficult for a second income earner to increase family income significantly. Because most married couples file joint federal and state individual income tax returns, there are no exemptions or deductions available to the second income earner plus their income is usually taxed at a higher marginal rate. In addition, their social security contributions may not provide a pension that exceeds the spousal benefits for which they have already qualified. Last, there can be substantial employment-related expenses, such as travel, clothing, meals, and child care, that reduce the income available to the family.

Although the financial-necessity argument for why married women are increasing their LFPR has broad appeal, it is not supported by the available data. Based on that argument, we would expect the LFPR to have climbed for women married to low-income workers. The evidence is exactly the reverse. Chinhui Juhn and Kevin Murphy found that whereas declines in employment and earnings of men have been greatest for low-wage men, employment and earnings gains have been greatest for wives of middle- and high-wage men.[116] For example, between

1969 and 1989, the LFPR increased by 16 percentage points for women married to men whose earnings were among the lowest 20 percent of married men. The percentage increase rose with earnings groups to 33 percentage points for women married to men within the group with the highest 20 percent of earnings. Juhn and Murphy concluded that these findings cast doubt on the rationale that married women have increased their labor supply in the recent decades to compensate for the disappointing earnings growth of their husbands.

Additional support for the conclusion that financial necessity does not have a dominant role in explaining the recent increase in the LFPR of married women is provided by Francine Blau, who showed that the LFPR for women rises with their education levels.[117] Due to assortative mating, the education level of spouses tends to be highly correlated; so highly educated women tend to marry men with higher levels of education and, therefore, higher income levels.[118] For women aged thirty-five to forty-four, for example, the LFPR increased from 40 percent in 1970 to 51 percent in 1995 for women with less than a high school education.[119] Meanwhile, for women with a college education or more, the LFPR for the same group rose from 58 percent to 84 percent.

No-fault divorce may have had an additional influence on the LFPR of married women due to the financial constraint imposed on families due to the housing market. No-fault divorce encouraged both spouses in many families to seek employment, which usually resulted in a higher income for their families. When a couple's income increases, their demand for many goods and services also increases. If the supply of these items can respond, there will probably not be a significant effect on market prices. That is a common phenomenon. The one market that is severely restricted in its ability to respond to an increase in demand is the housing market. The supply of houses in attractive locations often cannot respond to an increase in demand, so their prices rise. Much of the increase in the LFPR of married women was due to those married to middle- and higher-income husbands, usually resulting in an increase in their family income. Their increased expenditures did not affect many prices, but they did have a dramatic effect on housing prices. Between 1970 and 1996, the CPI rose by 412 percent, while the median sales price of new, privately owned, one-family houses increased by 598 percent.[120] The increase was particularly visible in the parts of the country in which there were attractive employment opportunities for educated women: the northeast and the west. In those areas, housing prices rose by 613 percent and 641 percent, respectively. Because of this rapid increase in house prices, families that otherwise would have preferred for one spouse to limit a career were pressured to have both spouses seek employment if they wanted a desirable house.

This empirical evidence provides support for a combination of better opportunities for women and concerns about divorce, rather than financial necessity, being the primary causes of the dramatic increase in the LFPR of married women during the past three decades. The problem facing married women is that they will sacrifice important on-the-job-training opportunities if they leave the labor force. On-the-job training consists of a broad range of formal and informal opportunities that employees encounter that increase their productivity and, therefore, their incomes. So not only do workers sacrifice income when they are not employed, they also sacrifice the opportunity to acquire additional training. The amount of on-the-job training that businesses give employees tends to increase with their educational level.[121] The sacrifice of this on-the-job training and the resulting income that it would produce is not the basis for substantial compensation at divorce, so married women have been reluctant to make this sacrifice.[122] The ones who would incur the largest sacrifice are those with the highest potential incomes, thereby explaining part of the increase in their labor market participation.

Rather than seeking employment, married women could use either pre- or postmarital agreements to deal with the lack of protection for sacrificed human capital during marriage. Traditionally, courts refused to enforce marital agreements that attempted to define the financial consequences of divorce on the grounds that these agreements encouraged divorce.[123] Some courts have become more willing to accept marital agreements that define the financial arrangements at divorce, a movement that has come through the courts themselves rather than by legislation;[124] and disagreement remains over enforcing agreements that limit alimony. An additional difficulty with using marital agreements to resolve the problems discussed in this book is the lack of recognition of the effects of no-fault divorce by many people: because most couples fail to recognize the impact of no-fault divorce, they are incapable of providing for it in a contract. For this reason, as well as because of problems of legal ambiguity, these agreements are not currently a reliable means for protecting spouses. They are more common and more appropriate for second marriages, when the parties have a greater amount of tangible separate property.

No-fault divorce imposed costs on many spouses who had committed themselves to an emphasis on domestic activities during marriage. With knowledge of that effect, married women, in particular, have an incentive to change their behavior. One reaction has been to place a higher emphasis on working outside the home during marriage. Another reaction has been to increase their human capital by pursuing additional education before and during marriage.

EDUCATION

Before the introduction of no-fault divorce, married women often specialized in work at home, ignoring employment outside the home and further education. Marriage was often the reason that women halted their education.[125] Because of this choice, women's income-earning capacity later in life was significantly less than it would have been if they had furthered their education during marriage. Often, additional education would have been a small investment compared to prior investments, but the joint decision of the spouses during marriage was that the family was better off not making that investment. Although these decisions reduced the human capital of married women, women made those decisions in an environment in which marriage was a fairly stable institution. Even if their marriage was dissolved, they anticipated being in a position to receive some compensation from their spouse as part of the negotiations necessary for any divorce.

This all changed with no-fault divorce. One reaction by married women has been to increase their employment outside the home to maintain their marketable skills in the event that their marriage is dissolved. An alternate method for maintaining or for enhancing their marketable skills is to continue their education during marriage. No-fault divorce also would influence unmarried women who recognize that marriage is no longer the stable institution it was in their mothers' time.

There has been a dramatic increase in the number of women attending postsecondary educational institutions. The percentage of all degrees being awarded to women rose from less than 25 percent in 1950 to over 50 percent by 1985,[126] and to 55 percent in 1995. With the exception of first professional degree programs, a majority of both undergraduate and graduate students are now women. Tremendous gains have occurred in what have traditionally been men's fields. For example, the percentage of bachelor degrees in business and management awarded to women rose from 9 percent in 1971 to 48 percent in 1995.[127] This trend was particularly evident among married women. Married women are spending more time in school.[128] Between 1970 and 1980, married women between the ages of eighteen and twenty-nine increased the number of years that they were in school by .30 years if they were childless and .14 years if they had children. This trend was most pronounced for married women with more than twelve years of education. Because they could qualify for higher-paying jobs, these were the women who had the most to lose from sacrificing employment or educational opportunities. They increased the proportion of their time enrolled in school from 16 percent to 22 percent while childless and from 6 percent to 13 percent when they had children.

As has been the case with other factors, there are links that go both ways between educational attainment and no-fault divorce. Better employment opportunities gave women incentives to invest more in education. The additional education, in turn, increased their potential income and their incentives to seek employment during marriage. If these changes are expected, they can contribute to making marriage a less-attractive institution. If these changes are unexpected, they can contribute to making marriage a less-stable institution. Thus, the increase in educational attainment of women could lead to fewer and less stable marriages.

No-fault divorce created incentives for women who wanted to marry to reject the earlier pattern of married women who ended their education. As the loss that they might experience if they specialized in working at home was not recognized by the courts at divorce, they had an incentive to maintain or to increase their human capital during marriage by furthering their education. With marriage being less predictable, unmarried women also had an incentive to seek more education.

THE QUALITY OF LIFE FOR MARRIED WOMEN

The deterioration in the financial condition and, therefore, potentially in the quality of life of many divorced women due to no-fault divorce has already been discussed. There also is evidence that no-fault divorce has reduced the quality of life for many married women. There are many potential criteria for judging quality of life, and some might argue that by accelerating a transition toward more self-reliance, no-fault divorce improved the quality of life of married women.[129] Here quality of life will be analyzed within the framework of hours worked. Victor Fuchs found that married women are working more hours per year under no-fault divorce than they had worked under fault divorce[130] and that when they work outside the home, their responsibilities at home are not absorbed by the other members of their families. Between 1960 and 1986, women increased the annual hours that they worked in the house and at a job by 7 percent, even as the hours spent by men in those two activities fell by the same percent.[131] From working 90 percent of the hours of men in 1960, women increased their hours of work to 105 percent of those of men in 1986. The difference was particularly noticeable for married couples: wives increased their total work by 4 hours per week, but husbands decreased theirs by 2.5 hours. Much of this shift was due to women continuing to assume most of the responsibility for child care. Fuchs attributed this role to women's stronger demand for children and their stronger concern for their children after they are born: "In short, there is a difference on the side of preferences, and this difference is a major source of women's economic disadvantage."[132]

The no-fault divorce laws provide an additional explanation for this process, which otherwise would border on the irrational: married women may feel compelled under no-fault divorce to work harder to maintain their marriages. The decision by married women to work outside the home should not necessarily result in an increase of total work hours. They might work outside the home as part of a plan to increase the overall welfare of the family and could expect the other members of the family to assume responsibility for providing some commodities that the women had been providing in the home. The specialization of labor during marriage can be a joint decision of the spouses. The arrangement is in the best interests of the spouses and the children, so they usually agree to it voluntarily. Labor market conditions may change to make it attractive for wives/mothers to shift some of their time to employment. This could occur either because husbands' earnings fell or those of wives rose. These women only would volunteer to make the shift if the benefits to them exceeded the costs. Family members may agree that the shift is also in their best interest, and some of the benefits to the wives should be other family members assuming responsibility for some commodities that had been provided by the women in the home. The husband or children might assume some of the responsibility for cooking or cleaning. If married women were working outside the home as part of family plans, we would not necessarily assume that their total hours of work would increase.

Alternatively, married women can pursue employment in an attempt to protect themselves from the adverse effects of no-fault divorce rather than necessarily to improve the welfare of their family. In this situation, the decisions are not part of a family plan, and the family members may be less willing to assume the responsibility for providing the commodities that had been provided by the wives/mothers. To be blunt, many married women find themselves between a rock and a hard place. They feel pressure to maintain their income-earning capacity in case their marriage is dissolved, but they may have to provide substantial household services to make the marriage attractive to their husband. One response might be, "Why bother?" Still, most people want to be married, and for mothers marriage may be particularly important because it is commonly viewed as a higher-quality environment for raising children.[133] So they respond by working longer hours in their employment and at home.

My research provides some support for this alternative hypothesis.[134] Using the most detailed data on people's time use, the *Time Use Longitudinal Panel Study, 1975–1981*, I estimated the impact of living in a no-fault divorce state on the work habits of married men and women. I anticipated that married women would work more hours in no-fault divorce states, in which they had only limited protection, than in fault divorce states, in which they had some protection. I did not anticipate that the state of residence would have any effect on the work habits of married men. Although living in a no-fault divorce state had no statistically significant effect on married men, it was shown to increase the total hours worked by married women by 4.5 hours per week. This occurred because married women in no-fault divorce states on average worked outside the home 6.5 hours more per week while only reducing their work in the home by 2 hours. Many married women were working harder to maintain the protection that they had under fault divorce—and still receiving less protection.

An additional effect of no-fault divorce may be on the distribution of the output of marriage.[135] People marry because they expect collectively to be better off married than single. That statement alone does not tell us how the gains from marriage are divided. No-fault divorce reduced the cost of divorce for spouses who feel they are better off divorced than married. Either spouse can pursue a divorce; but we have already observed that it is more likely to be a financial disaster for the wife, especially in established marriages. Wives may have reacted by attempting to make marriage more attractive to their husbands by providing them with more commodities by either working longer hours or by giving them a larger share of the gains from the marriage. In either case, they are worse off than they would be if they were more secure in the marriage.

Thus no-fault divorce not only made many divorced women worse off, it also may have made many married women worse off. Women's working outside the home to protect themselves from the adverse effects of no-fault divorce has not provided commensurate support at home; and in addition, they may have had to work longer hours or to accept fewer commodities to make marriage attractive to their husbands. Either way, their quality of life may have deteriorated.

These pressures on women may also help to explain the large percentage of women filing for divorce, as noted earlier. Some women initially may decide that it is in their best interest to accept the larger time burdens that appear to be common for married women and potentially to tolerate a smaller share of the rewards from marriage. Eventually they may conclude that they are better off divorcing. Meanwhile, the decision by many women to work so hard during marriage may in part explain why so many husbands who have been divorced wanted their marriage to continue. If couples had effective communication, they might in many cases find that they can resolve their differences. Unfortunately, if that communication does not occur, they can end up worse off divorced than they would have been if still married. Because most people who divorce remarry, a divorce is a rejection of a particular spouse rather than a rejection of marriage. Most people still view a happy marriage as one of the most important goals in life.

THE EFFECT ON INTACT FAMILIES

One of the most substantial, but subtle, effects of no-fault divorce probably has been on the quality of family life. Although the recent deterioration in the quality of family life is often attributed to a decline in family values and to a corresponding shift toward an emphasis on individuals' self-interest, the argument presented here focuses on a shift in incentives. The perspective that is accepted here is that people make decisions based on their perceived self-interest, so a change in it cannot be the basis for new outcomes. But the cost and the benefit of choices change over time, inducing people to change their behavior—based on their self-interest. No-fault divorce increased the cost and reduced the benefit of making a long-term commitment to a family.

So far we have observed the adverse effects of no-fault divorce on divorced men and women as well as on married women. In this section we will look at the impact of no-fault divorce on all family members. Although not as obvious as the trends already discussed, an important effect of no-fault divorce has probably been a reduction in the quality of family life for many Americans. Marriage can be an efficiency-enhancing arrangement that increases the welfare of all participants, with efficiency occurring when activities only continue as long as the incremental benefits exceed the incremental costs. In a family setting, the benefits and the costs are those of the members of the family. Often some costs or benefits of activities within families are external to the persons making decisions. The income earned by one spouse can benefit all members of the family. The meal cooked by the other spouse can benefit that person and the other members of the family. If these external effects are not considered by individuals, less-efficient outcomes will occur.

The economies of scale and the external effects of public goods can be important for the decisions made by individuals within families. As a consequence, altruism is very important within families.[136] People tend to make decisions in market situations based on narrowly defined self-interest, but the same people might base their decisions within the family on altruism. That is not to say that they are rational in one setting, but not in the other. Relationships in markets are often temporary. If a decision in a market confers uncompensated benefits on a stranger, the actor is not likely to receive anything in return.

Relationships within families can continue for a long time, with actions that benefit the other members often resulting in the other members acting similarly later. Love can be an important basis for altruism within a family, but economic analysis still recognizes that self-interest would eventually retard generous acts if there was no reciprocity. Consideration of these external effects is more likely when the people bestowing benefits on others anticipate that the other family members will reciprocate. This is more likely to occur when marriage is a long-term arrangement or, at least, when the people making the decisions know that they will eventually be compensated for any costs that they incur. Under those circumstances, the parties recognize that there is a quid pro quo: They act with the knowledge that their actions will benefit others and that they in turn will benefit from the acts of the other members of the family. The incentive for these activities is often the external benefits received from the other parties' activities.

If marriage can be dissolved unilaterally without adequate compensation, the incentive structure changes. This is especially true if the external benefits generated by the parties' actions are not concurrent, as is true with some of the services provided during marriage. For example, the child-rearing services frequently provided by wives tend to occur before husbands' peak earnings period. Both child rearing and income earning confer benefits on the other family members, but wives may question whether their marriage will continue long enough for them to receive the external benefits produced by their husband's future income and their children's love. If the wives do not have faith that their marriage will continue into that period, they do not have as much incentive to increase their specialization in child rearing.

A couple may want children and recognize that parental care is important for their welfare. Because mothers frequently earn less than fathers, in many cases

the couple may feel that the mother should be the parent to limit a career to accommodate this care. To obtain the mother's cooperation, the father may also want
to assure her that he is committed to their marriage. The problem is that it is difficult for a father—or for any spouse who has assumed the primary income-earning role in the family—to provide creditable assurances to the spouse because he
has no control over the grounds for the dissolution of the marriage that have been
established by the state. A repeated statement, even in writing, that the spouse
will never seek a divorce has no effect on the ability of a spouse to seek a divorce
under the no-fault grounds. Alternatives, such as marital contracts, can make the
spouses uncomfortable and are often difficult to enforce. With no credible assurances as to the durability of the marriage, both spouses reduce their specialization
in domestic production and increase their employment or education, potentially
leaving all the family members worse off.

This can be illustrated by reviewing the gains from economies of scale and
specialization. In chapter 3, it was assumed that husbands and wives specialized
completely in either income earning or household production during marriage.
There are many cases in which families would benefit from the spouses specializing, but not completely. The criterion for choosing how much time each party
should devote to working at home and to working at a job is the value of the
output in each setting. Efficiency occurs when an individual works at home as
long as the value of the output in that activity exceeds the value of what can be
bought with the income generated by being employed for the same period. The
increase in the wages available to women during this century has created an incentive for married women to shift some of their time to jobs outside the home.
Efficiency may not require a complete shift—the members of a family might find
that their collective welfare is maximized if the wife shifts 20 hours of labor from
the home to a part-time job. The value of the goods and services that can be
purchased with the earnings exceeds the value of the goods and services that she
can produce at home. The next 20 hours of labor, required to move to a full-time
job, may not produce goods that are as valuable as the household production
sacrificed. Overall, the family may be better off with her working outside the home
only part time.

If the marriage is not viewed as a long-term arrangement, conflicts arise between preferences of the family and those of individuals who worry about their
fate if the marriage is dissolved. Some individuals who limit their employment
opportunities may fear that they will not be compensated for any reduction in
their human capital that occurs if they work only part time because full-time jobs
provide opportunities for on-the-job training that are not available in part-time
jobs. Wives have incentives to evaluate the trade-off between working at home or
at a job by their welfare rather than the welfare of their family. Increasing their
work outside the home from 20 to 40 hours per week might impose more costs
than benefits on the family—the net benefits for the family are negative. Concep-

tually, the benefits include the psychic income of the wives from the jobs,[137] but from the wives' perspective, the extra hours of employment provide them with skills that would be beneficial if their marriages were dissolved. Therefore, the benefits of the jobs to the wives exceed the costs, and they decide to work full time.

As we observed earlier, the largest increase in the LFPR of married women has been among those with husbands with higher incomes. Many of these couples probably would be happy to trade some of their higher income for a more relaxed relationship with their spouses and their children. They would prefer that a spouse was more readily available during the week to handle chores so that weekends could be available for leisure activities. The problem is that neither partner can give credible assurance that the marriage will last. Therefore, couples are forced to make their own individual arrangements.[138] Both spouses might act differently if they felt that their reduced human capital due to working at home was protected. They would have a stronger incentive to choose the combination of working at home and at a job that was more likely to maximize family welfare. The protection could come either from negotiating power due to the grounds for divorce or by financial arrangements at divorce provided by law.

THE EFFECT ON CHILDREN

Although the discussion here has centered on adults, no-fault divorce also probably has had an adverse effect on the quality of life for many children. Certainly, children can benefit from the additional income and stimulation that come from their parents' employment.[139] This is most likely to occur when parents place primary importance on the welfare of their family when making decisions. However, no-fault divorce creates incentives for parents to interpret their self-interest more narrowly based on themselves and less on the welfare of their family. With marriage being a much more fragile institution, there are potentially fewer rewards for being concerned about the other family members. Most parents are deeply concerned about the welfare of their children, but—like all choices—parenting is influenced by its cost and its benefit. When employment opportunities outside the home were limited and sacrificed careers were protected to some extent by fault divorce, the cost of a parent placing an emphasis on child care was low. As the cost rose because employment opportunities increased and no-fault divorce reduced the protection for a sacrificed career, parents became less willing to make this sacrifice. Meanwhile, the high rate of marriage dissolution increased the likelihood that a parent—especially a father—might have a more limited interaction with his or her children, thereby reducing the benefit of parenthood.[140] With higher costs and lower benefits of parenthood, many parents have reduced their commitment to their children. As parents spend more time at jobs, they have less time to devote to their children.

Still, it should be no surprise that parents have a strong influence on the current and future welfare of their children. A particular concern has been the attachment between a child and a parent, which has important long-term effects.[141] Research finds that the great majority of physical brain development occurs by the age of three, with these findings being interpreted to suggest that early childhood furnishes a window of opportunity for enriching inputs and a window of vulnerability to such social stressors as a dysfunctional home environment.[142] In their systematic study of how family changes are related to a broad range of outcomes among offspring, Paul Amato and Alan Booth observed:

> Research has repeatedly demonstrated that a high level of parental support is associated with a variety of positive outcomes among children and adolescents, including psychological adjustment, academic achievement, high self-esteem, an internal locus of control, social competence, and the exhibition of considerate and altruistic behavior. Furthermore, a moderately high level of parental control—provided that it does not involve coercive methods of discipline, such as hitting—is associated with desirable outcomes among children and adolescents. However, if parental control is excessive, then its consequences for children and adolescents are problematic.[143]

Although parental involvement with their children is important, increasingly parents are turning responsibility for child care over to others. In 1990, more than half of American infants were in the care of someone other than their parents.[144] In 1994, in families in which the mother is either employed full time or has more than a college education or in which the family income is more than $50,000 a year, approximately 35 percent of preschool children are either in child care or a nursery school, and another 15 percent are being cared for by someone other than a relative in the provider's home.[145]

The quality and the impact of child care facilities have been heavily debated.[146] However, among professionals, there is a strong consensus that young children benefit from care by a parent. A 1990 poll of U.S. pediatricians conducted by the Thomas Jefferson School of Medicine in Philadelphia showed that 77 percent believed that infants six months of age or younger ought to be cared for only at home.[147] A different survey of 1,100 baby doctors carried out that same year by the American Academy of Pediatricians reported that a substantial majority of physicians consider full-time day care harmful for children under age four.

Most parents seem to understand the importance of a parent being with an infant, but many still choose to work outside the home. In a *Washington Post* survey, 68 percent of respondents agreed that it would be better if mothers looked after their children at home.[148] But parents face the dilemma that we have discussed here.

Michael Meyerhoff, director of the Center for Parent Education, noted that over 90 percent of the professionals with whom he deals would agree that full-time substitute care for children under age three is not ordinarily in the best interest of the child.[149] But many of these professionals who are parents are involved in situations where they feel that they cannot stay home.

There are also problems with the child care choices made by parents. Frequently the quality is not very good. The Cost, Quality and Child Outcomes in Child Care Centers study conducted in 1993–94 examined 401 child care centers in four states and concluded that 86 percent of the centers provided mediocre or poor quality services.[150] There was not much variation, on average, between fees for mediocre care and for good care, but parents frequently do not make the best choice for their child. Parents may be more concerned about the location, the hours, and the dependability of child care arrangements than they are about aspects of quality considered important by child development professionals.[151] Some studies suggest that parents place cost and convenience above warm interactions with caregivers.[152]

The importance of parents extends beyond just the preschool years; the importance of parents as a source of assistance and encouragement to older children later on can be frustrated when both parents have major obligations outside the home. The period of increased parent employment has been associated with the deterioration in the performance of children in school.[153]

Although, since the existence of no-fault divorce, children receive reduced amounts of attention in two-parent households, they get even less attention if their parents are divorced. We have already observed that no-fault divorce does appear to have a slight effect on the divorce rate, but it also appears to affect the *types* of families that divorce. Under fault divorce, people did not casually dissolve a marriage. There had to be a strong sense that the marriage was a failure, and at least one spouse frequently had to make major concessions to induce the other spouse to cooperate in a divorce. Knowing that it was going to be difficult to dissolve the marriage gave spouses an incentive to strive to make the marriage work. The durability of marriage frequently worked to the benefit of children.

No-fault divorce permits either parent to dissolve a marriage unilaterally based potentially on very flimsy motives. The vulnerability of marriage is compounded by the fact that no-fault divorce often makes marriages fragile by reducing the spouses' commitment to their marriage in the first place. Therefore, a marriage could be dissolved when there was still the potential for a successful and rewarding relationship for the spouses and their children. Paul Amato and Alan Booth found that between 1980 and 1992 only a minority of divorces that they reviewed involved high-conflict marriages.[154] Not having made a substantial commitment to their marriage, some spouses divorced after a minor provocation. Their weighing of the cost and the benefits of divorce might not adequately take into consideration the impact of the divorce on any children.

Although children are frequently hurt by disruptive families, they are usually better off in reasonably smoothly functioning two-parent households than in single-parent households or in stepfamilies. In single-parent households, the relations between the custodial parent—usually the mother—and their young children are often strained after divorce.[155] Being a single parent is a demanding and frustrating experience. Furthermore, because mothers are much more likely than fathers to receive custody of any children after a divorce, the end of a marriage can result in a reduction in the critical link between children and their father.[156]

THE EFFECTS ON PARENTS

Before we leave this discussion of the effect of no-fault divorce on children, let's consider the effect on the parents of the weaker commitment by many parents to their children. No-fault divorce creates incentives for both parents to seek employment, thereby frequently making parenting more difficult. Often the parents lose sight of the goals of parenthood. To use an economic perspective, the issue is whether children should be treated as an investment or as a source of consumption. Until recently, children were an important source of family labor and retirement support—they were an investment. Even then, the interaction between the parents and the children was an important source of enjoyment for both— the children were consumption. The investment incentive for parenthood is no longer important for most American families. So, consumption—the enjoyment received—would appear to be the primary motivation for parenthood. And yet, what do we observe? More and more often, both parents are working full time. Children's soccer games and parent-teacher conferences turn into obligations to be tolerated rather than a source of enjoyment. By the time that many parents realize that they have missed the opportunity to have had a more rewarding experience with their children, the children have grown up and that opportunity is gone.[156] In an environment in which marriage was viewed as a more durable institution, parents could take a longer-term perspective on their preferences. Many might decide that being able to spend more time with their children was far more rewarding than additional employment.

In summary, the effects of no-fault divorce have often been viewed as a zero-sum game—the losses experienced by the divorced spouses are balanced, or offset, by gains to divorcing spouses. It may be more appropriate to describe the effects of no-fault divorce as a negative-sum game—the sum of the effects is probably negative. Without adequate protection for the spouses who traditionally limited careers to work at home during marriage, these spouses have become less willing to devote their energies to those roles. The result has been a lower quality of life for all members of the affected families.

PROPERTY

As the deterioration in the financial condition of many divorced women was recognized, an attempt was made to use property settlements as a vehicle for reducing this effect. As we have seen, the introduction of no-fault divorce caused a new emphasis to be placed on the laws controlling the financial arrangements at divorce, and the courts' role in divorce proceedings increased.[157] Although couples could still negotiate, the laws placed a constraint on what the parties could demand. With the grounds for divorce less subject to negotiation, the spouses who did not want to dissolve their marriages had less to trade for more generous financial arrangements.

Without a negotiated settlement or a guilty party, many courts moved toward property settlements in which the parties shared the net assets of the marriage equally.[158] Traditionally, the laws in the community property states and the common law states took different approaches to the distribution of property at divorce.[159] In most community property states, each spouse had a one-half interest in all property acquired during the marriage. The common law states had often treated property rights as based on title, with the spouses accumulating their separate property during marriage and, if they divorced, each receiving his or her property. Gradually, all the common law states abandoned the title system and adopted some form of equitable distribution, based on the concept that marriage is a partnership or shared enterprise.[160] The introduction of equitable distribution in the common law states has resulted in the differences between the systems tending to disappear for divorce.[161] Because the community property system has a longer history, the common law states have been inclined to use community property precedents to interpret equitable distribution. Some common law courts have stated explicitly that they will attempt to construe their statutes consistently with community property principles.[162]

Accompanying the movement toward an equal division of marital property has been an expansion of the definition of the property subject to distribution. An equal division of marital property, along with limited spousal and child support, often resulted in a poor financial situation for divorced women. Some of the critics of no-fault divorce, such as Lenore Weitzman, have argued that the courts should consider "career assets" as property. Weitzman defined these assets as "the benefits of employment, such as pensions and health insurance coverage, as well as the capacity to earn future income."[163] Legislatures and courts also have attempted to expand the definition of property subject to division at divorce to include wage-continuation schemes such as pension, disability, and worker's compensation payments; the goodwill of individuals; and professional degrees and licenses. The recognition of these less-tangible assets has been an appropriate expansion of the definition of property, but the new laws are flawed by a lack of any clear understanding of how financial analysts identify assets and determine their value.

Wage-Continuation Schemes

Wage-continuation schemes include pension, disability, and worker's compensation payments, but most of the concern about these schemes has been directed to pensions.[164] With a reduction in the importance of the extended family and self-employment, the pensions provided by employers have become increasingly important assets for most families. Some pensions were recognized as marital property in community property states before no-fault divorce. In the common law states, pensions historically were treated as the separate property of the wage earner and were ignored at divorce; but a majority of both common law and community property states now accept the view that pension rights created during marriage may be divided at divorce.[165]

As states started to recognize pensions as marital property, a distinction continued to be maintained between vested pensions, for which an employee already had a guaranteed right, and nonvested pensions, for which the employee had to fulfill additional requirements—such as to work longer—to qualify. For example, when no-fault divorce was introduced in California, nonvested pensions were not property in that state because they were "mere expectancies."[166] This is a good example of the difference between the legal and the financial concepts of property. From a financial perspective, pensions, both vested and nonvested, should be treated as property. A vested pension can generate a future income stream, and, therefore, it is just as much property as a bond is. If funds were contributed to the pension during the marriage, the pension should be treated as marital property. Because a nonvested pension also has the potential to generate a stream of payments, it is just as much property as a vested pension. The payments from the nonvested pension are less certain than those for a vested pension, so the nonvested pension has a lower value than a vested pension. The lower value follows from applying a higher discount rate to the less-certain future payments that the nonvested pension may provide.[168] The appropriate discount rate for a nonvested pension can be speculative.

Recognizing the injustice to divorced women of not treating nonvested pension plans as marital property, the California courts in *In re Marriage of Brown*[168] expanded the definition of community property to include nonvested pension rights. In this case, the court retained jurisdiction until the pension vested to avoid the problem of valuation. In other jurisdictions, the courts have attempted to value nonvested pension plans at divorce so that the courts and the parties can have a clean break.

The valuation and allocation of a nonvested pension at divorce can result in consequences that may be socially unacceptable. For example, a wage earner may receive a highly discounted nonvested pension as part of the settlement at the dissolution of a marriage. If the employee leaves the current position, the pension never vests, and the employee receives nothing. But if the employee stays in the position and the pension vests, there may be a substantial increase in its value. It is appropriate to apply a lower discount rate to the payments from a vested pension than to those from a nonvested pension because the former are more predictable. The lower discount rate increases the value of the pension, and the result might be viewed as an unfair windfall for the wage earner. Therefore, the approach taken by the court in *Brown* is attractive: the pension can be allocated when it vests or when the wage earner retires. The courts have developed a number of approaches for determining the appropriate shares of the pension payments for the spouses.[169]

Federal pensions have a unique history.[170] The U.S. Supreme Court in recent years has been active in protecting federal rights and entitlements from division by state divorce courts. It held in 1979 that railroad retirement pensions were the property of the wage earner[171] and extended this interpretation to military pensions in 1981.[172] Congress then overturned both cases so that federal statutes now provide divorced spouses with an interest in certain federal pensions.[173] Civil service pensions have been divisible by statute since 1978.[174] Based on the provisions in the social security statute that provide benefits for non-employee spouses, most courts have determined that federal social security benefits cannot be divided at divorce.

Despite general recognition of pension rights as marital property, confusion remains about disability and worker's compensation payments.[175] Fewer courts have addressed the issue of whether these funds should be treated as separate property or as marital property. In most jurisdictions that have considered the issue, the conclusion has been that disability payments received after divorce are separate property. Worker's compensation payments are usually treated similarly. Both are insurance payments for which the premiums came from the worker's productivity irrespective of whether the insurance was purchased by the worker or the employer. The worker's productivity is based on the worker's human capital, most of which was acquired before marriage and therefore is separate property. This is especially true for workers who are not the beneficiaries of extensive education. Consequently, it is usually reasonable to treat these payments as a return to separate property.

Goodwill of an Individual

The concept of property also has been expanded to include intangible assets, such as the goodwill of an individual. An obvious injustice frequently occurs in divorces in which one spouse is a professional: the professional's high income continues after divorce, whereas the other spouse's financial condition plummets. A person who emphasized work in the home might not qualify for child support if any children have left home. Depending on the family's lifestyle, there might be little marital property, and the contemporary standards for spousal support might not justify substantial or long-term payments.

Searching for a way to expand the definition of property to allow a larger property award for spouses who would be adversely affected by divorce, the courts created a concept called "professional goodwill."[176] The courts expanded marital property to include not only the goodwill of businesses but also the goodwill of professionals themselves.[177] A business can be marital property, and courts have long recognized that a part of the value of a business can be goodwill: the goodwill of a business is an asset that reflects the higher profits that can be produced by an established business in contrast to a new business. The higher profits are based on the established relationships of the older business with both its workers and its customers. These relationships produce additional profits, and the additional profits can be converted to a present value that is an asset—goodwill. This goodwill is an asset of the business, not of any individual.

In steps that seemed logical to judges, but not to financial analysts, the concept of goodwill has been extended to individuals. Most courts agree that professional goodwill created during a marriage is marital property, but the future earning capacity of a spouse at divorce is not marital property.[178] Thus the courts have held that an asset can exist for which the future returns are not relevant in determining its value—a holding that, from a financial perspective, is deeply flawed. An asset is worthless if it does not have the capacity to generate future returns. An immobile house that is about to be destroyed and therefore will provide no future services is worthless even though it is solid and attractive today. Goodwill, either business or professional, has value based on its ability to produce future income.

The goodwill of an accounting practice and of the accountant as an individual, for example, are often viewed as synonymous in these cases,[179] but they are very different concepts. Although there are established methods for placing a value on the goodwill of a business, even an accounting practice, problems develop when the concept is expanded to individuals. First, there is no systematic way to value professional goodwill. By contrast, there is a standard approach for determining the goodwill of an ongoing business that is not being sold. The excess profits that the firm is expected to generate are converted to a present value based on a comparison of the profits of the firm to those of a similar business, usually new, without goodwill. The difference in their profits can be attributed to goodwill. This can be a difficult calculation under ordinary circumstances, but almost impossible when applied to individuals. With professionals, no two are alike because each is unique in his or her willingness to accept risk, qualifications, ambition, and so forth. Physicians in private practice cannot be compared with salaried physicians because of the inconveniences and risks inherent in private practice. What the courts have treated as professional goodwill is just the return to reputation. If that is the case, everyone has a reputation.

Second, a critical issue in determining whether property is separate or marital property is the date it was acquired. The education, training, and experience that result in older workers, including professionals, having higher incomes have occurred over many years of life; but most of the investments in human capital probably occurred in the people's earlier years as full-time students. In the professional goodwill cases, the timing of the acquisition of the professional goodwill is usually ignored, with the courts tending to assume that it was acquired during marriage.

Goodwill was expanded to professionals to attempt to correct for the financial problems faced by older divorced women under the existing divorce and property laws. The courts used professional goodwill to generate funds to cover the deficiencies that they found in the marital-property-allocation system. Many states do not distinguish between business goodwill and the goodwill of a professional individual in the business.[180] Meanwhile, some states attribute professional goodwill to the individual, thereby rejecting it as marital property.[181] Weitzman found that in California the goodwill value is often set to equal the equity in the family home.[182] It is unfortunate that an ad hoc system rather than a fundamental reform of the laws was developed for dealing with the deficiencies in the marital property laws.

Professional Degrees and Licenses

Traditionally, human capital created by education during marriage was not recognized as property subject to division at divorce.[183] Human capital can be acquired with the support of a spouse who pays some of a student spouse's expenses and provides household services. One of the injustices associated with divorce that is often noted becomes apparent in the case of wives who finance their husband's professional education. The increase in the number of women in higher education has increased the likelihood that the financing spouse is the husband. Still, the problem of what to do when education is funded by a spouse continues. Seldom are these sacrifices made with the intent that they are a gift: the supporting spouse is making an investment in the other spouse's human capital for the benefit of their family. There is an expectation that the supporting spouse will share in the increased income that the investment will produce. Often an analogy is made to business investments.

The courts started to recognize that an injustice was occurring when one spouse worked so that the other spouse could receive an education, but then the marriage was dissolved before the supporting spouse received a fair return on the investment. A few states recognize the professional degree or the license of a spouse as marital property. But the issue has not been addressed systematically. Some states have passed legislation, whereas others rely on case law.[184] There has been dispute over whether the education or license should be the basis for reimbursement to the supporting spouse or should be treated as marital property subject to division. A few states have divided the present value of the increased earnings attributable to the education.

Most states that recognize a degree or a license as property require reimbursement, with the amount of the reimbursement depending on the duration of the marriage. After a long marriage, the courts often have concluded that the supporting spouse has received an adequate return on the investment. In California, this is established by statute.[185] Some states also provide equitable remedies such as alimony or spousal support for the supporting spouse.

The issue of whether education is a marital property is often presented as one in which women are the victims,[186] and historically that was often the case. The number of women, married and unmarried, pursuing education has increased dramatically, however. By 1980, women students outnumbered the men in colleges.[187] In 1995, undergraduate women outnumbered men (6,831,000 versus 5,401,000) and graduate women outnumbered graduate men (965,000 versus 768,000). Only in professional education were there more men than women (174,000 versus 124,000), and those numbers were converging.[188] Married women have been spending more time in school during marriage,[189]and the problem of compensation for education during marriage is taking on unisex characteristics.

In summary, no-fault divorce has caused the courts and the legislatures to reconsider the definition of property subject to division at divorce. They have expanded the definition in a number of areas, but have given very little consideration to the financial analysis of property. Therefore, the expanded definition of property has not been systematic.

CONCLUSION

We live in a world that has experienced dramatic changes over the past few decades. No-fault divorce has influenced some of those changes. Although the divorce rate has fallen recently, research indicates that except for the change in the grounds for divorce, it would actually be lower. The change in the divorce laws contributed to the deterioration in the financial condition of many divorced women and the children of divorced parents as well as in the welfare of many divorced men. In response to the deteriorating conditions of divorced women, some married women increased their labor market participation and education, and some unmarried women delayed marriage. No-fault divorce also reduced the incentive for either spouse to specialize in domestic production and thus may have reduced the quality of life for many American families. No-fault divorce has caused this reaction because the compensation often provided to divorced spouses is inadequate. It is inadequate because some of the costs of divorce are not being recognized. Reforms necessary to correct for that omission and to make marriage a more welfare-enhancing institution are the subject of the following chapter.

NOTES

1. U.S. Bureau of the Census, *Statistical Abstract of the United States* (Washington, DC: U.S. Government Printing Office, various years).

2. See, for example, Victor R. Fuchs, *Women's Quest for Economic Equality* (Cambridge, MA: Harvard University Press, 1988), 28.

3. Robert T. Michael, "Why Did the U.S. Divorce Rate Double Within a Decade?" in T. Paul Schultz, ed., *Research in Population Economics* 6 (1988): 367–400.

4. Census, *Statistical Abstract*, various years.

5. President's Council of Economic Advisers, *Economic Report of the President, 1999* (Washington, DC: U.S. Government Printing Office, 1999), Table B-40, 374.

6. U.S. Bureau of the Census, *Statistical Abstract of the United States, 1998* (Washington, DC: U.S. Government Printing Office, 1998), Table 654, 409.

7. See Janice Peskin, "Measuring Household Production for the GNP," *Family Economics Review*, no. 3 (1982): 16–25.

8. Fuchs, *Women's Quest*, 78.

9. See Margaret F. Brinig and June Carbone, "The Reliance Interest in Marriage and Divorce," *Tulane Law Review* 62, no. 5 (May 1988): 866.

10. The ratio of women's-to-men's wages for median year-round earnings remained in the range from 0.57 to 0.61 during the 1960s and 1970s, but this ratio has had a steady increase in the 1980s, rising to 0.66 in 1987. See Claudia Goldin, *Understanding the Gender Gap* (Oxford, UK: Oxford University Press, 1990), 60–61. Among college graduates aged twenty-five to sixty-four, women's median annual earnings were 73 percent of men's in 1993. Daniel E. Hecker, "Earnings of College Graduates: Women Compared with Men," *Monthly Labor Review* 121, no. 3 (March 1998): 62–71. This women-men earnings ratio has continued to rise. Between 1969 and 1994, it increased from 0.60 to 0.72 for those in the twenty-five–to–thirty-four age bracket. The trend was particularly impressive for better-educated workers—the ratio rose from 0.66 to 0.83 for workers with at least a college education in that age bracket. See Francine D. Blau, "Trends in the Well-Being of American Women, 1970–95," *Journal of Economic Literature* 36, no. 1 (March 1998): 129.

11. Census, *Statistical Abstract*, various years.

12. Mary Ann Glendon, *Abortion and Divorce in Western Law* (Cambridge, MA: Harvard University Press, 1987), 81.

13. See Gary Becker, *A Treatise of the Family,* enl. ed., (Cambridge, MA: Harvard

University Press, 1991), 331–39. This argument is tested in H. Elizabeth Peters, "Marriage and Divorce: Informational Constraints and Private Contracting," *American Economic Review* 76, no. 3 (June 1986): 437–54.

14. Many of the commodities produced during marriage are joint or public goods. One of the reasons that people are collectively worse off after divorce is the reduction in these joint or public goods. For example, both parents enjoy the children at the same time when they are together, but when they divorce, the children can only be enjoyed by each parent separately. Martin Zelder, "Inefficient Dissolutions as a Consequence of Public Goods: The Case of No-Fault Divorce," *Journal of Legal Studies* 22, no. 2 (June 1993): 503–20.

15. Victor Fuchs noted that when women work outside the home, they do not reduce their work at home by a corresponding amount. See Victor R. Fuchs, *How We Live* (Cambridge, MA: Harvard University Press, 1983), 77–78. By working harder, married women can make marriage more attractive to their husband.

16. Richard Posner, *The Economic Analysis of Law*, 4th ed. (Boston: Little, Brown, 1992), 142. Robert T. Michael observed that between 1960 and 1970 the largest increases in the divorce rate were among younger women. See Robert T. Michael, "The Rise in Divorce Rates, 1960–1974: Age-Specific Components," *Demography* 15, no. 2 (May 1978): 345–47.

17. Becker, *Treatise*, 334. He found that the actual rates for California were higher than the "trend" in 1970–1972, but they returned to the long-term trend by 1973.

18. Peters, "Marriage and Divorce," 446.

19. Douglas W. Allen, "Marriage and Divorce: Comment," *American Economic Review* 82, no. 3 (June 1992): 679–85.

20. Zelder, "Inefficient," 516.

21. Jeffrey S. Gray, "Divorce-Law Changes, Household Bargaining, and Married Women's Labor Supply," *American Economic Review* 88, no. 3 (June 1998): 628–42.

22. Leora Friedberg, "Did Unilateral Divorce Raise Divorce Rates? Evidence from Panel Data," *American Economic Review* 88, no. 3 (June 1998): 608–27.

23. Margaret F. Brinig and F. H. Buckley, "No-Fault Laws and At-Fault People," *International Review of Law and Economics* 18 (1998): 325–40.

24. For a recent discussion of the evidence on this issue, see Robert Rowthorn, "Marriage and Trust: Some Lessons from Economics," *Cambridge Journal of Economics* 23 (1999): 661–91. Some of the other scholars who have addressed this issue are Steven J. Bahr, "Marital Dissolution Laws: Impact of Recent Changes for Women," *Journal of Family Issues* 4 (September 1983): 455–66; Gerald C. Wright and Dorothy M. Stetson, "The Impact of No-Fault Divorce Law Reform on Divorce in American States," *Journal of Marriage and the Family* 40 (August 1978): 575–80; and Robert Schoen, Harry N. Greenblatt, and Robert B. Mielke, "California's Experience with Non-Adversary Divorce," *Demography* 12 (May 1975): 223–44. Other economists have cautioned against broad economic conclusions about the effects of no-fault on the divorce rate because influences such as religion also influence the divorce rate. See Marianne A. Ferber and William Sander, "Of Women, Men, and Divorce: Not by Economics Alone," *Review of Social Economics* 47 (Spring 1989): 15–24. They found that religion as well as economic variables such as men's

and women's wages and the legal cost of divorce explained the percent of fifteen–to–fifty-four–year olds who were divorced in a state in 1980.

25.   For example, authors wrote about the deterioration in the income of divorced women long after the introduction of no-fault divorce without ever mentioning no-fault as contributing to that situation. See Thomas J. Espensade, "The Economic Consequences of Divorce," *Journal of Marriage and the Family* 41, (August 1979): 615–25.

26.   Lenore J. Weitzman, *The Divorce Revolution* (New York: Free Press, 1985). She published some of her results earlier in Lenore J. Weitzman, "The Economics of Divorce: Social and Economic Consequences of Property, Alimony, and Child Support Awards," *UCLA Law Review* 28 (1981): 1181–1268.

27.   Weitzman, *Divorce Revolution,* 19.

28.   Weitzman, *Divorce Revolution*, xi.

29.   Weitzman, *Divorce Revolution*, 8.

30.   Weitzman, *Divorce Revolution*, 12.

31.   There was a significant difference between the law on the books and the law in practice. While during the fault divorce era, divorce was supposed to be impossible without fault, collusion was common. See Max Rheinstein, *Marriage Stability, Divorce, and the Law,* (Chicago: University of Chicago Press, 1972), 55. The collusion was based on the couple's negotiations.

32.   Cal. Civ. Code, §§ 4000-5174 (West 1970 and Supp. 1981).

33.   Cal. Civ. Code, § 4800 (West Supp. 1981).

34.   Weitzman, *Divorce Revolution,* 30.

35.   The median duration of a marriage in 1970 was 6.7 years. U.S. Bureau of the Census, *Statistical Abstract of the United States, 1990* (Washington, DC: U.S. Government Printing Office, 1990), Table 124, 79.

36.   Weitzman, *Divorce Revolution,* 73. Weitzman noted that under the old law, the "innocent" plaintiff, usually the wife, was typically awarded a significantly larger share of the marital assets. Most of these awards allowed the wife to keep the family home and its furnishings, which often were the most valuable family assets. Weitzman, *Divorce Revolution,* 30.

37.   Between 1968 and 1972, that percentage rose in San Francisco from 12 percent to 59 percent and in Los Angeles from 26 percent to 64 percent. Weitzman, *Divorce Revolution,* 74. Over the same period, the percent of women receiving most of the property fell in San Francisco from 86 percent to 34 percent and in Los Angeles from 58 percent to 35 percent. By 1977, equal division of the property was typical.

38.   Between 1979 and 1990, the percentage of divorced women receiving property settlements fell from 44.5 percent to 32.3 percent. Gordon H. Lester, "Child Support and Alimony: 1989," *Current Population Reports*, U. S. Department of Commerce, Series P-60, No. 173 (September 1991): 14.

39.   Weitzman, *Divorce Revolution*, 143–83.

40.   Between 1968 and 1972, the percentage of divorced women awarded support fell from 20 percent to 15 percent in both Los Angeles and San Francisco. Weitzman, *Divorce*

Revolution, 167. In 1977, only 17 percent of divorced women in California were awarded support. Among those women receiving support, the median and average awards were about $2,500 and $4,000, respectively, per year. Weitzman, *Divorce Revolution*, 171.

41. Weitzman, *Divorce Revolution*, 34. In 1977, 54 percent of women married more than fifteen years were not awarded support. Weitzman, "Economics of Divorce," 1222.

42. Weitzman, *Divorce Revolution*, 265.

43. Weitzman, *Divorce Revolution*, 310.

44. Weitzman, "Economics of Divorce," 1234.

45. Weitzman, *Divorce Revolution*, 323.

46. Saul D. Hoffman and Greg J. Duncan, "What Are the Economic Consequences of Divorce?" *Demography* 25, no. 4 (November 1988): 641–45.

47. Greg J. Duncan and Saul D. Hoffman, "A Reconsideration of the Economic Consequences of Divorce," *Demography* 22, no. 4 (November 1985): 485–97.

48. Richard R. Peterson, "A Re-Evaluation of the Economic Consequences of Divorce," *American Sociological Review* 61 (June 1996): 528–36. He found a 27 percent decline in women's standard of living and a 10 percent increase in men's standard of living after divorce.

49. Peterson, "Re-Evaluation," 533.

50. Weitzman argued that the policy impact of her earlier research was not caused by its specific statistics. See Lenore J. Weitzman, "The Economic Consequences of Divorce Are Still Unequal: Comment on Peterson," *American Sociological Review* 61 (June 1996): 537–40.

51. Peters, "Marriage and Divorce," 449.

52. Eleanor E. Maccoby and Robert H. Mnookin, *Dividing the Child: Social and Legal Dilemmas of Custody* (Cambridge, MA: Harvard University Press, 1992), 260.

53. Maccoby and Mnookin, *Dividing*, 261.

54. Still, child support has been an important vehicle for reducing the income disparity between parents after divorce. See Judi Bartfeld, "Child Support and the Postdivorce Economic Well-Being of Mothers, Fathers, and Children," University of Wisconsin Institute for Research on Poverty Discussion Paper No. 1182-98, December 1998.

55. Mary Ann Glendon, *Abortion and Divorce*, 87.

56. Carol S. Bruch, "Developing Standards for Child Support Payments: A Critique of Current Practice," *UC-Davis Law Review* 16, no. 1 (Fall 1982): 49–64.

57. Mark Lino, "Income and Spending Patterns of Single-Mother Families," *Monthly Labor Review* 117, no. 5 (May 1994): 29–37. Part of the problem was that court-awarded child support and alimony were not being paid. In 1991, almost half of custodial parents did not receive the full amount of child support awarded, and no payments were made in a quarter of the cases in which it had been awarded. This problem becomes more pronounced when it is noted that barely half of custodial parents have awards calling for support payments. Census, *Statistical Abstract, 1998*, Table 632, 393.

58. Herbert Jacob, "Another Look at No-Fault Divorce and the Postdivorce Finances

of Women," *Law and Society Review* 23, no. 1 (1989): 95–115. The same arguments are generalized in Herbert Jacob, "Faulting No-Fault,"in "Review Symposium on Weitzman's *Divorce Revolution,*" ed. Howard S. Erlanger, *American Bar Foundation Research Journal* 1986, no. 4 (Fall 1986): 773–80; and Herbert Jacob, *Silent Revolution: The Transformation of Divorce Law in the United States* (Chicago: University of Chicago Press, 1988), 159–64.

59. Jacob, "Another Look," 105.

60. Jacob, "Another Look," 107.

61. Marygold S. Melli, "Constructing a Social Problem: The Post-Divorce Plight of Women and Children," in "Review Symposium," ed. Erlanger, 770.

62. Melli, "Constructing," 770.

63. Melli, "Constructing," 771.

64. Melli, "Constructing," 772.

65. Jana B. Singer, "Divorce Reform and Gender Justice," *North Carolina Law Review* 67 (1989): 1103–21.

66. Marsha Garrison, "The Economics of Divorce: Changing Rules, Changing Results," in *Divorce Reform at the Crossroads*, eds. Stephen D. Sugarman and Herma Hill Kay, (New Haven, CT: Yale University Press, 1990), 75–101.

67. Garrison, "Economics," 75.

68. Garrison, "Economics," 83.

69. Garrison, "Economics," 82.

70. Yoram Weiss and Robert J. Willis, "Transfers Among Divorced Couples: Evidence and Interpretation," *Journal of Labor Economics* 11, no. 4 (October 1993): 629–79.

71. Stephen D. Sugarman, "Dividing Financial Interests in Divorce," in *Divorce Reform,* ed. Sugarman and Kay, 130–65.

72. Sugarman, "Dividing," 135.

73. Sanford L. Braver, *Divorced Dads* (New York: Putnam, 1998), 55.

74. Ruth B. Dixon and Lenore J. Weitzman, "When Husbands File for Divorce," *Journal of Marriage and the Family* 44 (February 1982): 103–15. In an article that contradicts most other studies, B. G. Gunter and Doyle Johnson found that in a Florida county the percentage of divorces filed by men rose from 29 percent under fault divorce to 68 percent under no-fault divorce. B. G. Gunter and Doyle P. Johnson, "Divorce Filing as Role Behavior: Effect of No-Fault Law on Divorce Filing Patterns," *Journal of Marriage and the Family* 40 (August 1978): 571–74.

75. Maccoby and Mnookin, *Dividing,* 58.

76. Paula Mergenbagen DeWitt, "Breaking Up Is Hard to Do," *American Demographics* 14, no. 10 (October 1992): 53.

77. Braver, *Divorced Dads,* 124.

78. Linda J. Waite, "Does Marriage Matter?" *Demography* 32, no. 4 (November 1995): 483–507.

79. Allen M. Parkman, "Why Are Married Women Working So Hard?" *International Review of Law and Economics* 18, no. 1 (Winter 1998): 41–49.

80. William J. Goode, *After Divorce* (New York: Free Press, 1956).

81. William M. Kephart, *The Family, Society, and the Individual* (Boston: Houghton-Mifflin, 1977).

82. John M. Gottman, "Psychology and the Study of the Marital Process," *Annual Review of Psychology* 49 (1998): 184.

83. Margaret F. Brinig and Douglas W. Allen, "These Boots Are Made for Walking: Why Wives File for Divorce," presented at the 1998 meeting of the Canadian Law and Economics Association, Toronto, Ontario, September 27–28, 1998.

84. Allen M. Parkman, "Who Wants Out and Why," Anderson Schools of Management Working Paper, September 1999.

85. James A. Sweet and Larry L. Bumpass, *The National Survey of Families and Households—Wave 1 and 2: Data Description and Documentation* (Madison, WI: University of Wisconsin–Madison Center for Demography and Ecology, 1996).

86. Fiona M. McAllister, Penny Mansfield, and Duncan J. Dormor, "Expectations and Experiences of Marriage Today," *Journal of Social Work Practice* 5, no. 2 (Autumn 1991): 181–91.

87. Fuchs, *Women's Quest.*

88. Between 1970 and 1995, the ratio of women's wages to men's wages increased from .56 to .72 for full-time workers. Blau, "Trends." Although women college graduates made 73 percent as much as similar men in 1993, when earnings for women were compared with those of men in the same major field of study, at the same degree level, and in the same age group, about half of the women earned at least 87 percent as much as the men. Hecker, "Earnings of College Graduates," 62.

89. In 1970, most divorces were initiated by men. More recently, however, more than half of divorced women told the Gallup Organization that the divorce was their idea. See Paula Mergenbagen DeWitt, "Breaking Up Is Hard to Do," *American Demographics* 14, no. 10 (October 1992): 53. More recent research shows that women are twice as likely to initiate a divorce as men. See Braver, *Divorced Dads.* The data does not break down the responses by age, but I would be surprised if the percentage of women is anywhere near that high among women in longer-duration marriages.

90. When there is a conflict in the custodial preferences of fathers and mothers, the courts tend to respond to the mothers' preferences. See Maccoby and Mnookin, *Dividing,* 104.

91. See Braver, *Divorced Dads.*

92. Census, *Statistical Abstract,* various years.

93. U.S. Bureau of the Census, *Marital Status and Living Arrangements: March 1998,* December 1998, Table MS-2.

94. George F. Gilder, *Sexual Suicide* (New York: Quadrangle, 1973). More recently a similar point has been made by Lionel Tiger who argued that the sexual redundancy of

men wreaks social havoc as men who have lost their role as providers become sensation seekers. See Lionel Tiger, *The Decline of Males* (New York: Golden Books, 1999).

95.   Census, *Statistical Abstract, 1998,* Table 62, 58.

96.   William J. Bennett, John J. DiIulio, Jr., and John P. Walters, *Body Count* (New York: Simon & Schuster, 1996), 22.

97.   Census, *Statistical Abstract, 1998,* Table 750, 474.

98.   Not only does welfare permit women with poor employment opportunities to establish an independent household usually under poverty conditions, it acts as an inducement for women with employable skills to become mothers, often forsaking employment and, thereby, joining the ranks of the poor. Mwangi S. Kimenyi and John Mukum Mbaku, "Female Headship, Feminization of Poverty and Welfare," *Southern Economic Journal* 62, no. 1 (July 1995): 44–52.

99.   Steven L. Nock, "The Consequences of Premarital Fatherhood," *American Sociological Review* 63 (April 1998): 250–63.

100.   Kermit Daniel, "The Marriage Premium," in *The New Economics of Human Behavior,* ed. Mariano Tommasi and Kathryn Ierulli (Cambridge, UK: Cambridge University Press, 1994), 113–25; Frances K. Goldscheider and Linda J. Waite, *New Families, No Families?: Transformation of the American Home* (Berkeley, CA: University of California Press, 1991); Walter Gove, "Sex, Marital Status, and Mortality," *American Journal of Sociology* 79, no. 1 (July 1973): 45–68; Eugene Litwak and Peter Messeri, "Organizational Theory, Social Supports, and Mortality Rates: A Theoretical Convergence," *American Sociological Review* 54, no. 1 (February 1989): 49–66; and Linda J. Waite, "Does Marriage Matter?" *Demography* 32, no. 4 (November 1995): 483–507.

101.   Margaret F. Brinig and Steven M. Crafton, "Marriage and Opportunism," *Journal of Legal Studies* 23 (June 1994): 869–94.

102.   Census, *Statistical Abstract ,1998,* Table 66, 60.

103.   Paul C. Glick and Graham B. Spanier, "Married and Unmarried Cohabitation in the United States," *Journal of Marriage and the Family* 42 (1980): 19–30.

104.   Census, *Statistical Abstract, 1998,* Table 66, 60.

105.   Graham B. Spanier, "Cohabitation in the 1980s: Recent Changes in the United States," in *Contemporary Marriage,* ed. Kingsley Davis (New York: Russell Sage Foundation, 1985), 91–112 and especially 96.

106.   Steven L. Nock, "A Comparison of Marriages and Cohabiting Relationships," *Journal of Family Issues* 16, no. 1 (January 1995): 69.

107.   Census, *Marital Status.*

108.   Census, *Statistical Abstract,* various years.

109.   The labor-force-participation rate (LFPR) of women has been increasing for most of this century because of the increase in real wages. James P. Smith and Michael P. Ward, "Time-Series Growth in the Female Labor Force," *Journal of Labor Economics* 3, no. 1 (January 1985 Supplement): s59–s90.

110.   Peters, "Marriage and Divorce." Using data from 1972, Johnson and Skinner found that the probability of divorce increases the LFPR of married women, but the authors found

that living in a no-fault-divorce state had a negative effect on a married woman's labor supply. See William R. Johnson and Jonathan Skinner, "Labor Supply and Marital Separation," *American Economic Review* 76, no. 3 (June 1986): 455–69. 1972 was probably too early in the no-fault-divorce era to provide a reasonable test of its effect.

111.   Allen M. Parkman, "Unilateral Divorce and the Labor Force Participation Rate of Married Women, Revisited," *American Economic Review* 82, no. 3 (June 1992): 671–78.

112.   Larry L. Bumpass, "What's Happening to the Family? Interactions between Demographic and Institutional Change," *Demography* 27, no. 4 (November 1990): 489; Stephanie Coontz, *The Way We Really Are* (New York: BasicBooks, 1997), 57; and Paul R. Amato, "The Postdivorce Society: How Divorce Is Shaping the Family and Other Forms of Social Organization," in *The Post-divorce Family: Children, Parenting, and Society*, ed. Ross Thompson (Thousand Oaks, CA: Sage, 1999), 161–90.

113.   See Michael J. Boskin and Dale W. Jorgenson, "Implications of Overstating Inflation for Indexing Government Programs and Understanding Economic Progress," *American Economic Review* 87, no. 2 (May 1997): 89–93; and Charles R. Hulten, "Quality Change in the CPI," *Federal Reserve of St. Louis Review* (May/June 1997): 87–100.

114.   See W. Michael Cox, "What's Happening to Americans' Income?" *The Southwest Economy*, no. 2 (1995): 3–6.

115.   In 1969, women with husbands earning less than the median wage were much more likely to be working than those with husbands whose earnings were above the median. Chinhui Juhn and Kevin M. Murphy, "Wage Inequality and Family Labor Supply," *Journal of Labor Economics* 15, no. 1, pt. 1 (January 1997): 78.

116.   Juhn and Murphy, "Wage," 72–97.

117.   Blau, "Trends," 112–65.

118.   Becker, *Treatise*, 108–34.

119.   Blau, "Trends," 118.

120.   U.S. Bureau of the Census, *Statistical Abstract of the United States, 1997* (Washington, DC: U.S. Government Printing Office, 1997), Table 1189, 719.

121.   Gary S. Becker, *Human Capital*, 3d ed. (Chicago: University of Chicago Press, 1993), 233.

122.   One-sixth of wives would rather not work, including 10 percent of those employed full time; and of women who prefer to work, the vast majority want less than full-time employment. Bumpass, "What's Happening," 490.

123.   J. Thomas Oldham, *Divorce, Separation and the Distribution of Property* (New York: Law Journal Seminars-Press, 1997), 4-3–4-8.

124.   By May 1996, 26 jurisdictions had adopted the Uniform Premarital Agreement Act, which establishes standards for premarital agreements. See Brian Bix, "Bargaining in the Shadow of Love: The Enforcement of Premarital Agreements and How We Think about Marriage," *William and Mary Law Review* 40 (October 1998): 154.

125.   A. E. Bayer, "Marriage Plans and Educational Aspirations," *American Journal of Sociology* 75 (1969): 239–44.

126.   Census, *Statistical Abstract, 1998*, Table 298, 189.

127. Census, *Statistical Abstract, 1998*, Table 325, 200.

128. James A. Sweet and Ruy Teixeira, "Breaking Tradition: Schooling, Marriage, Work, and Childrearing in the Lives of Young Women, 1960–1980," Center for Demography and Ecology, University of Wisconsin-Madison, CDE Working Paper 84-13, 1984.

129. Herma Hill Kay, "Equality and Difference: A Perspective on No-Fault Divorce and Its Aftermath," *Cincinnati Law Review* 56, no. 1 (1987): 80.

130. Fuchs, *Women's Quest*, 77.

131. Comparing two years after no-fault divorce had become common, 1978 and 1988, Francine Blau observed that the total hours worked by the typical married woman increased by one hour over that period. See Francine D. Blau, "Trends in the Well-Being of American Women, 1970–1995," *Journal of Economic Literature* 36 (March 1998): 153.

132. Fuchs, *Women's Quest*, 68.

133. Having a good marriage continues to rank among the highest goals of most adults. See Norval D. Glenn, "Values, Attitudes, and the State of American Marriages," in *Promises to Keep*, ed. David Popenoe, Jean Bethke Elshtain, and David Blankenhorn (Lanham, MD: Rowman & Littlefield, 1996), 15–34. Moreover, a reasonably well functioning, two-parent household is far better for children than one with just one parent. See Sara McLanahan and Gary Sandefur, *Growing Up with a Single Parent* (Cambridge, MA: Harvard University Press, 1994). Finally, mothers tend to be more concerned about their children's quality of life than fathers are, which should cause the mothers to work harder to maintain a two-parent household. See Fuchs, *Women's Quest*, 68.

134. Parkman, "Why Are Married Women Working So Hard?"

135. The seminal contributions to this literature are Marilyn Manser and Murray Brown, "Marriage and Household Decision Making: A Bargaining Analysis," *International Economic Review* 21, no. 1 (February 1980): 31–44; and Marjorie B. McElroy and Mary Jean Horney, "Nash Bargained Household Decisions," *International Economic Review* 22, no. 2 (June 1981): 333–49. A recent survey of the literature is provided in Shelly Lundberg and Robert A. Pollak, "Bargaining and Distribution in Marriage," *Journal of Economic Perspectives* 10, no. 4 (Fall 1996): 139–58.

136. Becker, *Treatise*, 277–306. People who feel that a divorce is more likely make a weaker commitment to their marriage, thereby experiencing a lower quality of family life. See Paul R. Amato and Stacy Rogers, "Do Attitudes toward Divorce Affect Marital Quality?" *Journal of Family Issues* 20, no. 1 (January 1999): 69–87.

137. Many studies show positive effects of paid employment on women's mental health, and multiple roles have been found to have beneficial rather than adverse effects on mental health. See Lorraine Dennerstein, "Mental Health, Work, and Gender," *International Journal of Health Services* 25, no. 3 (1995): 503–09. As with most activities, the incremented benefits of work probably decline as the amount of work increases. Generally, women with families do not work full time as Claudia Goldin found that only 22 percent of women were combining a full time career and a family. See Claudia D. Goldin, "Career and Family: College Women Look to the Past," in *Gender and Family Issues in the Workplace*, ed. Francine D. Blau and Ronald G. Ehrenberg (New York: Russell Sage Foundation, 1997), 20–58. Just as men do, women can experience depression if their career goals are not

realized. See Deborah Carr, "The Fulfillment of Career Dreams at Midlife: Does It Matter for Women's Mental Health?" *Journal of Health and Social Behavior* 38, no. 4 (December 1997): 331–44. Sometimes the psychic income of employment is overestimated. As retirement benefits increase, many workers elect to take early retirement, which indicates that they prefer leisure to their jobs. Better-educated workers are more likely to find interesting jobs and, therefore, work longer. See Fuchs, *How We Live,* 160.

138.   Both spouses often feel compelled to aggressively pursue a career without understanding the reasons why and the costs incurred. For example, because jobs can be more structured than work in the home, some adults are finding a job to be a tranquil retreat from a hectic home life. See Arlie Russell Hochschild, *The Time Bind: When Work Becomes Home and Home Becomes Work* (New York: Metropolitan Books, 1997). Men and women feel their time squeezed because in dual-earner households there is no one at home assuming primary responsibility for domestic activities. Jerry A. Jacobs and Kathleen Gerson, "Who Are the Overworked Americans?" *Review of Social Economy* 56, no. 4 (1998): 456.

139.   For support for this position, see Susan Chira, *A Mother's Place* (New York: HarperCollins, 1998); and Joan K. Peters, *When Mothers Work* (Reading, MA: Addison-Wesley, 1997).

140.   Margaret F. Brinig and Frank H. Buckley, "Joint Custody: Bonding and Monitoring Theories," *Indiana Law Journal* 73 (Spring 1998): 393–423.

141.   "The Effects of Infant Child Care on Infant-Mother Attachment Security: Results of the NICHD Study of Early Child Care," *Child Development* 68, no. 5 (1997): 860–79.

142.   Lynn A. Karoly, Peter W. Greenwood, Susan S. Everingham, Jill Hoube, M. Rebecca Kilburn, C. Peter Rydell, Matthew Sanders, and James Chiesa, *Investing in Our Children: What We Know and Don't Know about the Costs and Benefits of Early Childhood Interventions* (Santa Monica, CA: Rand, 1998), xi.

143.   Paul R. Amato and Alan Booth, *A Generation at Risk* (Cambridge, MA: Harvard University Press, 1997), 17.

144.   Shannon Brownlee and Matthew Miller, "Lies Parents Tell Themselves about Why They Work," *U.S. News & World Report* 122, no. 18, May 12, 1997, 58–64.

145.   Lynne M. Casper, "Who's Minding Our Preschoolers? Fall 1994" (Update), U.S. Bureau of the Census, *Current Population Reports*, P70-62, November 1997.

146.   Some early research suggested that children suffer emotionally and cognitively when placed in child care for more than 20 hours per week before age two, but these findings have been criticized because of their small samples and failure to account for selection factors. Jay Belsky, "Parental and Nonparental Child Care and Children's Socioemotional Development: A Decade in Review," in *Contemporary Families: Looking Forward, Looking Back,* ed. Alan Booth (Minneapolis, MN: National Council on Family Relations, 1991), 122–40. Jay Belsky and David Eggebeen attempted to correct for these problems by using a much larger sample. They conclude that there is little support for the contention that early nonparental care is a risk factor for aggression but do suggest that child compliance is strongly associated with early and extensive nonparental care. Although maternal employment is not confirmed as a cause of child development problems, it is confirmed as a risk factor. Jay Belsky and David Eggebeen, "Early and Extensive Material

Employment and Young Children's Socioemotional Development: Children of the National Longitudinal Survey on Youth," *Journal of Marriage and the Family* 53, no. 4 (November 1991): 1083–98. For a summary of the debate, see William T. Gormley, Jr., *Everybody's Children: Child Care as a Public Problem* (Washington, DC: The Brookings Institution, 1995).

147.   Karl Zinsmeister, "Longstanding Warnings from Experts," *The American Enterprise* 9, no. 3 (May-June 1998): 34–35.

148.   Zinsmeister, "Longstanding."

149.   Zinsmeister, "Longstanding."

150.   Suzanne W. Helburn, *Cost, Quality, and Child Outcomes in Child Care Centers: Technical Report.* Department of Economics, Center for Research in Economic and Social Policy, University of Colorado–Denver, 1995.

151.   Freya L. Sonenstein, "The Child Care Preferences of Parents with Young Children," in *Parental Leave and Child Care: Setting a Research and Policy Agenda*, ed. Janet Hyde and Marilyn Essex (Philadelphia: Temple University Press, 1991), 337–50.

152.   Ellen Kisker and Rebecca Maynard, "Quality, Cost and Parental Choice of Child Care," in *The Economics of Child Care*, ed. David M. Blau (New York: Russell Sage Foundation, 1991), 127–43.

153.   Between 1967 and 1997, the average score on the verbal component of the Scholastic Assessment Test (SAT) fell from 543 to 505, while the math score fell from 516 to 511. During intervening years, these scores were even lower. Census, *Statistical Abstract, 1998*, Table 290, 183.

154.   Booth and Amato, *A Generation at Risk*, 220.

155.   Divorced mothers, compared with married mothers, are less affectionate with their children, punish them more harshly, and monitor their behavior less carefully. E. Mavis Hetherington and W. Glenn Clingempeel, "Coping with Marital Transitions," *Monographs of the Society for Research in Child Development* 57, nos. 2 and 3 (1992): 6.

156.   Much of the discontent with long hours of employment is in dual-income couples, particularly those with children. See Jacobs and Gerson, "Overworked," 456.

157.   With a decline in the importance of alimony, the property settlement became particularly important. Homer H. Clark, Jr., *The Law of Domestic Relations in the United States*, 2nd ed. (St. Paul, MN: West, 1988), 589.

158.   Joan M. Krauskopf, "Theories of Property Division/Spousal Support: Searching for Solutions to the Mystery," *Family Law Quarterly* 23, no. 2 (Summer 1989): 253–78 and especially 258.

159.   Oldham, *Property*, 3-11.

160.   Lawrence J. Golden, *Equitable Distribution of Property* (Colorado Springs, CO: Shepard's/McGraw-Hill, 1983).

161.   Oldham, *Property*, 3-12.

162.   Oldham, *Property*, 3-15.

163.   Weitzman, *Divorce Revolution*, 61.

164. For a more detailed discussion of this topic, see Grace Ganz Blumberg, "Marital Property Treatment of Pensions, Disability Pay, Workers' Compensation, and Other Wage Substitutes: An Insurance, or Replacement, Analysis," *UCLA Law Review* 33 (1986): 1250–1308 and especially 1260.

165. See Harry D. Krause, *Family Law,* 3d ed. (St. Paul, MN: West, 1995), 444; Oldham, *Property,* 7-60.

166. *French v. French,* 17 Cal.2d 775, 112 P.2d 235 (1941).

167. Using a 10 percent discount rate, a $1,000 payment that is anticipated a year from now is worth $909 now; using a 20 percent discount rate, the $1,000 payment a year from now is worth $833 now.

168. *In re Marriage of Brown,* 15 Cal.3d 838, 844, 544 P.2d 561, 564, 126 Cal.Rptr. 633, 636(1976).

169. The different approaches taken to the valuation of pensions is discussed in Oldham, *Property,* 7-65–7-109.

170. John Dewitt Gregory, Peter N. Swisher, and Sheryl L. Scheible-Wolf, *Understanding Family Law* (New York: Matthew Bender, 1993), 342.

171. *Hisquierdo v. Hisquierdo,* 439 U.S. 572, 99 S.Ct. 802, 59 L.Ed.2d 1 (1979).

172. *McCarty v. McCarty,* 453 U.S. 210, 101 S.Ct. 2728, 69 L.Ed.2d 589 (1981).

173. The Railroad Retirement Act was amended to clarify that certain retirement benefits are divisible at divorce. 45 U.S.C. 231(b)(2). Military pensions not based on disability were made divisible by the Uniformed Services Former Spouses' Protection Act, 10 U.S.C. 1408.

174. 5 U.S.C. 8345(j)(l).

175. Oldham, *Property,* 8-22 and 8-23; and Blumberg, "Marital Property."

176. See Allen M. Parkman, "A Systematic Approach to Valuing the Goodwill of Professional Practices," in *Valuing Professional Practices and Licenses, 3d ed.,* ed. Ronald L. Brown (Gaithersburg, NY: Aspen Law & Business, 1998), 6-1–6-18; and Allen M. Parkman, "The Treatment of Professional Goodwill in Divorce Proceedings," *Family Law Quarterly* 18, no. 2 (Summer 1984): 213–24.

177. A special case of individual goodwill occurs with celebrities. See Allen M. Parkman, "Valuing and Allocating Celebrity Status at Divorce," in *Valuing Professional Practices,* ed. Brown, 42-1–42-32.

178. Oldham, *Property,* 10-32.

179. Weitzman found that the Los Angeles judges had found goodwill in the professional practices of an accountant, an architect, a banker, a consultant, a dentist, a doctor, an engineer, an insurance agent, a lawyer, a pharmacist, a professor, a sales representative, and a social worker, as well as a wide range of small and large businesses, including a barber shop, a hardware store, a restaurant, an indoor sign business, and a beauty salon chain. Weitzman, "Economics of Divorce," 1214.

180. Oldham, *Property,* 10-32.

181. Oldham, *Property,* 10-41.

182.   Weitzman, "Economics of Divorce," 1216, n. 124. She reported that one judge said that he was personally in favor of goodwill because it allowed him to give the wife the home.

183.   Allen M. Parkman, "Bringing Consistency to the Financial Arrangements at Divorce," *Kentucky Law Journal* 87, no. 1 (1998–99): 51–93; Allen M. Parkman, "An Investment Approach to Valuing Spousal Support of Education," in *Valuing Profession Practices,* ed. Brown, 32-1–26; and Allen M. Parkman, "Human Capital as Property in Divorce Settlements," *Arkansas Law Review* 40, no. 3 (1987): 439–67.

184.   For a discussion of the treatment of professional education by the courts, see Oldham, *Property,* 9-1–9-28.

185.   Cal. Civ. Code, § 4800.3 (West Supp. 1987).

186.   Weitzman perpetuates this stereotype by identifying the problem as being the situation when the wife typically supports the husband through graduate school. Weitzman, *Divorce Revolution,* 1216. A number of cases have involved wives who acquired medical degrees during marriage. See *Korman v. Korman,* 12 *Family Law Reporter* (BNA) 1611 (N.Y. Supp. 1986), and *Freyer v. Freyer,* 524 N.Y.S.2d 147 (N.Y. Supp. 1987).

187.   Census, *Statistical Abstract, 1998,* Table 250, 161.

188.   Census, *Statistical Abstract, 1998,* Table 306, 191.

189.   Between 1960 and 1980, married women between the ages of eighteen and twenty-nine increased the number of years in school on average from .12 year to .33 year. See Sweet and Teixeira, "Breaking Tradition."

6

The Reform of No-Fault Divorce

No-fault divorce has had an impact on society that extends far beyond the changes foreseen by its initial proponents. It was expected to improve the welfare of divorced couples and their children by eliminating the hypocrisy and the ill feelings produced by the fault grounds for divorce; but many who argued that an improvement in welfare would follow from removing the hypocritical fault grounds for divorce gave little consideration to the other laws affecting divorce. Others proposed additional changes to the divorce laws, such as conciliation procedures, but these were rejected by most states. The rejection of these other laws, however, has not been the primary source of the problems with no-fault. This chapter discusses recent reform efforts and then analyzes why a combination of no-fault, mutual consent, and fault grounds for divorce would be an improvement over the current laws.

The primary problem with no-fault divorce is that it ignores some costs of divorce and the incentives that these costs create. The most obvious examples of these omissions are the inadequate financial awards received at divorce by a spouse who made sacrifices—such as limiting a career—for the benefit of the family, frequently causing injustices and often a response by both spouses that reduces their family's welfare. Until recently, the financial impact was almost exclusively on women. These financial awards are often meager because of the limited definition of property used in divorce proceedings. The original no-fault divorce debate included no significant discussion of the definition of property subject to division at divorce, but there has subsequently been recognition that there is a need to reform the financial arrangement at divorce. Some of this reform movement has focused on the expansion of the definition of property, but so far this expansion has been unsystematic. The impact of no-fault divorce would be significantly improved if the definition of property were expanded to include human capital. The financial awards at divorce have been the most obvious problem with no-fault divorce, but other costs have also been ignored, including the cost of the loss of companionship and the cost of the additional search process by the divorced spouse, along with the costs to the children.

The reform of no-fault divorce is the subject of this chapter. This reform can occur at two levels: A *limited* reform of the no-fault divorce laws would retain the no-fault grounds for divorce with a change in the financial arrangements at divorce to recognize the effects of marriage and divorce on human capital. A more *systematic* reform would recognize that no-fault divorce is fundamentally flawed. Mutual consent offers a more desirable standard for the dissolution of most established marriages, with no-fault still appropriate early in a marriage and fault when there is an abusive relationship.

For these changes in the grounds for divorce to improve the incentives facing married couples, spouses have to have more control over the basis on which their marriage is going to be dissolved. From a legal perspective, marriage is currently treated as a status that attaches to the spouses and that gives a state in which either spouse is domiciled the jurisdiction to grant a divorce. The grounds for that divorce will be those of the state with jurisdiction, rather than the one in which the couple had been married, the one in which they had lived, or the one in which the divorced spouse continues to live. Therefore, if a few states made it more difficult for a couple to divorce, that would have very little effect on the incentives facing adults because they have very little control over the grounds for divorce that may be applied to their marriage. Even if a couple was married in and lived for a long duration in a state that had divorce laws that encouraged couples to make a long-term commitment to their marriage, either spouse could, for example, move to a state with no-fault grounds for divorce and obtain a divorce that probably would have to be honored in all the other states. Given that uncertainty, adults have to continue to react to the uncertainty and to the incentives caused by no-fault divorce. This situation could be improved if marriage is treated as a contract rather than as a status. Then the grounds for any divorce—preferably the ones that will be presented in the following discussion—could be established at marriage.

THE RECOGNITION OF THE PROBLEM

The initial no-fault divorce law enacted in California in 1969 was broadly accepted as an improvement over the existing fault-based statutes. This broad support continued as no-fault was passed in the other states. Eventually, however, it was recognized that its proponents had been too optimistic, and no-fault divorce has been subjected to increasing criticism as its adverse effects on families in general and divorced women and the children of divorced parents in particular have become more apparent.[1] The reformers became aware that it was easier to condemn the fault divorce system than it has been to find an adequate replacement.[2]

The hypocrisy of the fault divorce era is gone, but the ill feelings associated with divorce remain. The ill feelings are particularly acute among divorced people who feel that they have not been compensated for the commitment that they made to their marriage and for the sacrifices that they made for its benefit. The visible examples have been divorced women who find that their financial condition has deteriorated. This deterioration goes beyond the fact that two households cannot live as cheaply as one to include the smaller financial settlements that frequently followed from the shift from negotiated settlements under fault divorce to settlements that reflect the legal standards under no-fault. Most divorce cases continue to be settled rather than litigated,[3] but the negotiated settlements under no-fault divorce can be radically different from those that occurred under fault divorce. Under no-fault, neither spouse has the veto power that often existed under fault divorce, and, therefore, the negotiated outcomes under no-fault divorce are strongly influenced by the outcomes that the parties expect if they litigate. These financial arrangements usually consist of half of marital property, child support for any minor children, and limited spousal support. Without the veto power that existed under fault divorce, it is difficult for a party to obtain a negotiated settlement that is a substantial deviation from the outcome expected from a trial. With no-fault divorce, the criteria for spousal support and property division emphasize need, rather than fault, or contribution with an attempt to achieve as clean a break between the spouses as possible at divorce. Property settlements rather than support awards have been encouraged as the preferred method for dealing with the parties' needs after dissolution.[4] The criteria for child support have not changed dramatically, but the amount of child support is now more likely to reflect the legal standards than the outcome of private negotiations.[5]

Although no-fault divorce has not lived up to its expectations, there have only been limited attempts at reform. A major problem with any reform of no-fault divorce is that the conditions that led to the shift from fault to no-fault divorce no longer exist. The problems with fault divorce were obvious: The laws were hypocritical in forcing people to fabricate testimony to establish the grounds for a divorce to dissolve a marriage that had failed for other reasons. People were lying to get a divorce, and, to add to the discomfort, they were lying under oath—they were committing perjury. In addition, there were some very vocal advocacy groups. Because the problems with fault were obvious, no-fault had strong support among academics.[6] In addition, the matrimonial bar was very uncomfortable suggesting perjury to its clients, which gave the bar a strong impetus to change the grounds for divorce.[7] Last, divorced people—the most vocal being men—were often unhappy with the negotiations necessary for their divorce.[8]

The problem with no-fault divorce is that its repercussions are subtle, while not being hypocritical. It is subtle because the primary reaction has been a reduction in the commitment by adults to their family. Few people recognize that both spouses frequently are making a weaker commitment to each other and a stronger commitment to employment, not because of dire financial circumstances or wonderful and fulfilling jobs, but because of concerns about their circumstances if their marriage is dissolved. Although there is broad concern about the state of the American family, seldom is no-fault divorce recognized as a significant contributing factor.[9] Because no-fault divorce is effectively unilateral divorce in most states, there is no opportunity for hypocrisy. If someone wants out of a marriage, they no longer have to rationalize why—they just file for divorce. Without recognition of the problem and a committed advocacy group, the reform of no-fault divorce has not progressed very far.

It is regrettable that the debate so far represents the triumph of the obvious over the subtle coupled with a lack of appreciation for the trade-off between policy alternatives. No-fault divorce is defended because it protects people who have made a miscalculation by marrying someone with whom they no longer want to live—the obvious.[10] Concerns are often expressed about unfortunate spouses who would be locked into loveless marriages if we did not have no-fault grounds for divorce. Frequently ignored when these concerns are addressed—because they are a great deal subtler—are the gains from encouraging and rewarding those who have made or are attempting to make better decisions. They want to search diligently for the best spouse, and then after marriage they want to make the decisions that increase their and their family's gains from marriage. No-fault divorce does not encourage or reward success in this process.

Most proponents of no-fault divorce see few costs associated with permitting people to easily dissolve marriages—especially the unfortunate, long-term, but loveless ones just mentioned. But the argument here is that there are costs—and they are substantial—associated with always making it easy to dissolve a marriage. There are trade-offs between making it easy to dissolve marriages and encouraging sacrifices during marriage based on the spouses' long-term commitments. No set of divorce laws is perfect. But the costs as well as the benefits of alternative proposals have to be addressed. When that is done later in this chapter, I think that a combination of no-fault, mutual consent, and fault grounds for divorce would be a substantial improvement over the current no-fault grounds for divorce.

No-fault divorce is an example of *moral hazard*, the tendency of a person who buys insurance to relax his or her efforts to prevent the occurrence of the risk against which he or she has insured.[11] Automobile drivers with insurance have incentives to drive less carefully than those with none. In a similar manner, no-fault divorce is a form of insurance against bad decisions, and as a result it encourages bad decisions.[12] Because no-fault divorce—relative to fault or to mutual consent divorce—reduces the cost of poor judgment when choosing a spouse, we would expect a less diligent search for a spouse and, consequently, poorer matches and more divorces. Rather than reducing the cost of poor decisions, this book argues that the preferred solution would be to encourage wiser decisions.

The debate about divorce reform also represents an unfortunate use of the English language. The problem with the current divorce laws is not that they are necessarily no-fault, but rather that they permit unilateral divorce. In fact, it is interesting to consider whether the divorce reforms that we have observed over recent decades would have been as warmly received if the proposed legislation had been called "unilateral divorce" rather than "no-fault" divorce. If the true problem with the current laws is recognized to be the permitting of unilateral divorce, then the appropriate alternative to consider is mutual consent, rather than fault divorce.

REFORM OF THE NO-FAULT GROUNDS FOR DIVORCE

Whereas there has been substantial criticism of the effects of the current divorce laws, the reform of the no-fault divorce statutes has been very limited.[13] Surveys show that roughly half of all Americans favor changes that would make it more difficult to get a divorce,[14] which is a significant increase from a decade ago. But it was almost thirty years after the passage of no-fault divorce in California before states seriously considered alternatives. In 1996, at least twenty states considered divorce reform, including proposals in twelve states to modify or eliminate no-fault divorce statutes.[15] The reform movement got its start in the Midwest, where legislators in Michigan and Iowa sought to create a divorce system that would prohibit no-fault dissolution in cases in which one spouse contests the divorce or minor children are involved. On Valentine's Day 1996, Michigan State Representative Jessie Dalman launched the divorce counterrevolution. In an announcement made on the steps of the Michigan capital building, Representative Dalman unveiled a series of bills designed to strengthen the institution of marriage by ending unilateral divorce.[16] Under these bills, if one spouse opposed the divorce, the divorcing spouse would be required to prove fault, consisting of desertion, infidelity, abuse, a prison sentence of more than three years, alcoholism, or drug addiction.[17] If both the husband and the wife agree to dissolve the marriage, the no-fault grounds would remain. However, if minor children still live at home, the couple would be required to get counseling and a parenting plan first. This proposed legislation also encouraged premarital counseling by having a lower fee and a shorter waiting period for those people who had gone through sessions with a minister, a psychologist, or a family therapist.

Representative Dalman's bills have not been passed, and similar bills have fared no better in other states. The first bill to be voted on was in Washington State; the bill would have permitted couples the option to sign a prenuptial contract excluding no-fault divorce.[18] Common among the opponents of any change in the no-fault divorce laws has been concern for the people who made a poor decision when they married. For example, the minority leader of the Washington legislature, who was a family lawyer, argued that the bill might induce many couples to sign prenuptial contracts they would later regret. Ignored, because it is subtle, was the argument made here that many people want and are willing to make a long-term commitment to their spouses, which is not permitted in most states under current legislation. The Washington bill did not pass. Iowa did pass legislation in 1996 that requires parents to take classes on how to protect their children from the pain of divorce.[19]

In 1997, Louisiana became the first state to enact a major revision of its no-fault divorce statute when it passed the Covenant Marriage Act.[20] This Act gives those planning to marry in Louisiana a choice between two options: (1) a standard marriage with the potential for a no-fault divorce or (2) a covenant marriage.[21] The covenant marriage differs from the standard marriage in several ways: Most fundamentally, those choosing a covenant marriage must receive counseling prior to the wedding,[22] must agree to pursue additional counseling if the marriage encounters difficulty,[23] and cannot obtain a no-fault divorce without a lengthy separation.[24] Under these covenant marriages, the grounds for divorce are limited. A spouse in a covenant marriage may obtain a judgment of divorce only with proof of one of the following: (1) the other spouse has committed adultery;[25] (2) the other spouse has committed a felony and has been sentenced to death or imprisonment at hard labor;[26] (3) the other spouse has abandoned the matrimonial domicile for a period of one year and constantly refuses to return;[27] (4) the other spouse has physically or sexually abused the spouse seeking the divorce or has abused a child of one of the spouses;[28] or (5) the spouses have been living separate and apart continuously without reconciliation for a period of two years, if there is no separation agreement.[29] If a separation agreement has been obtained, the parties can obtain a divorce after one year of separation if there are no minor children[30] and after one year and six months of separation if there are minor children.[31] Separation judgments can be obtained for the same fault-based reasons as the divorce, as well as for the "habitual intemperance of the other spouse, or excesses, cruel treatment, or outrages" if such behavior is "of such a nature to render their living together insupportable."[32] So far, the covenant marriage has not been warmly received by couples in Louisiana. After one year, only one percent of Louisiana newlyweds have chosen it.[33] Similar covenant marriage legislation was passed in Arizona in 1998.[34] Meanwhile, states such as Pennsylvania, Illinois, Virginia, Georgia, and a handful of other states are also considering legislation.

These reform efforts would not be expected to change the incentives facing adults. The primary problem with covenant marriage is that an agreement entered into in Louisiana or Arizona is not binding on the spouses if either spouse becomes a resident of another state.[35] The incentive for couples to make a long-term commitment to their marriage is still severely restricted because people do not know where they will live in the future. Covenant marriage also has additional problems. So long as there is a no-fault divorce option, couples will weigh the costs and benefits of those options. Covenant marriage starts out with the requirement for marriage counseling that may be viewed as having only limited value. Marriage was durable in the past because of physical attraction, pragmatic gains for the spouses, a social stigma associated with divorce, and laws that made it difficult to divorce. All of these occurred without counseling. Unless the counseling addresses the pragmatic realities of married life, especially those associated with living in a no-fault divorce environment, the counseling will be perceived to be of little value and just costly enough to induce the couple to take the no-fault divorce option.

Moreover, although people might eventually prefer a covenant marriage, it may be more than they are willing to commit to initially. We live in a world in which the gains from marriage have been reduced for many people. Whether two people will gain from marriage is less certain than it was in the past. It is a big jump for a couple to make a lifelong commitment when there is an easy-out option under no-fault divorce. Last, the requirement of living separate and apart for two years to dissolve a marriage is inordinately long if both spouses agree that the marriage is a failure.[36] If the benefits of the divorce clearly exceed the costs, then—subject to legal protection for the interests of any children—social welfare is improved by permitting the couple to dissolve the marriage by mutual agreement. As to the other legal changes, the new requirements in Iowa do not address the concerns discussed in this book.

REFORM OF THE FINANCIAL ARRANGEMENTS AT DIVORCE

Whereas there has been only a limited reform of the grounds for divorce, there has been some improvement in the financial arrangements at divorce. Under no-fault divorce, property settlements have become the primary device for resolving the spouses' financial arrangements at divorce. For example, the Uniform Marriage and Divorce Act limits the awarding of alimony to a spouse in two situations:[37] (1) the spouse does not have sufficient property to provide for his or her reasonable needs, and (2) the spouse is unable to support himself or herself through appropriate employment or has custody of a child whose circumstances make it appropriate that he or she not seek a job outside the home. In both the community property and common law states, the property settlements now tend to return the parties' separate properties and then divide their marital property equally.[38] With this emphasis on an equal distribution of marital property at divorce, the advantages of the community property system have been recognized.[39] From the perspective of the community property system, marriage is a partnership to which the parties bring different but equal contributions. Because both parties make essentially equal contributions to the creation of marital property, they should share equally in its distribution at divorce. For example, the California Family Law Act requires the court to divide the community assets and liabilities equally.[40]

Traditionally under the common law system, the ownership of property was determined by the name or names on the title to the property. Even though substantial property had been acquired during a long marriage, a marriage could end with little or no official marital property, and the courts of many common law states lacked the power to order transfers or divisions of property at dissolution. Although these common law rules often produced unfair results, they were not subjected to a concerted challenge during the fault divorce era because most actual property divisions at divorce in those states under fault divorce were based on negotiations and only secondarily on the law. With no-fault, as we have seen, the emphasis in property settlements shifted to the legal standards.

With the introduction of no-fault divorce and a reduction in the financial settlements received by many wives, unjust outcomes became more frequent in some common law states. If the property acquired by the family during the marriage was held only in the name of the husband, he received that property at divorce. Recognizing the injustice of that outcome, the common law states enacted statutes that required an equitable distribution of property at dissolution. The property division was to assume part of the role that alimony had played in addressing the needs of the divorced individuals, but it has been argued that property settlements seldom have been adequately adjusted to reflect the needs of divorced women.[41] The usual result has been an equal division of the marital property,[42] which has been touted as a victory for divorced women.

That victory was an illusion. Soon it was recognized that "equal" was not necessarily "just," and some obvious injustices were not covered by existing laws. Marriages were being dissolved in which working spouses had financed the education of student spouses. Long-term marriages were being dissolved in which there was little officially designated marital property, no right to child support, and only limited provision for spousal support. Yet professionals were leaving long-term marriages with their high income essentially intact. The prevailing rules for the financial arrangements at divorce did not fairly handle these situations.

Concern about these situations was less when the parties negotiated a settlement under fault divorce. In negotiations, the parties were free to use any method that they chose to identify and value the property; but the flexibility of that situation changed under no-fault divorce when the legal rules for identifying and valuing marital property came to control the proceedings. These rules could not be easily adapted to new situations. If one spouse has a property interest in the business that is operated by the other spouse, should he or she also have an interest in the *profession* of the spouse? What is the appropriate method for valuing a profession? These were difficult questions that had not been addressed under fault divorce.

Reform in the Courts and Legislatures

Most reform efforts in the courts and the legislatures have focused on the items that are treated as property, including those that are clearly assets from a financial perspective, such as pensions. The limited relevance of the legal definition of property under fault divorce is reflected in these reform decisions. All pensions had not been recognized as property under fault divorce, even though they had become increasingly important components of families' wealth. This omission had not been subjected to a systematic challenge because of the private financial arrangements at divorce. The new emphasis on the legal definition of property under no-fault divorce quickly exposed the limitations of the current statutes when people dealt with these obvious financial assets.

The reform did not stop with these financial assets. A major focus of the ensuing reform movement in the courts and legislatures consisted of expanding the financial arrangements at divorce to include consideration of earning capacity.[43] The injustice of no-fault divorce often was associated with the higher income of the spouse who had focused on income earning during marriage. To capture part of the value of this income-earning capacity, the definition of marital property was expanded in some states to include educational degrees, licenses, and professional goodwill.[44] When a spouse's earnings increased during marriage, it was often concluded that property was created at that time, and the issue of whether the underlying property was separate or marital was often ignored. Although most of these deliberations occurred in the courts, some legislatures addressed these issues. In California, legislation was passed that required compensation for the contribution made by working spouses to the education of a student spouse.[45]

Procedures already existed for valuing businesses, but they were often ignored when legal rules were established for valuing earning capacity. Principles have been borrowed from the fields of taxation, wrongful death, antitrust, and business litigation,[46] but there has been little uniformity or certainty in the valuation methods utilized by the courts. Although financial theory provides standard methods for valuing assets, some courts have turned to rules of thumb, such as "one times gross revenues" for valuing professional businesses. These rule-of-thumb techniques often have no analytical foundation.

The difficulties the courts have with earning capacity can be illustrated by the manner of their recognition of professional goodwill as marital property.[47] *Pro-*

fessional goodwill is the excess earnings of a professional business, usually represented by an individual or individuals, that parallels the goodwill concept for other businesses. *Business goodwill* is a commonly recognized intangible asset of an established business. The recognition of professional goodwill as property was often a reaction to the financial situation of some older married women. At divorce, a professional husband might leave his marriage with an expectation of a high future income, but the income of his wife might decline dramatically. To supplement the meager financial awards that the wives would otherwise receive at divorce, the courts started to recognize the intangible asset of professional goodwill as marital property.

Professional goodwill created problems because the courts had difficulty conceptualizing intangible assets. Physical evidence accompanies the tangible marital property traditionally recognized at divorce: the family has a title to the house; there are stock and bond certificates. At divorce, these items can be documented and readily dated as to when they were acquired. Attempting to maintain a parallel, the courts required that the value of the professional goodwill should be determined at divorce by evidence that was already in existence and with no regard for the potential or continuing income of the professional spouse.[48]

In making this determination, the courts had no clear idea of the process that creates value. From a financial perspective, which is the only appropriate framework for valuing assets or property, property has no value if there will be no future income or services provided by the property. A solid, but unmovable, house that is about to be destroyed has no value. Its price, as a house, is zero. Similarly, professional goodwill has no value if the analyst is required to ignore the future. Commenting on a California professional goodwill case, Joan Krauskopf noted, "A certain amount of fictionalization is involved in arriving at a present value of the expectation of future patronage while at the same time forbidding consideration of future efforts."[49]

Among the states that recognize professional goodwill in a law practice, for example, there is no agreement on the appropriate method for valuing the goodwill.[50] Because law practices cannot be sold, the courts have reverted either to partnership agreements or to an accounting formula approach. Partnership agreements are created for a number of reasons, including potential divorce of the partners, and the value that is placed on goodwill in those agreements may be an unreliable measure of its true value. Large law firms, for example, can expect repeat business that is the essence of goodwill. In one of the most frequently cited cases on professional goodwill, a court held that if the shareholders' agreement in a large law firm stated that goodwill and other intangible assets were worth one dollar, that was their value for purposes of a divorce proceeding.[51] The accounting formula approach is more in line with normal business valuation in which goodwill is estimated by capitalizing the excess earnings of an established business compared with a similar, but new, business. The problem with applying this technique to a law firm is finding a similar business. Often the courts compare the income of partners to salaries of lawyers in the public sector to determine the excess earnings. That is like comparing apples to oranges because these practices are so different from each other.

Licenses and academic degrees were recognized in some states as a basis for an adjustment in the financial arrangements at divorce, but the parties found themselves with a variety of outcomes, depending on the state in which their divorce was occurring.[52] Only a limited number of states recognized these items as property, in some cases including them in the property settlement, in others making them the basis for additional spousal support. Where recognized as property, the value of these items was based on reimbursement of the supporting spouse in some states and on a share of the discounted value of increased earnings in others. Seldom was there an attempt to place the items into a systematic financial framework.

Expanding the definition of marital property to include professional goodwill, licenses, and academic degrees seldom included any objective analysis. Some commentators viewed this movement as an attempt to restore alimony through the property division.[53] The issue of what was property often arose when there was little traditional marital property and when the wife's attorney was looking for a method for increasing the financial award.[54] The expanded legal definition of property was driven by the lack of other assets for division rather than by any determination that the current definition was too restrictive.[55]

Reforms by the American Law Institute

An important addition to the analysis of the financial repercussions of divorce has been the deliberations of the American Law Institute (ALI), which issued its Proposed Final Draft: Part 1 of the *Principles of the Law of Family Dissolution* (*Principles*) on February 14, 1997.[56] The *Principles* seek to achieve an equitable sharing of the losses from the dissolution of the family relationship,[57] and also recognize that the process of family dissolution ordinarily is based on negotiation rather than on litigation. This project deals with the issues of property division, postdissolution support, and child custody.

The *Principles* reject the inclusion of such intangible assets as spousal earning capacity among the items considered in property settlements, rather assigning their relevance to be considered in alimony awards.[58] In general, the *Principles* assume that the traditionally recognized property should be divided equally,[59] except when there is financial misconduct.[60] The primary emphasis in adjustments at divorce is given to alimony, or compensatory spousal payments, that is based on compensating a spouse rather than on need.[61] These payments would provide compensation for a loss in living standard and in earning capacity, for an investment in the other spouse's earning capacity, and for assistance in recovering the spouse's premarital living standard after the dissolution of a short marriage.[62] Under the *Principles,* compensatory spousal payments for a loss in living standard or in earning capacity, like alimony, generally end with remarriage or death[63] and can be modified.[64] Compensation is based on a sharing of the spouses' postdissolution incomes, although the income transfer often has only a very limited link to the loss incurred.[65] Alternatively, compensation for investments in the other spouse's earning capacity and to assist the spouse in recovering his or her premarital living standard after the dissolution of a short marriage is more directly related to the actual losses incurred. These losses cannot be modified and do not terminate with remarriage or death.[66] To date, the influence that the *Principles* will have on state statutes is not clear.

Academic Contributions to the Reform Movement

Along with the efforts of the courts, the legislatures, and the ALI, suggestions for reforming the financial arrangements at divorce were presented by academics. The academic reformers tended to deal directly with the financial problems facing divorced women and children of divorced parents, but the resulting programs again have not been systematic. The deterioration in the financial condition of divorced women and children of divorced parents caused Lenore Weitzman, for example, to direct her concerns to four groups: (1) children, (2) the long-married older housewife with little or no experience in the paid labor force, (3) the mother with primary responsibility for the care of minor children, and (4) the transitional generation of middle-aged women.[67] Concern for these groups suggests a variety of reforms. One reform would give the custodial parent a special preference in the family home. This may not be unreasonable, but it is no substitute for an accurate calculation of the true costs of acting as custodial parent. The primary problems with child support have been an inadequate recognition of the costs incurred by the custodial parent and a lack of satisfactory enforcement.

Weitzman's second reform would expand the definition of marital property to include career assets and to divide those assets as part of the property settlement. *Career assets* are defined as

> the tangible and intangible assets that are acquired in the course of a marriage as part of either spouse's career or career potential—pensions and retirement benefits, a professional education, license to practice a profession or trade, enhanced earning capacity, the goodwill value of a business or professional, medical and hospital insurance, and other benefits and entitlement.[68]

The fact that Weitzman has to argue that pensions and business goodwill should be added to the list of items considered as property divided at divorce illustrates the limited challenges that were made to the definition of property during the fault divorce era. A couple can save for retirement by acquiring a portfolio of stocks and bonds. Alternatively, a pension right can be created by the employment of the spouses. Both are clearly assets from a financial perspective, but the courts seldom treated the pension as marital property.

Weitzman's concerns are less valid when it comes to human capital. She implied that the creation of a career is associated with the time that income flows occurred: a career established before marriage would be recognized as separate property, but a career partially or wholly built during the marriage should be viewed as a product of the marital partnership.[69] If only part of a career is developed during marriage, Weitzman argued, the courts should acknowledge that there are separate and community property interests in the career. A review of the process by which human capital is created shows, however, that the skills that result in individuals having the ability to generate high incomes are usually acquired over their lifetime. Any skills that were acquired during marriage built on others that had been acquired earlier. To recognize every increase in income during marriage as being a direct result of the marriage partnership would overcompensate the couple at the expense of the individual. Without further guidance, I do not believe this reform would be an improvement over the current conditions.

Weitzman's third reform attempted to correct the injustices experienced by older women by using spousal support to equalize the standard of living of the two parties after divorce.[70] Although this suggestion has an aura of fairness, it is unrealistic and potentially extremely unfair. It would reduce the incentive for income earners to work, while leaving the people who had emphasized work at home with little incentive to increase their paid employment.

Weitzman's last reform dealt with child support, essentially basing it on income sharing. Weitzman assumed that children are entitled to maintain the standard of living of the higher-income parent to the extent possible. It is difficult to object to this reform, but I believe reform of child support would benefit more from a recognition of the true costs of custody. The current rules do not recognize the human capital costs of custody incurred by the custodial parent. The costs of custody should include not only the support of the child but also the reduced social and employment opportunities of the custodial parent. The psychological costs of divorce to the children are not recognized as a cost of the divorce. Moreover, a cost is not a cost unless it is incurred by the person making the decision. In many cases, child support is not a cost because it is not paid. The lack of enforcement for court-ordered child support obligations is a critical problem.

Weitzman's policy recommendations focused on legislative reforms. She recognized the need for education of both judges and lawyers,[71] but part of the problem in educating judges and lawyers is the lack of a clear program. Other than identifying the financial problems faced by divorced women and the children of divorced parents, Weitzman did not provide a systematic program for reform.

Because of her experiences with the judicial system, she concluded, "The route to divorce law reform must have a strong legislative focus."[72] Her concern is shared by many feminists; judges tend to be older males, and feminists fear that permitting these men discretion will work to the detriment of women.

Other academics have addressed reforms to specific problems faced by divorced women. One area of potential injustice occurs when education is acquired during marriage. Joan Krauskopf calculated a formula for determining the value of education acquired during marriage, subtracting the present value of the pre-education earning capacity and the present value of the cost of the education from the present value of the posteducation earning capacity.[73] The difference is the return on the investment, which Krauskopf argued is marital property. This process would give each spouse an equal interest in the income produced by the education.

This approach conflicts with methods normally used to determine the value of investments in businesses. First, it ignores whether the investors acquired a debt or an equity interest in the education.[74] A debt interest would require reimbursement, whereas an equity interest would create a claim on a share of the profits. Second, this approach overestimates the return to the education because it underestimates the value of the individual's human capital before the additional education. A person who is admitted to a highly competitive program, such as medical school, is clearly an above-average college graduate. Therefore, it is inaccurate to estimate the gain from medical school by comparing the average doctor to the average person with a bachelor's degree.

Mary Ann Glendon, an authority on comparative legal systems, has also contributed to the debate about the reform of no-fault. She reported that the reformers soon realized that the shift to no-fault divorce required more consideration of the financial aspects of divorce.[75] The financial problems experienced by divorced women in the United States under no-fault divorce have not been unique. European women experienced similar problems when many European countries introduced no-fault divorce laws at the same time as the United States. To European reformers, it was intolerable that one spouse could obtain a divorce if either the other spouse or the children of the marriage were not fully protected from adverse financial consequences, and in Europe as in the United States, a reexamination of the legal regulation of the financial aspects of divorce occurred. Glendon identified three responses: (1) Most European countries retained considerations of fault and emphasized the financial obligations of the former income earner, supplemented with assistance by the state. (2) In the Scandinavian countries, the idea of fault was minimized, with the emphasis instead on the spouses becoming self-sufficient; parents retain child support obligations, but there also are major programs of public benefits for families with children. Both of these European models include relatively rigid and predictable formulas for child support and an equal property division. (3) In the United States and Great Britain, both the parties and the courts have much broader discretion. The courts have broader discretion over both property distribution and child support, and the spouses often are permitted to determine the amount of child support. Glendon included no discussion of whether the different environments have considered whether the definition of property is accurate.

Glendon identified most of the problem in the United States as centered on child support, with the awards being too small, not adjusted for inflation, and generally unenforced.[76] She advocated that the state become much more involved in establishing rules for child support that cannot be altered by the agreement of the spouses. She also called for special consideration for short, childless marriages, advocating a fixed rule for marital property—she was less concerned with the particulars of the rule than with reducing judicial discretion.

Glendon summarized her criticism of the current situation, "In sum, the idea of effecting a clean break by dividing property between the spouses and excluding maintenance after divorce does not come to grips with the fact that no legal system has been able to achieve this result on a widespread basis because, in most divorce cases, children are present and there is insufficient property."[77] She advocated an approach that she called the "children-first principle": Having children imposes "a lien upon all of the parents' income and property to the extent necessary to provide for the children's decent subsistence at least until those children reach the age of majority."[78] She argued that this principle has the twin virtues of being relatively noncontroversial and easily applicable to most cases, but she admitted that she does not provide detailed specifications for its implementation.

Marriage contracts also have been advocated to remedy the outcomes dictated by the no-fault divorce statutes.[79] Glendon noted that marriage contracts are an established institution in the civil law in European countries, although they have been discouraged in the United States. Weitzman argued that women would benefit from premarital agreements that address the property division and support obligations in case of divorce. Subject to government regulation to protect the interests of the children, the expanded use of marriage contracts is very appealing. They are not an ideal solution because, at the time of marriage, people are often unaware of the issues that they will need to address later in life. Just as the Uniform Commercial Code provides rules to cover outcomes that often were not contemplated when commercial agreements were initiated, statutes are probably still necessary to cover similar outcomes of a marriage agreement.[80]

In summary, there has been substantial discussion about reforming no-fault divorce to improve the dire financial conditions of many divorced women and children of divorced parents. Numerous programs have been advocated in the courts and legislatures or by academics, generally emphasizing a shift of financial resources to the women and children who have been viewed as the victims of no-fault. These programs suffer from not being systematic and from failing to recognize all the costs of divorce.

A PROPOSAL TO REFORM THE FINANCIAL
ARRANGEMENTS AT DIVORCE

As the emphasis in the financial arrangements at divorce have shifted toward the property settlement, the primary reason that less-than-satisfactory results have occurred is because property itself is not appropriately defined.[81] Although a common concern at divorce is the property division, the statutes do not clearly define property. The equitable distribution statutes in the vast majority of jurisdictions define *marital property*, but usually ignore the more basic definition of *property*.[82] The community property principles leave open the issue of what items should be treated as property. The recently developed *Principles* of ALI do not provide any clarification. When the *Principles* consider the division of property at the dissolution of marriage, they define marital and separate property, but not property itself.[83] Furthermore, the *Principles* state that they would have to define *property*,

> if the term was meant to have a special meaning different from its meaning in other areas of the law, but no such special definition is necessary or desirable. The most frequent occasion for debate over the definition involves the law's treatment of earning capacity and goodwill, but the characterization of these assets involves policy choices whose analysis is not aided by appeal to a general definition of property. The definition of marital property must follow from the policy choice; the policy choice is not determined by the definition.[84]

Nothing could be further from the truth. When people were making their own financial arrangements at divorce, a clear definition of property was not essential or, for that matter, very important. However, that is no longer the case. There are numerous reasons why a clear understanding of what property is and how it is affected by marriage and divorce is important. It is not an acceptable conclusion that the law's treatment of earning capacity and goodwill, for example, should be based on policy choices. If something is an asset and, therefore, property, it should be recognized as such with the normal standards for its identification and valuation. Public choices may then determine whether there are reasons for modifying the general rules for the allocation of property at divorce. Much of the confusion about how earning capacity and professional goodwill, for example, should be treated at divorce is due to the lack of a clear definition and understanding of property, something that can be remedied easily by using the language of the financial and economic analysts who usually identify and value property. *Property* is just another word for *assets*, and the obligations between spouses can often be viewed as *debts*.[85]

Still, lawyers and economists would recognize most items that are property, such as physical and financial assets. They would agree that automobiles and bonds are property. But economists also recognize individuals' income-earning capacity as their property—their human capital. Human capital is the major asset possessed by most individuals, but it has not been recognized as property by the law in an orderly manner. Human capital is property just like a house or a portfolio of stocks and bonds, and, therefore, the tools of financial analysis can be applied to its identification and valuation.

Human capital exists when individuals have an income-earning capacity. It is normally created by a process that is not dissimilar from the investment process that results in the creation of a portfolio of stocks and bonds. For example, parents can buy shares of common stock that they give to their child, or they can pay for the child's education. The student is wealthier due to the education just as he or she would be wealthier on receiving shares of stock: the child will have a higher income in the future due to either investment. The investments that produce human capital usually occur through education or employment. They can be financed by parents, by taxpayers, or by the individuals.

The value of a person's human capital is frequently only minimally related to that person's current income. This is especially true at the normal age at which people marry for the first time. Human capital increases when individuals' expected future earnings rise; and these individuals can have substantial human capital, even though their current earnings might be low. To go one step further, there can be an inverse relationship between individuals' income and their human capital. People who leave school to find a job usually have higher earnings over the subsequent couple of years than their contemporaries who remain in school. Education, however, is a primary source of higher future earnings. Eventually, the people who remain in school will usually have more human capital than their higher-income contemporaries who are not in school.

The value of an individual's human capital is based on that individual's anticipated future net earnings. The usual assumption is that those earnings will increase over time.[86] This occurs for a number of reasons: First, their earnings increase as they apply to particular occupations the education and training that they received early. The increases in productivity and earnings tend to be higher for better-educated workers. Second, the earlier education opens up the opportunity for additional training, which often occurs on the job. The time and, therefore, the investment spent on this additional training will usually be small compared to the time and the resources invested in human capital earlier. High school graduates have a minimum of twelve years of essentially full-time education. Without this prior education, workers usually do not qualify for additional training. Although this additional training is important, the critical investments in human capital usually occur early in an individual's life—generally before marriage. An individual's income at marriage is often a poor gauge of that individual's human capital at that time.

Human capital could be formally incorporated into property considered at divorce by modifying the property section of the Uniform Marriage and Divorce

Act. The recognition of human capital may not require complex calculations. Human capital has a value that reflects the individual's expected future earnings. The human capital possessed before marriage is separate property, just like any other asset acquired before marriage. When third-year medical students marry, it is reasonable to assume that they will receive their medical degree and pursue a medical career. There is no need to know the exact amounts that they will earn. All that is necessary is the recognition that the investments by parents, by taxpayers, and by the individual before marriage were substantial. The career pattern was established, and a medical career is essentially separate property. Although the funding of the acquisition of this separate property may require compensation to a spouse, the property itself is essentially separate. Alternatively, any human capital acquired during marriage should be treated as marital property.

Adjustments in Property Settlements at Divorce

The value of the spouses' human capital can change during marriage so that an adjustment becomes necessary if there is a divorce.[87] If spouses can expect to have earnings after a divorce that could have been anticipated at marriage, the marriage has not affected their human capital. Consequently, they leave the marriage with that component of their separate property intact. But when the spouses' human capital has increased or decreased during marriage, adjustments are required in the property settlement at divorce. If the expected future earnings have increased, human capital has been created that should be treated as marital property. Alternatively, if the expected earnings have decreased, the individuals' separate properties have been diminished, and they should be compensated for this loss.

An Increase in Human Capital

The expected earnings of spouses can increase during marriage for a number of reasons. One spouse can help the other in ways that would not have occurred if they had not been married. Opera singer Frederica von Stade's husband argued in their November 1990 dissolution proceeding that he was her voice coach and teacher during their seventeen-year marriage.[88] He claimed that he was responsible for her success. The court held that her voice was marital property.[89] One spouse can provide financial assistance that is unobtainable from any other source for the graduate education of the other spouse. The individuals' expected earnings and, therefore, their human capital have increased. Marital property has been created. The increased earnings during the marriage were enjoyed by both spouses, so they are not an issue at divorce.[90]

A word of caution is in order. Even if an individual's earnings are above those of his or her contemporaries at divorce, that is not prima facie evidence that marital property has been created. The earnings of individuals vary for a number of reasons, with the obvious ones being level of intelligence, quality of education, disposition toward work, and willingness to accept risks. Because these characteristics are so fundamental, the usual presumption should be that they were acquired before the marriage, and thus an individual's human capital is separate property.

When human capital was created during marriage, its value can be estimated by discounting the increase in the expected future earnings that are a result of the marriage.[91] This is a process similar to that used by economists to estimate lost profits in commercial cases or lost earnings in personal injury cases. Using a rate of return on similar cash flows, the economist discounts the expected increase in future earnings back to the present—the discounted present value method.

This process can be illustrated by estimating the value of the professional goodwill created during a marriage. Suppose a professional's wife has been instrumental in his meeting people, so that at divorce he can expect to earn more than before he met those influential people. The increase in his earnings is $25,000 per year. Because these business relationships are uncertain and unmarketable, an annual discount rate of 50 percent might be reasonable. Applying this discount rate to the excess earnings would give a value to his professional goodwill of $50,000.[92] It is a marital asset because it was created during the marriage.

A Decrease in Human Capital

Many of the injustices at divorce occur because a decline in a spouse's human capital has occurred during a marriage. Individuals' expected future earnings also can decrease during marriage. The investment process before marriage gives individuals skills, which can be used to generate earnings. But if these skills are not used or updated, their value depreciates. Often spouses will decide that their family will benefit from one spouse limiting his or her participation in the labor force to specialize in household production. (That traditionally resulted in wives assuming roles as homemakers and mothers.) This decision can cause the homemaker's human capital to depreciate. If the marriage is later dissolved, the homemaker will find that he or she no longer can expect future earnings as large as those that could have been expected if he or she had not limited participation in the labor force.[93] If the marriage lasts, the homemaker is compensated for the reduction in human capital by actions taken for his or her benefit by the other family members. But if the marriage is dissolved, the homemaker is often the one who has to incur most of the long-term costs of the decisions that resulted in the specialization in household production and the reduction in the value of his or her human capital.

The lack of recognition of the reduction in the human capital of spouses who increase their emphasis on work in the home during marriage is a significant injustice that occurs due to the nature of the financial arrangements under the current no-fault divorce laws. Many states recognize the contributions of spouses who work in the home to the acquisition of marital property.[94] Even in those states, this calculation is not made in a systematic manner. This injustice could be reduced by recognizing human capital as property by statute. The human capital possessed by individuals at marriage could be acknowledged as separate property, and the reduction in the value of separate property human capital could be shared between the spouses at divorce.

As an alternative to a statutory approach, the reduction in the human capital of spouses who specialize in household production could be recognized by the courts as creating implied contracts of indemnification. If their marriages are dissolved, these parties have a right to compensation for the reduced value of their human capital. Their actions fulfilled the requirements of an implied contract. Their limited participation in the labor force conferred benefits on their families through services provided at home. The decisions that produced those actions were made with the expectation of compensation, that is, a sharing of family income and services. The people who worked at home were not acting as volunteers because marriage is a partnership. To allow the primary income-earning spouse to have the benefits of the other spouse's past services without compensating him or her for the reduction in human capital would result in an unjust enrichment of some spouses at the expense of others. If the sacrifice was made by the wife, this implied contract of indemnification would result in a debt of the couple to the wife if the marriage is dissolved. In effect, the husband would be required, as part of the property settlement, to compensate the wife for half her loss.[95]

The value of the reduced future earnings due to limited participation in the labor force during marriage can be estimated using the discounted present value method described earlier. Let us assume that a divorced woman can now earn $10,000 per year less than she would have been earning if she had never limited her employment during marriage. It will take ten years of experience in the labor force for her earnings to reach the level that she could have expected without the limitations. If her loss dropped from $10,000 in the first year to $1,000 in the tenth, her limiting her employment during marriage reduced her human capital by $42,410, assuming a 10 percent discount rate.[96] Her loss is a debt of the marriage to her personally. The effect would be that husbands and wives would share the losses equally.

Working in the home does not have the same impact on all worker's human capital. People enter marriage with different amounts of human capital. In addition, limiting their employment during marriage has different effects on human capital.[97] A third-year medical student has much more to lose from leaving medical school than a waitress has from leaving her job. The third-year medical student may find that she cannot return to medical school if she divorces later in life. The decision to leave medical school has a substantial effect on her human capital. She will now earn much less than if she had completed medical school and pursued a career in medicine. But being a homemaker and mother may have only a limited effect on the human capital of the waitress. She may be able to find a job after divorce that provides earnings similar to those of women who worked continuously over the intervening period. The marriage did not affect her human capital.

Educational Support

The recognition of individuals' human capital at marriage as separate property also will clarify how educational support should be handled if a marriage is dissolved.[98] The earnings from the separate property human capital of the spouses are usually used during the marriage for current consumption and for the acquisition of marital property. The relative contributions of the spouses to the marriage normally are not a concern of the courts at divorce. Most products and services purchased during marriage are for the benefit of both spouses or their children.

This is not universally true. Some of the earnings during marriage from one spouse's separate property human capital may be used to increase the human capital of the other spouse. Education is an obvious example. The spouse providing the funds is making an investment. An initial question is the nature of the property interest created by the investment. The funding can result in either a debt or an equity interest in the student spouse's human capital. Equity funding is essential to the student. As equity does not guarantee a return, it is usually required before debt financing. An equity lender is entitled to a share of the profits of an enterprise. Debt funding comes later when the investment is more secure, and the debt lender is entitled only to a market rate of return on the investment. Given the prior investments in human capital, the funds provided by supporting spouses for graduate or professional education are usually in the form of debt financing. These funds usually replace loans, parental support, or student earnings. If the marriage lasts a sufficient time for the supporting spouse to receive a fair return on the investment, no compensation is necessary.

If the marriage does not last long enough for the supporting spouse to receive an adequate return on the investment, then the beneficiary of the investment should pay the supporting spouse the unamortized amount of the investment plus interest. The investment by the working spouse consists of the student spouse's living expenses and the direct cost of the education. The funds came from the working spouse's separate property, and he or she should be reimbursed. The foregone income of the student spouse is also a cost of the education, and the working spouse incurred half of the cost of this reduced income. The current legal rules that limit the reimbursement for investments in human capital at divorce tend to result in suboptimal levels of investment in human capital during marriage.[99]

On-the-Job Training

On-the-job training also can result in the need for an adjustment at divorce. Economists have identified on-the-job training as an important factor that influences workers' future earnings. To induce an employer to provide on-the-job training that has broad applications, workers often have to accept wages below those offered in other positions. After these special skills are acquired, the current employer has to meet the higher wages that the increased productivity would command from other employers. For example, some of the highest-qualified law graduates accept positions in government agencies that pay less than they could receive in the private sector. These lawyers are not irrational, nor are they necessarily altruistic. They often view the experience that they will receive in the government as an investment because they will ultimately receive a higher income in the private sector if they are familiar with the procedures and standards of the agencies before which they will represent clients. Of course, the lawyers might stay with the government if the government compensation was similar to that available to them in the private sector after they acquire the new skills. Thus one spouse can increase his or her human capital by reducing the family's standard of living temporarily. If the reduction in the family's standard of living was substantial and the family has not received an adequate return on the investment, then indemnification of the other spouse would be appropriate.

Human Capital and Other Financial Arrangements at Divorce

An understanding of human capital can also assist in the understanding of when adjustments are necessary in the other financial arrangements at divorce. The standards for alimony have often been vague, whereas those for child support have become much more structured.

Alimony

The introduction of human capital into property settlements at divorce reduces the need for alimony. Alimony has traditionally been just one component of the financial arrangements at divorce, usually not even evaluated on its own, for the spouses are generally more concerned about the overall package than the components. The division of the financial settlements into separate components is as likely to be driven by tax considerations as by legal requirements. Alimony has had an ambiguous role at divorce, with the standards being very broad. Alimony decisions tend to be ad hoc with few clearly articulated principles and only occasional disclosure of the underlying reasons.[100] Without a systematic framework for awarding alimony, awards have predictably been highly arbitrary. This arbitrariness has not been a major problem because alimony has been awarded only in a limited number of cases, and its duration usually has been limited as well.[101] Under no-fault, alimony, or spousal support, has shifted toward rehabilitation.[102]

Potentially, alimony serves three distinct functions:[103] (1) awarding damages for breach of the marriage contract, (2) repaying the divorced spouse his or her share of the marital partnership assets, or (3) providing the spouse with a form of severance pay or unemployment benefits. Alimony thus compensates for property settlements that underestimate the losses incurred by many spouses at divorce. A recognition of human capital as property would provide a more equitable solution to these concerns.

It might be tempting to use alimony, or spousal support, to deal with a special problem that occurs when, even with the recognition of human capital, a divorced spouse does not qualify for either a substantial property settlement or child support. If a woman with limited human capital at marriage is divorced, she may only qualify for a small adjustment in her property settlement at divorce if the marriage had only a limited effect on her human capital and if she could still obtain a job similar to the job that she had before marriage. Suppose she was, and still is, qualified to be a supermarket clerk. The income generated by her best job may be very low and disproportionate to the husband's, but this concern is best addressed as the societywide problem of low-income workers rather than as an issue in family law.

The recommendations contained in the ALI's *Principles* reemphasize compensatory spousal payments based on losses rather than on meeting needs.[104] These payments are to cover "financial claims between spouses arising in the dissolution of their marriage, other than claims for a share in their property or for support of their children."[105] Because of the lack of a clear understanding of property, the losses covered are not recognized as property claims, which they are in most cases. The ad hoc nature of these provisions is evidenced by some awards being fixed at dissolution, whereas others can be modified and terminated with remarriage or death. Compensation is provided for the loss of marital living standard,[106] for being the primary caretaker who incurs a loss in earning capacity,[107] for the loss of earning capacity arising from the care of third parties,[108] for contributions to the other spouse's education or training,[109] and for the restoration of the premarital living standard after a short marriage.[110] Compensatory spousal payments for a loss in living standard or in earning capacity, like alimony, generally end with remarriage or death[111] and can be modified.[112] In these cases, this compensation is based on a sharing of the spouse's postdissolution income, which often has only a very limited link to the loss incurred.[113]

Economists would be deeply concerned that income sharing might create disincentives for ex-spouses to seek their best employment opportunities because they would have to share their income with their ex-spouses. Working at home during marriage is only a basis for compensation if the couple has children.[114] If a talented woman marries a man with lower earnings and they elect for her to work in the home even without children, thereby limiting her career, she may receive no compensation if the marriage is dissolved even if she has to reenter the labor force at a much lower income level than she would have had without the disruption in her employment. Moreover, if the primary caretaker has a higher potential income after dissolution than the other spouse does, he or she will receive no compensation for any reduction in his or her income due to working in the home. Maintaining the ad hoc nature of the law in this area, the *Principles* note that it is contrary to existing law for the lower-income spouse to compensate the higher-income spouse, even though it is the latter spouse who incurred a sacrifice because of the marriage.[115] Sacrificing or limiting a career affects that spouse's human capital and, therefore, should be recognized in the property division, not as a basis for alimony. In sum, the recommendations in the *Principles* are not an improvement over the current system.

Child Support

An understanding of human capital can provide insights into the adjustments that are necessary in the current provisions for child support. Efficient outcomes require confronting individuals with the benefits and the costs of their actions. The current child support guidelines tend to underestimate at least one cost of child custody.[116] The cost of raising a child consists of the direct costs, such as clothing and food, plus the indirect costs incurred by the custodial parent. The custodial parent may have to limit employment opportunities because he or she lacks the flexibility of employees without child care obligations. As a result, the custodial parent may have to reject jobs involving extensive travel or overtime. Another cost to the custodial parent is the reduced probability that the custodial parent will be able to remarry. The custody of the children reduces social interaction and may be viewed as a negative attribute by potential new partners. Of course, the costs incurred by the custodial parent have to be balanced against the consumptive value to the parent of having custody. Both costs and benefits are likely to be difficult to calculate, but they should not be disregarded.

The support of children is the responsibility of children's parents. Given the large number of children born to unwed mothers, child support is clearly an issue that goes beyond marriage. Aid to Families with Dependent Children (AFDC)—and more recently the Temporary Aid for Needy Families program that replaced AFDC in 1996—has become an important public program for helping women and children, but it cannot and should not replace the obligations of the parents.[117] While the marriage lasted, the children were enjoyed by both parents. Some authors argue that child support and the property settlement should be combined,[118] but the two are conceptually separate issues. For the best outcomes, I believe the usual assumption should be that the true costs of custody should be shared equally. If the human capital costs of the custodial parent are recognized, this allocation would tend to require larger financial contributions from the noncustodial parent. All periodic payments, such as those for child support, must be adjusted to their current costs, which should, as a minimum, include a cost-of-living adjustment.

Remarriage Prospects

The human capital analysis can be used, *with caution*, for individuals whose "marketability" declined during a marriage. This might be particularly true for especially physically attractive people. Because their physical attraction may procure them a higher-income spouse, it can increase their anticipated income, thereby enhancing their human capital. Fault divorce provided some protection for these individuals in that if they became less attractive, their spouses were forced to continue the marriage or to pay compensation. No-fault divorce removed much of that protection. For example, divorced men find it easier to find new spouses than divorced women. Between ages twenty-five and forty-four, the remarriage rates for men are almost twice as those high as for women.[119] Victor Fuchs noted that remarriage prospects fall with age.[120] There tends to be a larger difference in age between grooms and brides in remarriages than in first marriages. Fuchs noted a trend toward divorced women remaining unmarried for a longer period of time even if they eventually did remarry, which he attributed to the supply side of the marriage market because divorced women have other alternatives to marriage, such as better employment opportunities and government transfer programs. Lloyd Cohen observed that the slower remarriage rate of divorced women is also reflected in the demand side of the marriage market because men generally have a relative preference for younger women.[121] He argued that fault divorce never provided perfect protection, and women traditionally protected themselves by marrying older men.[122] Therefore, the attraction of both spouses probably declines at similar rates. Such unusual cases are probably better dealt with through premarital agreements than statutes.

OTHER COSTS OF DIVORCE

Although the recognition of the effect of divorce on the spouses' human capital would certainly be an improvement over the current laws, there are other costs of divorce that are not being adequately addressed. A divorcing spouse is not required to consider other financial and psychological costs of divorce, such as the costs of lost companionship, of searching for an alternative spouse or companion, and of disrupting the lives of the children. The fact that the divorcing spouse no longer wants to be married to the divorced spouse tends to reduce the value that the divorced spouse places on the companionship of the divorcing spouse; but that companionship and that of any children affected by the divorce may retain substantial value to the divorced spouse that may be lost if the marriage is dissolved. Separation and divorce have been shown to have strong negative consequences for the mental and physical health of spouses.[123]

Divorce also imposes a search cost on the divorced spouse. The marriage was the result of a search process by the spouses, who searched as long as they individually believed that the benefit of additional search exceeded the cost. At divorce, the divorcing spouses have decided that they want out of their current marriage. This choice might mean that they are no longer interested in being married to anyone, but it is common for people to remarry after divorce.[124] The divorcing spouses may have decided that their costs of searching for a new spouse will be low or zero. For example, suppose a wife seeks a divorce. Through her employment, she has discovered a new circle of stimulating and attentive men. She believes that with a limited search she can find a better mate than her current spouse. Of course, in some cases, she has already located her next spouse, and her search costs are zero. Whether or not the divorcing spouses incur new search costs, they impose costs of new searches on the divorced spouses. For some divorced spouses seeking a new mate, the costs of these new searches are so high that they never remarry.[125] These search costs recognize that one of the main costs of marriage and divorce is the sacrificed opportunity to have married someone else at an earlier date. Even if the divorced spouse has no desire to remarry, there are costs in establishing a social life that compares favorably to the marriage.

A major cost of divorce is the one imposed on the children.[126] The courts attempt to recognize the financial costs of divorce on the children, but other costs to the children are often ignored. Clearly, it is not in the best interest of the children to force their hostile parents to live together; but there are situations in which the parents do not hate each other—they are just no longer as strongly attracted to each other as they once were. Researchers have noted that frequently divorces have occurred when the conflict level between the spouses was not high.[127] The children would be much better off in this marriage environment than they would be if they were being shuffled between divorced parents. The cost of the divorce to the children is often underestimated by the divorcing spouse, who tends to see the children as relatively well adjusted to the new situation.[128]

This adjustment process is especially a problem if the children's new household has only one parent. Research consistently indicates that children from divorced, one-parent families tend to have more problematic relationships with parents and other family members than do children from two-parent families.[129] The relations between custodial parents—usually mothers—and their young children are often strained after divorce. Growing up with a single parent, which often occurs after divorce, is also associated with a broad range of children's problems in school and in society.[130] All of these costs should be recognized at divorce. If these costs are underestimated, as is common under no-fault, divorces can occur when the collective costs exceed the benefits.

THE GOAL OF REFORM

Systematic reform of the divorce laws requires a more clearly defined goal, and the goal presented here is efficiency.[131] Economists champion efficiency as the goal of human action, but given the common image of a smoothly functioning factory as the model of efficiency, people may reasonably question the relevance of efficiency as a goal for the divorce laws. Properly applied, the concept of efficiency has broad applications. Any action for which the benefit exceeds the cost increases efficiency—efficient decisions therefore increase social welfare. Efficiency is important because we live in a world in which resources—time as well as money—are limited relative to wants, and, therefore, we have to make choices. Marriage and divorce are the result of these choices. Our primary concern with no-fault divorce is that it is less efficient than other grounds for divorce because it does not encourage welfare-enhancing decisions during marriage. Often efficiency is viewed as conflicting with other goals, such as fairness and equality; but for divorce reform, that may not be a problem. A reform that is more efficient also may be fairer and may produce more equal results.

Applying the concept of *efficiency* to marriage and divorce requires that people marry when they collectively will be better off and divorce when that is no longer true. In both cases, the outcomes are efficient. During marriage, efficiency is enhanced when the parties have incentives to make choices for which the benefits to the family members exceed the costs.

Fairness—defined as outcomes conforming to established rules—and efficiency are very closely related ideas. Efficient outcomes usually are fair. Both types of outcomes benefit from predictability—people are saved from wasting valuable resources by preparing for alternate outcomes. Receiving what one reasonably expects from an exchange is the essence of fairness. When two people participate in a mutually advantageous exchange, the outcome will tend to be both efficient and fair: the benefits will exceed the costs, and the exchange that the people will receive will be the one for which they bargained.

Efficient rules also tend to promote equality. The characteristics of the participants in a transaction usually are not relevant in efficient decisions. There is much popular support in the United States for individuals to be treated equally, but in actual practice, *equality* can be a vague term. There is often confusion between equality of opportunity versus equality of outcome. Our present goal is narrower: Equality would occur if all spouses were treated similarly during marriage and at divorce.

The financial arrangements under no-fault divorce are inefficient, unfair, and unequal. They are *inefficient* in that divorces can occur in which the collective benefits do not exceed the costs, primarily because divorcing spouses are not confronted with the complete costs, both financial and psychological, of divorce. The current arrangements at divorce seldom consider sacrificed careers or the psychological concerns of the divorced spouse and any children.No-fault divorce is inefficient, too, because resources are often wasted by married people trying to protect themselves from the potentially adverse effects of divorce. Out of their concern about their situation if their marriage is dissolved, both spouses may pursue employment or education when the benefits to the family may not exceed the costs. Improved legislation could provide financial protection to spouses who specialize in household production at a lower cost.

No-fault divorce is *unfair* to many spouses who assumed that their commitment to their marriage was protected by the de facto requirement of mutual consent under fault divorce. Because no-fault divorce did not adequately address these conditions, it has not been fair. It changed the rules under which these persons married without providing adequate compensation.

Last, no-fault divorce produces *unequal* results. In the area of property settlements, equal results can be accomplished by returning any separate property to the owner of record and dividing equally the marital property. Because the current laws do not systematically recognize human capital as property, the financial arrangements at divorce often do not treat the spouses equally. When spouses provide funds that are separate property for the down payment on a house during marriage, those funds generally will be returned at divorce. Similarly, individuals can have income-earning capacities—human capital—at marriage. This human capital is conceptually separate property, just like the money used as a down payment on the house. An individual can sacrifice part of his or her human capital to the marriage by limiting employment outside the home. In other words, the individual's human capital is worth less at divorce than if he or she had maintained a more active role in the labor force during marriage, but these people usually do not receive adequate compensation for that contribution at divorce. The rules under no-fault divorce produce unequal results because contributions of financial property to marriages are treated differently from contributions of human capital property. Although either spouse can provide financial property, women are more likely to contribute separate property in the form of human capital to their marriages. The result has been a different treatment at divorce for wage earners in contrast to people who work at home.

To produce efficient, fair, and equal outcomes, any reform of the divorce laws has to attempt to recognize all the costs of divorce. In the next section, a reform program is presented.

A PROGRAM FOR THE REFORM OF DIVORCE

Any reform of no-fault divorce should attempt to increase efficiency, fairness, and equality by recognizing all the costs of divorce. This is more likely to occur if adults have incentives to screen potential mates more carefully and to work more diligently to pursue activities during marriage that optimize the gains from that arrangement for all parties. For some valuable insights about how to improve the divorce laws, we can look to the incentives that contract law provides for people to make efficient decisions.[132]

A *contract* is a voluntary exchange that all parties anticipate will make them better off. When the agreed exchanges occur simultaneously, the need for long-term protection of contractual rights is slight. But when the obligations under an agreement are not simultaneous, the danger arises of opportunistic behavior and unforeseen contingencies.[137] *Opportunistic behavior* occurs when, for example, one party to a contract attempts to take advantage of a party who has already performed part or all of a contractual obligation. After a painter paints a house, for example, the homeowner may be tempted to renegotiate the price of the job. The painter is in a weaker negotiating position than before he or she painted the house because the work is complete and cannot be withheld. Only if unfair behavior like the homeowner's is restricted can the parties to contracts have faith that future obligations will be fulfilled and refrain from wasting resources providing themselves with self-protection.

As no agreement can contemplate all the potential alternate outcomes, contract law also provides guidance for the effects of unforeseen contingencies on the parties' obligations.[134] The longer the duration of the obligations, the greater is the importance of contract law. As conditions change, contract rules also can change. Predictability is important, but adjustments to the common law can make for compensating improvements. For example, it has been argued that the evolution of the idea of mutual mistake as a ground for voiding contracts creates desirable incentives for contracting parties to generate the efficient level of information.[135]

The contractual outcomes that are efficient for the parties may not necessarily be efficient for society because the actions of the contracting parties may impose costs or benefits on third parties. The government has established additional guidelines to recognize these third-party effects, such as pollution regulations that require correction or compensation for the costs that producers and consumers can impose on third parties.

Contract law also encourages people to breach a contract when it is efficient. People are encouraged to not comply with the contract when the costs exceed the benefits. Under the common law, contractual obligations normally are not absolute. It has been the policy of contract law not to require adherence to an agreement, but only to require the parties to choose between performing in accordance with the contract or compensating the other party for any injury from a failure to perform. Participants are encouraged to breach contracts when the performance is no longer efficient and the benefits fail to exceed the costs. When a breach of a contract occurs, the issue becomes one of the proper remedy—either damages or specific performance. Damages can be based on the expected gain of the victim, on the costs incurred by the victim in reliance on the contract, on restitution that returns any money or other compensation paid by the victim, or on liquidated damages specified in the agreement. Alternatively, specific performance gives both parties a right to the performance that they expected. The subject of the contract rather than the preferences of the parties usually determines the applicable remedy, and the usual remedy for the breach of a contract is damages.

An Efficient Breach

The process by which damages based on the parties' expectations induces parties to make efficient decisions can be illustrated with an example. A grocer promises to sell a customer 5 pounds of fish at $10 per pound for delivery tomorrow. The grocer has an expectation that a particular delivery will occur that will cost her $8 per pound. The customer wants to buy the fish because he values it at $15 per pound. For simplicity, we also assume that the customer can buy the fish today for $15 somewhere else. Both parties expect to gain from this transaction. The expected gain to the customer is ($15 – $10) × 5, or $25; the expected gain for the seller is ($10 – $8) × 5, or $10.

If the delivery does not occur, the fish may only be acquired by the grocer for $25 per pound. Social welfare is increased by permitting the grocer to breach the contract: The fish would cost the grocer more than it is worth to the buyer. The customer expects a gain of $25 from the transaction. The grocer will incur a loss of ($25 – $10) × 5. or $75, if she completes the transaction. Therefore, social welfare is increased by permitting the grocer to reimburse the customer for his loss—$25—rather than forcing her to comply with the contract and incur a loss of $75. An award of damages to the customer, rather than requiring completion of the contract, leaves the customer just as well off as if he had the fish. Meanwhile, the grocer is better off because she does not have to comply with the contract.

A breach of a contract is efficient when the benefit to the breaching party exceeds the cost to the injured party. This efficient outcome occurs in an impersonal manner if the damages accurately reflect the loss experienced by the injured party. If the damages awarded nonbreaching parties under the law are either too high or too low, the outcomes may not be efficient.[136] Under the initial assumptions made by the contracting parties in the example, they are both better off if the transaction takes place. If the cost to the seller rose to $13 per pound, they are collectively still better off if the transaction takes place: The gain to the customer, $25, is greater than the loss to the seller, ($13 – $10) × 5, or $15. If the measure of damages is accurate, the seller is confronted with the choice of incurring a $15 loss on the transaction or paying damages of $25. Given these options, the seller should complete the sale and collectively the parties are better off. Alternatively, the damages could be based on the fish being worth only $12 per pound to the consumer. The seller then has an incentive to breach the contract and pay damages of ($12 – $10) × 5, or $10, when compliance with the contract would produce a more socially desirable result, that is, a gain for the customer of $25.

The underestimation of damages also affects the individual welfare of the parties: the seller is better off, but the customer is worse off. With knowledge of these imperfections in the law, the parties can fashion provisions around them to produce efficient results. For example, many contracts specify the damages that will be awarded if there is a breach; but in a complicated world, it is impossible to write a contract that covers every potential outcome. Therefore, legal rules that inaccurately estimate damages due to the breach of a contract will tend to produce inefficient outcomes.

Damages are the normal remedy for the breach of a contract, but the courts can require specific performance as an alternative remedy. Specific performance is a preferred remedy when there is no accurate external measure of the loss to the injured party, as can occur when the subject of the contract is unique. In that case, specific performance is more likely to produce efficient results than damages.[137] Suppose an individual agrees to buy a house with a unique view. Before the closing on the transaction, the seller finds a second buyer who is willing to pay a higher price. The seller attempts to renege on the first agreement. The difference between the selling price of this house and the price of a comparable house could be used to calculate money damages, but if this house is unique in the eyes of the first buyer, no amount of money will enable its replacement. In addition, the buyer will incur additional costs locating another house.

The usual method used to estimate damages is probably not an accurate gauge of this buyer's loss. That is not to say that the first buyer will always want to take possession of the house. Even with specific performance, if the first buyer is offered a higher price for the house, he may decide not to exercise his right under the agreement. This price could be paid by the seller or by the second buyer. One of the major attractions of specific performance is its ability to force the parties to estimate their costs—psychological as well as financial—due to the breach. The house is eventually acquired by the party who places the highest value on it.

Specific performance is a right rather than an outcome. Under *specific performance*, the nonbreaching party has a right to the exchange contained in the contract. This right can be waived by mutual agreement, however. The usual reason for waiver is compensation. One party may want to avoid the conditions of the contract more than the other party wants the contract completed. A financial transfer, rather than performance, will leave them both better off.

Specific performance might be appropriate in our fish example if there was no accurate way to estimate the customer's loss. The grocer can buy her way out of the contract if her gain from that action exceeds the cost incurred by the injured party. Both specific performance and damages, when accurately estimated, tend to force the contracting parties to reach efficient outcomes.

In actual practice, neither damages nor specific performance are perfect remedies.[138] Because actual damages are legally constrained, they will often underestimate the loss of the victim. As a result, damages as a remedy tend to result in excessive breaches. Specific performance gives substantial power to the party wanting performance. If that party is motivated by spite, for example, specific performance can result in excessive performance. It has been argued that damages are the normal remedy for a breach because they can usually be administered at a lower cost.[139] Specific performance requires mutual consent to terminate a contract. This can cause substantial negotiating. Suppose that the seller of a house is willing to pay $100,000 to have a sales contract canceled and that the buyer, who has a right to specific performance, would surrender the right to buy the house for $50,000. The contract will be canceled if the seller pays the buyer between $50,000 and $100,000, with the actual outcome depending on the parties' negotiations. These negotiations can be long and involved and often are wasteful, merely shifting wealth rather than creating it. In contrast, the calculation of damages often can be much more straightforward.

In addition to the negotiating costs, there can be higher enforcement costs with specific performance. When damages are paid, the court's involvement in the dispute is over. With specific performance, the court's oversight obligation can go on for an extended period. Considering these trade-offs, U.S. courts have decided that damages will usually be preferred as a remedy in contract cases.[140] The preferred remedy in a situation in which the expectations of the contracting parties are not realized is a breachable contract and accurate estimates of the injured party's loss. Without accurate estimates of damages, the second-best outcome would require specific performance with the option for the parties to negotiate a settlement.

Reliance

Contract law also can encourage an optimal reliance under a contract. The parties to a contract often change their position in reliance on the contract. These changes should occur as long as the benefits exceed the costs. Often the costs of reliance are current and predictable, but the benefits are in the future and speculative. Optimal decisions require that the assessment of the benefits be adjusted for these factors. Because distant, speculative outcomes are less attractive than current, certain outcomes, the value of the distant, speculative outcomes have to be reduced when making decisions.

Contract law not only encourages efficient outcomes, it also tends to produce fair and equal results. Contract law promotes predictability, so it tends to be fair. Contract law is impersonal and therefore tends to produce similar results for all types of people—it generates equality. Therefore, contract law remedies tend to produce results that are efficient, fair, and equal.[141]

Marital Law and Contract Law

The parallels between marital law and contract law should be obvious.[142] A marriage agreement has all the elements of a common law contract: offer, acceptance, and consideration. Generally, the principles of contract law that deal with capacity, for example, apply to marriage laws.[143] Parties to marriage have to be of sound mind at the time of marriage. When a marriage is based on fraud, annulment provides the contractual remedy of rescission—"taking back" the agreement. During marriage, the parties experience concerns similar to those addressed by contract law, such as opportunistic behavior and unexpected contingencies. The timing of the contributions of spouses to marriage, with the women's contribution often preceding the men's, can create incentives for opportunistic behavior by men. The fault divorce laws acted to protect women from this opportunistic behavior. When people say "I do" and thereby enter into an agreement, there are likely to be many issues that can affect that agreement that the parties never contemplated or discussed.[144] Marital law attempts to provide for these unforeseen contingencies.

As with commercial contracts, individuals do not have complete freedom to draft their marriage agreement. Traditionally, marriage has been viewed as a status based on contract and established by law because it constituted an institution involving the highest interests of society, thereby making it subject to state regulation.[145] However, the government interest in marriage agreements is not unique because it plays a major role in the parties to and subjects of most other contracts. Child labor laws, for example, limit the parties who can enter labor contracts, and drug laws limit the subject of contracts. Similar restrictions apply to marriage agreements. During most of the Christian era, marriage has been an agreement that, by law, could not easily be dissolved by the parties. Many obligations of the husband and the wife cannot be altered or modified by their agreement. Government regulations also have limited the rights of parties to contract when there are effects on third parties such as in zoning. The marriage laws have similar restrictions. Children are third-party beneficiaries of the marriage agreement, so statutes define the obligations of the parents to their children. These obligations once only occurred if the father and the mother were married, but they have been extended to parents who are not married. In summary, a marriage agreement is clearly similar to other contracts.

Contract remedies have a parallel in divorce law. Our normal expectation in contractual disputes is that permitting dissolution of the contract accompanied by payment of damages is preferable to specific performance; but for most of the history of the United States, marriage agreements were subject to specific performance. Each spouse who complied with the marriage agreement had a right to the continuation of the marriage. Historically, specific performance of marital agreements was a logical policy. First, each marriage was unique. Second, the costs of divorce were very high for society. The specialization of labor during marriage was much more extensive than it is today, with very few married women working outside the home. Married women's commitments to household production were evidenced by the much larger number of children per family. Under these circumstances, divorces could impose large, but indeterminate, costs on women and children. Also, in that less affluent society, men were less likely to be able to establish new households while adequately compensating the old households for their damages. In that environment, the fault grounds for divorce had the effect of making specific performance the normal remedy in a divorce case.

The requirement of specific performance made divorce difficult but not impossible. With the tacit approval of the courts, the parties gradually were permitted to reach negotiated settlements that permitted them to dissolve their marriage. These agreements could only be reached if the injured parties received compensation to cover their losses. If the gains to the party who wanted to dissolve the marriage did not exceed the losses to the injured party due to the dissolution, no agreement could be reached and no divorce would normally occur. The outcomes tended to coincide with the best interests of society.

Conditions changed. As women's wages increased, the labor-force-participation rate of women rose, with the result that the specialization of activities during marriage decreased. The number of children per family decreased. The demand for children fell as the opportunity cost of children rose, due in part to higher wages available to women. Overall, society became more affluent. Some of the logic behind specific performance of marriage contracts started to erode. There were pressures for procedures that would permit marriages to be dissolved more easily. The product of these pressures was no-fault divorce, replacing specific performance with damages as the remedy in dissolution cases. This situation is similar to contract remedies that permit parties to breach most contracts subject to the payment of compensation to the nonbreaching party.

Specific Performance and a Marriage Contract

Still, specific performance as the remedy for breach of a marriage contract is particularly attractive for established marriages because the costs of divorce can be large and indeterminate, especially by any one other than the spouses. First, consider the effect of marriage on the spouses' income-earning capacities—their human capital.[146] At marriage, individuals have already acquired some separate property. For many people, their most valuable asset then is their human capital. The value of this human capital is the discounted value of earnings that reasonably can be expected in the future, net of any future investments. During marriage, human capital can increase or decrease. If it increases, marital property is created. Alternatively, if a spouse's human capital decreases during marriage due to mutual decisions by the spouses, that loss is similar to a contribution of separate property to the marriage. Often a couple decides that the family will benefit from one spouse—the wife—limiting her career to assume a primary role as a homemaker and a mother. At divorce, this person's human capital is worth less than if she had not limited her career.[147] But by how much? It is difficult to determine the career that someone would have had, if they did not have it. The couple is probably in a better position to accurately gauge the magnitude of this sacrifice than any judge or jury would be.

The incorporation of human capital into the property considered at divorce would still not recognize other subjective costs due to a divorce. Although the knowledge that the divorcing spouse no longer wants to live with the divorced spouse might reduce that person's attraction to the divorcing spouse, there is still a potential loss to that person due to the desire for a continuing relationship with that person.

Another important source of costs for the divorced spouse are those associated with search.[148] Both parties incurred search costs to identify each other initially. Now, one spouse has decided that he or she either has already found a person that he or she prefers to the current spouse or is willing to incur additional costs searching for a better spouse or situation. The divorced spouse must involuntarily incur the cost of searching for another mate or living situation. Often, this cost can be very high.

Last, a major cost can occur because a divorce may be harmful to the couple's children.[149] The quality of life can deteriorate for children shared by two parents—living separately—compared to the conditions still possible living with both parents. If divorce were more difficult to obtain, some parents would probably try to make their marriage work and, thereby, provide benefits to their children. The parent, usually the mother, who expects custody of the children after divorce is more likely to recognize the costs that the children will incur because they will be less happy when they live only with her. These companionship, search, and children's costs are difficult to calculate and, therefore, are not completely included in awards at divorce. As a result, the awards at divorce tend to underestimate the costs of divorce. When the costs of divorce are underestimated, the probability increases that a divorce will occur when the net benefits are negative. These divorces reduce social welfare.

In summary, a marriage agreement is similar to other contracts. Because the costs of divorce would be difficult for anyone other than the spouses to estimate, specific performance is the preferred remedy for established marriages. This would increase the likelihood that the marriage agreement would be breached—the marriage dissolved—only when the collective net benefits are positive. Also, by being able to rely on the agreement, the spouses would also be able to lower their costs of protecting themselves against a unilateral termination of the agreement.

A MARRIAGE CONTRACT PROPOSAL

The marriage contract proposed here starts out with the idea that for established marriages the spouses should have a right to specific performance of their agreement for the marriage to continue for their lives. Early in the marriage, no-fault divorce would still be permitted, although extreme behavior would be the basis for a divorce based on fault.

A very simple statute is proposed here. It only prescribes the default grounds for divorce and financial arrangements at divorce, leaving the couple with the opportunity to modify their contract either before or during marriage. The statute should also state that the couple is entering into a contract and that, if a divorce action is ever initiated, the couple is choosing the laws of the state of marriage or potentially of some other state to govern the aspects of divorce covered by the contract. States have traditionally been reluctant to become involved in the normal interactions within a family, and that is a position that is supported here.[150] At the same time, the states' interest in marriage itself has been held to be so large that the states have had the right to control the marital status of spouses domiciled there.[151]

This preemption of the grounds for divorce by the states has become increasingly questionable. The imposition by essentially all states of a no-fault divorce agreement on all spouses has been a disaster in many cases. Social welfare would be improved by giving adults more freedom to create their own marriage contracts, while the states still maintain control where it is important. The state's role in protecting children is obvious, so it is appropriate for states to have statutes that establish rules for protecting children during and after a marriage. It is important to recognize that the conditions that accompany the dissolution of marriage have far greater effect on the quality of the marriage itself than has been commonly accepted because the conditions strongly influence the commitment that the spouses make to their marriage.[152]

A basic marriage contract consisting of a combination of no-fault, mutual consent, and fault grounds for divorce will provide a major improvement in the incentives facing adults. At the same time, it is important to recognize that adults have more realistic living arrangements than in the past. Living alone or with another person of either sex is much more common than in the past. A marriage contract continues to be the appropriate choice for people who anticipate making sacrifices based on the expectation that a relationship is going to be long-term. For others, marriage may be attractive as a form of commitment, whereas for some people, it may not be attractive at all. We should recognize that this is not a contract that is appropriate for all relationships but just for the large number of people who want a long-term relationship that they feel would be improved by having incentives to make sacrifices that benefit their family or that are evidence of a commitment to their relationship.

The default financial arrangements at divorce, which traditionally consisted of a property settlement, alimony, and child support, should be based on "debts" incurred during marriage.[153] Choices during marriage result in obligations that are best treated as debts. Child support can be viewed as a debt to the child that the parents incur when they elect to become parents. This component of the financial arrangements should be subjected to close scrutiny by the state with it establishing minimum levels, for example. Because the reasons for and the level of alimony are very ambiguous,[154] the primary emphasis in the financial arrangements between the spouses at divorce should be on the property settlement. The property settlement should be based on partnership principles, with the items being considered expanding to include the spouses' income-earning capacities, their human capital. Couples can acquire marital property such as mutual fund shares by saving, which is the sacrifice of current consumption, that should be treated as a debt of the couple to each other as individuals if the marriage is dissolved. Other acts, such as limiting a career or providing uncompensated educational support, create a debt between the spouses that should be recognized at divorce. When the couple's assets, such as their human capital, cannot easily be sold, the property distribution should be based on periodic payments.

Mutual Consent Divorce

Mutual consent should be the primary ground for divorce. Because mutual consent gives either spouse the right to the continuation of the marriage, it is similar to specific performance of other types of contracts. Traditionally, the understanding was that when a couple married they were entering into an agreement that was expected to last for the lifetime of at least one of the spouses,[155] and, for those who continue to have that expectation, that is the agreement that is proposed here. It is attractive because many of the costs of dissolution are difficult for persons other than the spouses to estimate—and even the spouses may find the process challenging. The opponents of fault divorce—and more recently those who support no-fault divorce—do not appear to have given serious consideration to mutual consent divorce.[156] However, mutual consent is more likely to produce welfare-enhancing outcomes than either fault or no-fault grounds.

Among those willing to consider a change, the normal alternative to no-fault divorce that is considered is fault divorce rather than mutual consent divorce.[157] If we recognize that the true problem with the current laws is their permitting unilateral divorce, then the appropriate alternative to consider is mutual consent divorce rather than fault divorce. Knowing that the ground for divorce for established marriages is mutual consent would encourage spouses to make sacrifices that benefit their marriage. Meanwhile, not all established marriages are successful; and if a couple is questioning the durability of their marriage, mutual consent would increase the incentives for them to recognize and to place a value on the collective benefits and costs of continuing the marriage or of pursuing a divorce. Both benefits and costs are broad concepts that include both financial and psychological factors. The costs of divorce include those of the effects on the spouses' human capital as well as the costs associated with lost companionship, the search for a new spouse or companions, and the disruption in the lives of the children. These costs can be substantial. Under mutual consent divorce, the party who does not want the divorce would have an incentive to ask for compensation for these costs as a basis for agreeing to the divorce.

This point can be illustrated with an example: A husband is being asked for a divorce by his wife. On the one hand, he may feel that he is no longer strongly attracted to her, that he can find someone just as attractive with a limited amount of effort, and that any children would not be adversely affected by a divorce. Therefore, he might be willing to reach a divorce agreement at a small cost to his wife. Because the benefit of the divorce exceeds the cost, social welfare would be improved by permitting the divorce. On the other hand, he might still be strongly attracted to his spouse, feel that only a long and costly search would find another comparable spouse or situation, and believe that the children would suffer compared with the quality of life that is still possible if the parents stay together. He might under those circumstances ask for a level of compensation that the other spouse is unwilling to provide. In other words, the party who wants the divorce does not value the divorce as much as the other spouse and the children value the continuation of the marriage. In that case, social welfare is improved by continuing the marriage.

One of the attractive aspects of mutual consent divorce is the increased likelihood that both parents will address the costs incurred by their children due to a divorce. These costs go far beyond just maintenance, which is covered by child support. If the divorcing spouse is forced to recognize the full costs of divorce, he or she might be able to make the marriage work and thereby provide benefits to the children.[158] The parent, usually the mother, who expects custody of the children after divorce is most likely to recognize the costs that the children will incur. If the children are less happy after divorce, their attitudes will impact the welfare of the custodial parent. These changes in the welfare of the children and the custodial parent are a cost. The custodial parent has incentives to take these costs into consideration when considering whether to agree to divorce. These companionship, search, and children's costs would be difficult for anyone other than the spouses to estimate and include in any award at divorce.

Another attraction of mutual consent divorce is the incentives it creates for couples to consider the rules that are appropriate for their marriage. If people considering marriage knew that mutual consent was the primary ground for dissolving an established marriage, that knowledge might increase the incentive for them to negotiate premarital agreements. Neither fault divorce nor no-fault divorce provides marrying individuals with the opportunity to construct their own grounds for the dissolution of their marriage. With mutual consent divorce, the dissolution of marriage would be based on the parties' criteria rather than that of the state. Under those circumstances, the parties might be more inclined to specify their own grounds at the time of marriage; for example, some might feel that adultery should be a ground for dissolution, whereas others might not.

Because the divorce would be based on the mutual agreement of the spouses, the default financial arrangements suggested earlier could be ignored by the spouses. If a spouse expected a divorce to be extremely costly, that person could ask for substantially more than would be provided by the default financial arrangements. Any agreement of the spouses should be subject to regulations that attempt to protect the interests of any children.[159]

Mutual consent is not a perfect solution. It can result in the continuation of a marriage if one party wants to ignore the costs imposed on all parties by the marriage.[160] This can occur when a spouse who bases a decision on spite is opposed to a divorce under any circumstances. However, people can be surprisingly rational even when dealing with emotional issues such as marriage and divorce. Most divorces involve at least one spouse who initially wanted the marriage to continue;[161] but when the collective benefits of divorce exceed the costs, divorce increases social welfare. Under those circumstances, the parties have incentives to construct an agreement that leaves them both better off. The large number of divorces based on mutual consent under the fault grounds illustrates the willingness of spouses to negotiate even under trying conditions.

Although mutual consent as a basis for divorce is unappealing to some people because it appears to lock people into unsuccessful and potentially abusive marriages, the provisions for no-fault and fault grounds for divorce discussed later should address many of those concerns. No-fault divorce is appropriate early in a marriage because a couple are still evaluating each other. Fault divorce is appropriate when extremely abusive behavior occurs. However, we need to recognize the limited ability of mutual consent divorce to keep an antagonist couple together. Either spouse can always leave the relationship with the only restrictions being the response of others, any financial obligations imposed by law on the spouses to each other and to their children and, of course, the ability to marry anyone else.

No-Fault Divorce

No-fault divorce is still attractive during the early period of a marriage. Mutual consent divorce gives substantial power to spouses who do not want a divorce. To limit abuse of this power, it would appear to be attractive to permit no-fault divorce when the potential costs of divorce are likely to be low, as they tend to be early in a marriage, and when there are no children. Early in marriage, a couple is still involved in an evaluation process. Because the gains from marriage can be smaller today for many couples than they were in the past, a relevant question is, does one party still want to make a long-term commitment to this other party?[162] During this period of evaluation, no-fault divorce should continue to be the grounds for divorce.

Eventually, at least one spouse may make sacrifices based on a long-term commitment to the marriage, and then the grounds for divorce should shift to mutual consent. These sacrifices will usually occur because a spouse is limiting a career or because the couple is having a child. In our highly mobile society, it is common for a couple to relocate. Frequently, in this process, a spouse is forced to relinquish a desirable situation so that the other spouse can take advantage of an employment opportunity that appears to be in the couple's long-term best interest.[163] This sacrifice is a cost of the change. In addition, children usually require one parent to adjust his or her career to assist in child care. With these changes in the couple's circumstances, the ground for divorce would shift to mutual consent. Because accommodations for the long-term benefit of the marriage may be subtle, setting a predetermined period, such as five years, as the basis for the shift from no-fault to mutual consent divorce would seem to be reasonable. Recognizing that the grounds for divorce are going to change under certain circumstances—

a relocation, a child, or a specified time period—will force a couple to reevaluate their commitment to each other. If they are uncomfortable with the restrictions that will accompany mutual consent divorce, they can mutually agree to maintain no-fault grounds for divorce.

Because no-fault divorce limits the incentives for couples to negotiate, the default financial arrangements would apply to these divorces, if the couple has not agreed to alternative arrangements. Since no-fault divorce would only be permitted early in a marriage, the property issues should not be complicated. The major sacrifices such as limiting a career due to a relocation or the assumption of child care responsibilities would already have shifted the grounds for divorce to mutual consent.

The most vocal defense of no-fault grounds for divorce throughout a marriage is based on protecting people who eventually realize that they made a mistake in their choice of a spouse.[164] Seldom is recognition given to the benefits of mutual consent that would flow to people willing to make a long-term commitment. Therefore, this combination of no-fault divorce early in a marriage followed by mutual consent attempts to address both of those concerns. We need to recognize that using no-fault divorce to protect people from their own poor judgment or unfortunate choices is not the proverbial "free lunch" because it imposes substantial costs on the people who want to make a long-term commitment.

Fault Divorce

Fault divorce can still have a role in dissolving marriages. Mutual consent can create problems when someone is "driven out" of a marriage rather than "wanting out." It is often difficult for anyone, including the spouses and judges, to clearly identify fault. Being driven out of a marriage raises concerns similar to those addressed with the fault divorce statutes. Under fault divorce, the "guilty" spouse did something that gave the "innocent" spouse a right to dissolve the marriage: the innocent spouse was driven out of the marriage. Mutual consent would not provide a solution for the situation in which one spouse is the victim of acts such as cruelty or adultery, but in which the "guilty" spouse does not want a divorce. Courts during the fault divorce era showed little skill, however, at making determinations in these cases. Often the grounds given for fault divorce were hypocritical, and the marriage had failed for other reasons.[165] And even when the fault grounds could be proven, the reasons why a marriage failed were probably a great deal more complicated than just the acts that established the grounds. Still, fault divorce would appear to be appropriate when there is clear evidence of fault such as abuse of a spouse or any children. Because abuse is socially unacceptable behavior and should be discouraged, it should also be the basis for an adjustment in the default financial and custodial arrangements at divorce.

In sum, mutual consent as the ground for the dissolution of most marriages is not a perfect solution to problems facing the family, but it is superior to the alternatives, especially no-fault divorce for all marriages. No-fault divorce early in marriages provides spouses with an opportunity to evaluate their commitment to each other at a fairly low cost. Fault divorce can still be appropriate when a spouse is forced out of a marriage under extreme circumstances. The program advocated here has a logical foundation and would be a substantial improvement over the current divorce laws. However, for these reforms to be effective, marriage has to be recognized as a contract entered into at marriage and upon which a dissolution has to be based, thereby overcoming the current Constitutional limits on divorce reform.

CONSTITUTIONAL LIMITS ON REFORM

Even if the grounds for divorce were changed in a few states in the manner just suggested, the impact would be feeble at best. Standing in the path of an effective reform of the divorce laws is federal law, which holds that a marriage is a status that gives the state in which either spouse is domiciled jurisdiction to grant a divorce that usually will be honored in the other states due to the Full Faith and Credit Clause of the U.S. Constitution. When most states had similar fault grounds for divorce, seldom was it advantageous for a spouse to move to another state to obtain a divorce. Moreover, in 1905, the U.S. Supreme Court in *Haddock v. Haddock*[166] held that a divorce obtained by a spouse in a proceeding in which his or her spouse, who was domiciled in another state, did not participate was not enforceable in other states under the Full Faith and Credit Clause.

The trend toward migratory divorces continued, especially because some states discovered that easy divorces and short-term residency requirements could attract new business. This trend was particularly apparent in Nevada. In 1942, the U.S. Supreme Court reconsidered the credit to be given migratory divorces in *Williams v. North Carolina (Williams I)*.[167] In that case, Mr. Williams and Mrs. Hendrix left their spouses in North Carolina and went to Nevada, where they each obtained a divorce after establishing a domicile there based on the minimum period required for residency. The Supreme Court overturned its prior ruling in *Haddock v. Haddock* by holding that the domicile of one or both spouses is sufficient to confer divorce jurisdiction to a state court, stating that "each state, by virtue of its command over its domiciliaries and its large interest in the institution of marriage, can alter within its own borders the marriage status of the spouse domiciled there."[168] Meanwhile, the Court noted that its opinion did not address the issue of the power of the divorced spouse's domicile to refuse full faith and credit to the divorce if, contrary to the findings of the court granting the divorce, that divorced spouse's state of domicile—in this case, North Carolina—found that no bona fide domicile was acquired in Nevada.

This issue was addressed by the U.S. Supreme Court in *Williams v. North Carolina* (*Williams II*),[169] which followed the conviction of the new Mr. and Mrs. Williams for bigamy in North Carolina when a North Carolina court rejected Nevada's determination that they had established a valid domicile in Nevada and decided, therefore, their divorces were not valid in North Carolina. The Supreme Court emphasized the important role of the states in the regulation of marriage by stating,

> Divorce, like marriage, is of concern not merely to the immediate parties. It affects personal rights of the deepest significance. It also touches basic interests of society. Since divorce, like marriage, creases a new status, every consideration of policy makes it desirable that the effect should be the same wherever the question arises.[170]

Nevada clearly had the right to determine the marital status of its domiciliaries, but North Carolina could independently review that decision to determine whether a valid domicile had been established. The U.S. Supreme Court upheld North Carolina's determination that a valid domicile had not been established in Nevada and that, therefore, Mr. Williams and Mrs. Hendrix were still domiciled in North Carolina, where they continued to be married to others, making their cohabitation bigamous.[171]

Although we are concerned with the honoring of divorce decrees in jurisdictions other than the one in which they are granted, the courts have continued to require an actual domicile in a state as a condition necessary for a valid divorce decree based on due process. In 1953, the U.S. Court of Appeals for the Third Circuit held in *Alton v. Alton*[172] that a statute that determined domicile based on a period of residency without additional requirements addressing the intent of the party was invalid under the Due Process Clause of the U.S. Constitution.[173] Because of marriage being a status, domicile continued to be the key issue. The court concluded that "[a]n attempt by another jurisdiction to affect the relation of a foreign domiciliary is unconstitutional even though both parties are in court and neither one raises the question."[174] Moreover, the court "believe[d] it to be lack of due process for one state to take to itself the readjustment of domestic relations between those domiciled elsewhere."[175]

Although the decisions in *Williams II* and *Alton* might lead one to the conclusion that migratory divorces were going to be scrutinized closely and, therefore, become much less attractive, that did not occur because state courts generally applied a very generous standard toward the acts and duration necessary for establishing domicile.[176] A particular concern has been for the position in which an innocent new spouse would be if divorces obtained in other states were frequently overturned based on a lack of domicile.

With the introduction of no-fault divorce making the divorce laws in most states similar, the need for migratory divorces has been reduced and with it any litigation as to whether divorces granted to a spouse in one state should be honored in other states. Still, the decisions in *Williams I* and *II* present major problems for divorce reform. Migratory divorce was perceived to be a problem when most states had strict divorce laws and a few had lenient laws. One can imagine the problems that proponents of stricter divorce laws have if most states have lenient laws. So long as marriage is treated as a status, this problem is almost insurmountable.

Full Faith and Credit

Whether marriage is a contract or a status is crucial, because the Full Faith and Credit Clause of Article IV of the U.S. Constitution requires states to recognize the public acts, records, and judicial proceedings of other states. Congress is prohibited from passing legislation that limits the effects of a state's divorce decrees in other states. If marriage is treated as a status, people cannot know the grounds for divorce that will be applied to their marriage if their spouse ever wants to dissolve it. Then, a decree granted in another state will probably have to be honored in all the other states.

It makes it virtually impossible for some states to make marriage more durable by making divorce more difficult, so long as marriage is treated as a status and many states have no-fault divorce laws. Not knowing where a couple will eventually reside will force many spouses to protect themselves against a no-fault divorce even though they either were married in or are living in a state in which divorce is more difficult. Frequently spouses establish residency in a state other than the one in which they were married. A divorce obtained in a no-fault divorce state has to be given full faith and credit in all other states, including the one in which the other spouse lives or the one in which they were married. Domicile is not difficult to establish either due to a legitimate move or for the purpose of pursuing a divorce. Most states impose a durational requirement ranging from six weeks to one year to meet the domicile requirement to file for divorce.[177] The most common durational requirement for divorce is six months.[178]

Whether a marriage is a status or a contract is more than a philosophical debate because treating marriage as a contract is an essential step toward an effective reform of the divorce laws. This can be accomplished either judicially or legislatively: The U.S. Supreme Court could overrule or modify its decision in *Williams I* to recognize that marriage is a contract rather than a status.[179] Alternatively, Congress could enact legislation establishing that condition. The enforcement of contracts, especially if they include a choice of law provision, is usually based on the law chosen by the parties and otherwise is determined by an interest analysis.[180] Then full faith and credit would have to be given to a judgment based on the contract agreed to at marriage rather than to a divorce decree obtained unilaterally in a state in which the other spouse may never have lived. More than just more accurately reflecting the couple's situation, treating a marriage as based on a contract would correct for the problems that have been created by treating marriage as a status. Uncertainty about the conditions associated with a dissolution of the marriage will be reduced because the agreement at the time of the marriage, subject to any mutually agreed upon modifications, will continue for the duration of the marriage.[181]

The critical attraction of recognizing marriage to be a contract is that it would bind the couple no matter where they lived. People seldom think about the grounds for divorce now because there is so little variation in them among the states. If there were a variety of statutes, then couples would be encouraged to consider the effects of the different contracts available to them. Often people are concerned about young, uninformed couples entering into a contract that does not conform to their views later.[182] Bear in mind that the average age at marriage has increased significantly over the past decades with the typical person now being in the mid-twenties at first marriage. Also, subsequent marriages among older people have become much more common. Certainly, under the marriage contract proposed here some people might find that they are unhappy with their contract, but at least they would have a choice. Today, a person who initially—or eventually—wants to make a creditable long-term commitment to a spouse is precluded from that because marriage is treated as a status rather than as a contract, and most states permit unilateral divorce.

The Enforceability of Marriage Contracts

Presuming that marriage is recognized as a contract, the last concern is the enforceability of the contract in states other than the one in which it was created. Until recently, contracts between spouses were seldom enforced even in the state in which they were created.[183] Some recent trends suggest that the likelihood is increasing that states other than the marriage state will honor these contracts, especially if they include a choice of laws provision.

The Restatement (Second) of Conflict of Laws, which is an attempt by the American Law Institute to present an authoritative statement of each area of the common law, gives support to enforcing the law of the state chosen by contracting parties.[184] These laws will be applied unless two conditions exist: First, the chosen state has no substantial relationship to the parties and there is no reasonable basis for the parties' choice.[185] Although an argument can be made that this requirement has been met by the marriage state even if residency there was brief, couples probably would be advised to more carefully choose their marriage state, even if it is a source of inconvenience for others. That is currently not an issue because the laws of the marriage state are not relevant if a spouse seeks a divorce in another state.

Second, a state can reject the law chosen by a couple if the application of the law of the chosen state would be contrary to a fundamental policy of a state that has a materially greater interest than the chosen state in the determination of the particular issue and that, under another section of the Restatement, would be the state of the applicable law in the absence of an effective choice of law by the parties.[186] This section would have created a major problem if some states had the contract proposed in this discussion when most states had only fault divorce. If the couple attempted to enforce the contract in a fault divorce state, the courts in that state probably would have concluded that its concern for its domiciliaries was a "materially greater interest," thereby permitting the fault divorce state to apply its laws rather than those chosen by the couple.

The states' central role in marriage, which often was interpreted as having precedence over the spouses' interests, has declined dramatically over the past few decades, as is evidenced by the passage of no-fault divorce statutes. Because most states have effectively acknowledged that their "fundamental policy" is to let one spouse dissolve his or her marriage unilaterally even in the face of the opposition of the other spouse, the states would be hard pressed to impose their laws on spouses who had elected to make it more difficult to divorce. No-fault divorce is a reflection of the states' willingness to permit couples to decide for themselves when their marriage has failed.[187]

Further evidence of the decline in the paternalistic role of states toward marriage is provided by the growing willingness to give spouses greater freedom to draft pre- and postmarital contracts.[188] Many see *Posner v. Posner*[189] as the turning point in the trend toward permitting couples more flexibility in drawing up their own marriage contracts.[190] In that case, the court upheld an award of alimony that had been prescribed in a prenuptial agreement. The court acknowledged that some states were retreating from the position that the state's interests in marriage take precedence over the private interests of spouses.[191] In particular, the court noted the passage of no-fault divorce statutes as a reflection of this trend.[192] Subject to fair disclosure, the court held that the antenuptial agreement that addressed the alimony after divorce was valid and binding.[193]

The enforceability of premarital agreements became much more predictable with the approval of the Uniform Premarital Agreement Act (UPAA),[194] which has been adopted by half of the states.[195] Under the UPAA, an agreement is unenforceable under only two sets of circumstances: (1) if there was a lack of voluntariness[196] or (2) if the agreement was substantially unreasonable at the time of execution and if the aggrieved party did not have adequate knowledge of the other party's financial position.[197]

The willingness of states to enforce contracting parties' choice of law even as applied to marriage is reflected in a recent Connecticut case, *Elgar v. Elgar*.[198] In that case, the couple married in New York, having signed a prenuptial agreement containing a choice of law provision specifying that the agreement was being made pursuant to New York law and would be interpreted accordingly. During the marriage, the wife remained a New York resident, whereas the husband continued to be a Connecticut resident, with their sharing time in both places. When the husband died, the wife challenged the validity and enforceability of the agreement. A referee concluded that the parties' expressed choice of New York law was valid and that under New York law the agreement was enforceable.[199] The trial court found that the referee's findings of fact were supported by the evidence and that the conclusions of law were legally and logically correct.

That decision was upheld on appeal. Particularly important here is the court's consideration of the choice of law provision based on the Restatement. The court took special notice of the importance of protecting the justified expectations of the parties.[200] It then went on to conclude that the law selected had a substantial relationship to the parties and that there was a reasonable basis for their choice. In addition, Connecticut did not have a greater material interest in the determination of the issue than New York, the laws of which had been chosen by the couple.

In summary, in the past thirty years, there has been not only a shift from fault to no-fault grounds for divorce, but also a reduction in the states' role in matrimonial decisions. Couples are being permitted to include a broader range of provisions in antenuptial agreements; and, either through statutes such as the UPAA or through court cases, it is much more likely that the couples' preferences will be enforced by the courts. It is a logical step to extend this trend to permit couples to contract as to the grounds for divorce, either through statutes or case law.

LIVING WITH NO-FAULT DIVORCE

No-fault divorce—with all its problems—probably will continue to be the law in most states for the foreseeable future, so people are going to be forced to live with it. The most important lesson that this book has attempted to teach is that no-fault divorce has subtly warped incentives to induce adults often to make decisions that are against their best interests and the best interests of those that they love the most. A recognition of these incentives is the first step toward learning how to live with no-fault divorce. If spouses enjoy their careers, which do not conflict with each other, and if they do not want any children, then a recognition of the effect of no-fault divorce probably will not change their behavior.

Most couples face conflicts between their careers and between their careers and their children. This can occur if one spouse has an opportunity to relocate, but it can also occur when the spouses travel or have different work schedules. These conflicts become more apparent when spouses consider having the children that most adults want. Then, it is time to be realistic about whether—with the additional information gained during the marriage—the spouses feel comfortable that the relationship is durable. If they feel committed to each other, then decisions have to be made about the activities that increase their family's welfare.[201] With improved opportunities for women, it is not realistic for many couples to have one spouse working exclusively in the home throughout the marriage. The challenge is to find the preferred combination of employment and work in the home for both spouses.

The gains to a family from a spouse limiting a career are particularly high when there are young children in the family, so couples should decide which parent is in the best position to assume primary responsibility for child care. This person is not necessarily the earner of the lower income, but rather the one with the lower "economic rent." Economists have a concept called *rent*, which has nothing to do with apartments. It reflects the difference between what is paid for something and what is necessary to make it available in the first place. Think about this concept from your perspective. Rent is the difference between what you are paid in a job and the minimum amount necessary to induce you to take the job. If you are being paid $50,000 in a job that you would be willing do for $30,000, your rent is $20,000.

Sometimes family welfare does not benefit from encouraging the higher-income spouse to emphasize a career while the other spouse places a more significant emphasis on working in the home. Subject to a reasonable income level, the better strategy should be for the spouse with the larger rent to be the one who is employed full time. For example, a husband might have the potential to earn $60,000 a year in a stressful and unpleasant job that he would not consider for less than $50,000; his rent is $10,000. Meanwhile, his wife might have the potential to earn $50,000 a year in a job that she enjoys and would be willing to consider for $20,000, so her rent is $30,000. Knowing that the family will have the $50,000 from the wife's job might permit the husband to get a part-time job that accommodated his child care responsibilities for $15,000. If he was willing to work in this part-time job for free, he is getting more rent—$15,000 versus $10,000—than he would have had in the higher paying job. Even though the family's income has fallen from $105,000 to $65,000, the couple is providing child care while actually increasing their rents.

Because the minimum salary that each parent requires to consider a job is often influenced by the satisfaction that they expect from child care responsibilities, the parent who prefers child care is likely to be the one with the lower rent from full-time employment, thereby making him or her the obvious choice to emphasize that role within a marriage. As an alternative to the preceding example, consider the situation in which the minimum income necessary for the wife to continue in her full-time job increases to $45,000 after she became a mother, whereas the arrival of the child may not have had any effect on the minimum required by the father. Now her rent from full-time employment is only $5,000, and a part-time job has the potential for increasing the family's rents and potentially its overall welfare.

As child care responsibilities decline, the couple can consider other alterna-tives. They may feel that the welfare of their children is so important that free time is best used with other children-oriented activities, such as volunteering in school. Alternatively, the spouse who worked part time might consider full-time employment that still accommodates the needs of the children. The couple should continue to recognize the reciprocity of their actions so that their self-interest should guide them to activities that benefit each other and their family.

Marriage still can have uncertain outcomes, so parents emphasizing work in the home may still want to consider strategies that will enhance their human capi-tal. This would protect them if the marriage ended or it potentially would increase their employment opportunities and family's income if the marriage continued. Often these investments can occur at a small cost to the family. An obvious choice is education—university classes may be offered at a time that coincides with a morning nursery school for the children. Another choice is part-time employment. Different jobs provide different types of opportunities to enhance human capital. Licking envelopes for ten hours a week does not leave the licker with any skills that he did not have before the experience. However, using an accounting pack-age to maintain a company's books for the same period will give that person new skills when—or if—he wants to make a more substantial commitment to the la-bor force later.

An understanding of the effects of no-fault divorce can even be beneficial for couples without children. No-fault divorce has created incentives for essentially all adults to make a major commitment to a career. Still, it is common for people to view their jobs more positively than candor would warrant. Not all jobs are fulfilling and rewarding.[202] Someone who is content with his or her spouse's commitment to their marriage might benefit from the recognition that others may not be working for the usually articulated reasons, such as financial necessity or psychic income, but rather to protect themselves from the potentially adverse effects of divorce. With that recognition, more content couples might be happy to trade some of their higher income for a more relaxed relationship in their mar-riage. They would prefer that a spouse was more readily available during the week to work in the home so that weekends could be available for leisure activities.

In sum, the best protection against the adverse effects of no-fault divorce is making good decisions, especially about whom to marry. Next, spouses have to recognize the changes that will occur in their lives, especially if they become par-ents, and whether and how they can adapt to those changes. They need to recognize that their self-interest is often best served by considering others. Last, it is appropriate to take steps to protect oneself from the adverse effects of divorce because, properly planned, these strategies often will benefit an ongoing marriage.

CONCLUSION

This chapter discusses the need for divorce reform and the steps that have been taken so far toward reform. The progress on that front has not been impressive. One alternative suggested here is to make property settlements much more systematic by recognizing all the property, including human capital, affected by divorce. A preferred reform program would address the more fundamental problem with the current divorce laws in the United States that do not force divorcing spouses to consider all the costs of divorce. This program would make mutual consent the ground for divorce in established marriages in which at least one spouse has made a significant sacrifice based on the expectation that the marriage is going to last for a substantial period. Prior to those sacrifices, no-fault divorce would be the basis for divorce. Fault divorce would be available in extreme cases. The impact of any reform is limited because the Full Faith and Credit Clause of the U.S. Constitution currently requires states to honor divorces acquired in other states. This impediment can be resolved by recognizing that a marriage creates a contract rather than a status. However, these reforms are not imminent, so couples need to develop strategies that minimize the adverse effect of the incentives created by no-fault divorce.

NOTES

1. See Maggie Gallagher, *The Abolition of Marriage* (Washington, DC: Regnery Publishing, 1996).

2. Lynne Carol Halem, *Divorce Reform* (New York: Free Press, 1980), 288.

3. Eleanor E. Maccoby and Robert H. Mnookin, *Dividing the Child: Social and Legal Dilemmas of Custody* (Cambridge, MA: Harvard University Press, 1992), 19–57; and Robert H. Mnookin and Lewis Kornhauser, "Bargaining in the Shadow of the Law: The Case of Divorce," *Yale Law Journal* 88 (April 1979): 951, n. 3.

4. The comment to Uniform Marriage and Divorce Act, § 308 (Section 9A, Uniform Laws Annotated, 1973) on maintenance states: "The dual intention of this section and Section 307 (property division) is to encourage the court to provide for the financial needs of the spouses by property disposition rather than by an award of maintenance. Only if the available property is insufficient for the purpose and if the spouse who seeks maintenance is unable to secure employment appropriate to his skills and interests or is occupied with child care may an award of maintenance be ordered."

5. Title IV-D of the Social Security Act now requires states to develop child support guidelines; and those guidelines are sometimes treated as refutable presumptions. See Carl E. Schneider and Margaret F. Brinig, *An Invitation to Family Law* (St. Paul, MN: West, 1996), 972.

6. See Herma Hill Kay, "A Family Court: The California Proposal," *California Law Review* 56)1968): 1205–48; and Walter Wadlington, "Divorce without Fault without Perjury," *Virginia Law Review* 52 (1966): 32–87.

7. Professor Grace Blumberg argued that the primary beneficiaries of the no-fault divorce reform were lawyers and judges who had previously been forced to compromise professional ideals in the routine management of divorce cases. See Grace Blumberg, "New Models of Marriage and Divorce," in *Contemporary Marriage: Comparative Perspectives on a Changing Institution*, ed. Kingsley Davis (New York : Russell Sage Foundation, 1985), 352.

8. The concern of divorced men can be illustrated with James A. Hayes, who was discussed in Chapter 4 and who was the chairman of the California Assembly Judiciary Committee that drafted the California no-fault divorce act. He had negotiated a divorce settlement prior to the passage of the act, which he eventually had modified based on the act and on the Assembly's Report that he wrote.

9. For a discussion of concerns about the family, see Elizabeth Gleick, "Should This Marriage Be Saved?" *Time Magazine,* February 27, 1995, 48.

10. For example, Stephanie Coontz, *The Way We Really Are: Coming to Terms with America's Changing Families* (New York: BasicBooks, 1997), 82. Some authors argue that no-fault divorce protects children from the mistakes of their parents without those authors recognizing the benefits to children from parents having incentives to make better decisions. See Robert M. Gordon, "The Limits of Limits on Divorce," *Yale Law Journal* 107 (1998): 1435–65.

11. See Richard A. Posner, *Economic Analysis of Law, 4th ed* .(Boston: Little, Brown, 1992), 108.

12. With no-fault divorce making it easy to limit the costs of poor judgment as to a choice of a spouse, it should be no surprise that adults are less likely to search diligently for a spouse, which often results in poor matches. See Bruno S. Frey and Reiner Eichenberger, "Marriage Paradoxes," *Rationality & Society* 8, no. 2 (May 1996): 187–206.

13. Laura Bradford, "The Counterrevolution: A Critique of Recent Proposals to Reform No-Fault Divorce Laws," *Stanford Law Review* 49 (February 1997): 607–36.

14. Ann Scott Tyson, "States Put Minor Speed Bumps in Divorce Path," *The Christian Science Monitor*, September 10, 1996, 1.

15. Maggie Gallagher, "Time to 'Fess Up to Messing Up," *USA TODAY*, January 23, 1997, 15A.

16. H.B. 4432, 88th Leg., 1995 Reg. Sess. (LEXIS, States Library, MIBill File, Mich. 1995).

17. Kenneth Cole, "Bills Would Make Divorce Harder," *Detroit News*, February 13, 1996.

18. Cole, "Bills."

19. Katherine Shaw Spaht, "Propter Honoris Prestum: For the Sake of the Children: Recapturing the Meaning of Marriage," *Notre Dame Law Review* 73 (May 1998): 1547–79; and Jenifer Warren, "No-Fault Divorce under Fire in State, Nation," *Los Angeles Times*, April 12, 1998, A1.

20. La. Rev. Stat. Ann. 9:272(West Supp. 1998). For a discussion of covenant marriage, see Steven L. Nock, James D. Wright, and Laura Sanchez, "America's Divorce Problem," *Society* 36, no. 4 (May/June 1999): 43–52.

21. La. Rev. Stat. Ann. 9:272, 9:273.

22. La. Rev. Stat. Ann. 9:273(A)(2)(a).

23. La. Rev. Stat. Ann. 9:273(A)(2)(a).

24. La. Rev. Stat. Ann. 9:307.

25. La. Rev. Stat. Ann. 9:307(A)(1).

26. La. Rev. Stat. Ann. 9:307(A)(2).

27. La. Rev. Stat. Ann. 9:307(A)(3).

28. La. Rev. Stat. Ann. 9:307(A)(4).

29. La. Rev. Stat. Ann. 9:307(A)(5).

30. La. Rev. Stat. Ann. 9:307(A)(6)(a).

31. La. Rev. Stat. Ann. 9:307(A)(6)(b).

32. La. Rev. Stat. Ann. 9:307(A)(6).

33. Christine B. Whelan, "No Honeymoon for Covenant Marriage," *Wall Street Journal*, August 17, 1998, A12. During the last six months of 1998, data collected by Steven Nock, a sociologist at the University of Virginia, indicated that the percentage of couples selecting a covenant marriage had increased to approximately 3 percent. He also determined that people in Louisiana were only gradually becoming aware of the covenant marriage alternative. Conversation with Steven Nock on February 22, 1999.

34. Ariz. Rev. Stat. § 25-901.

35. Margaret F. Brinig, "The Law and Economics of Covenant Marriage," *Gender Issues* 16, nos. 1 and 2 (Winter-Spring 1998) : 4–33.

36. The Arizona covenant marriage statute provides for divorce based on mutual consent. Ariz. Rev. Stat. 25-903(8).

37. Uniform Marriage and Divorce Act § 308(a), 9A Unif.L.Ann 160 (1979).

38. Numerous common law states continue to weigh fault, and not all community property states disregard fault in the allocation of marital or community property upon divorce. See Harry D. Krause, *Family Law,* 3d ed. (St. Paul, MN: West, 1995), 440.

39. Mary Ann Glendon, *The New Family and the New Property* (Toronto: Butterworths, 1981), 63; Mary Ann Glendon, "Family Law Reform in the 1980s," *Louisiana Law Review* 44, no. 6 (July 1984): 1561; and Joan M. Krauskopf, "A Theory for 'Just' Division of Marital Property in Missouri," *Missouri Law Review* 41 (1976): 165–78.

40. Lenore J. Weitzman, "The Economics of Divorce: Social and Economic Consequences of Property, Alimony, and Child Support Awards," *UCLA Law Review* 28 (1981): 1199.

41. Although alimony has become a less important source of financial support for divorced women, property settlements have not increased in importance by a corresponding amount. Suzanne Reynolds has argued that the "need" standard for division of property has been underutilized because of a lack of a consensus on what constitutes need. See Suzanne Reynolds, "The Relationship of Property Division and Alimony: The Division of Property to Address Need," *Fordham Law Review* 56, no. 5 (April 1988): 830.

42. Doris J. Freed and Timothy B. Walker, "Family Law in the Fifty States: An Overview," *Family Law Quarterly* 18, no. 4 (Winter 1985): 392.

43. Annual summaries are provided in the American Bar Association's *Family Law Quarterly.* For example, see Linda D. Elrod and Robert G. Spector, "A Review of the Year in Family Law: A Search for Definitions and Policy," *Family Law Quarterly* 31, no. 4 (Winter 1998): 613–66.

44. For a review of the law as applied to professional education and closely held businesses, see J. Thomas Oldham, *Divorce, Separation, and the Distribution of Property* (New York: Law Journal Seminars-Press, 1997), 9-1–10-51.

45. Cal. Civ. Code, § 4800.3[b][1] and [c], [c][1], [c][2],[c][3] effective January 1, 1985 [West Supp. 1985, added by Stats 1984, C. 1661, Section 2]. If the divorce occurs at least ten years after the contribution was made, the assumption is made that the contributing spouse has received adequate compensation for the investment, and no further compensation is required. See Lenore J. Weitzman, *The Divorce Revolution* (New York: Free Press, 1985), 128.

46. Harriet N. Cohen and Patricia Hennessey, "Valuation of Property in Marital Dissolutions," *Family Law Quarterly* 23, no. 2 (Summer 1989): 380.

47. Allen M. Parkman, "A Systematic Approach to Valuing the Goodwill of Professional Practices", in *Valuing Professional Practices and License, 3d ed.,*, ed. Ronald L. Brown (Gaithersburg, NY: Aspen, 1998), 6-1–6-18; and Allen M. Parkman, "The Treatment of Professional Goodwill in Divorce Proceedings," *Family Law Quarterly* 18, no. 2 (Summer 1984): 213–24.

48. *Hurley v. Hurley*, 94 N.M. 641, 615 P.2d 256 (1980).

49. Krauskopf, "Marital Property," 170.

50. Cohen and Hennessey, "Valuation," 367.

51. *Hertz v. Hertz*, 99 N.M. 320, 657 P.2d 1169 (1983).

52. Oldham, *Property*, 9-1–9-29.

53. Glendon, *New Family,* 68.

54. Krauskopf, "Marital Property," 167.

55. Weitzman, "Economics of Divorce," 1220 and Weitzman, *Divorce Revolution,* 53.

56. American Law Institute, *Principles of the Law of Family Dissolution: Analysis*

and Recommendations, Proposed Final Draft, Part 1 (Philadelphia, PA: American Law Institute, 1997), xiii.

57.   American Law Institute, *Principles*, xiii.

58.   American Law Institute, *Principles*, 146, § 4.07.

59.   American Law Institute, *Principles*, 196, § 4.15(b).

60.   American Law Institute, *Principles*, 213, § 4.16.

61.   American Law Institute, *Principles*, 259, § 5.02.

62.   American Law Institute, *Principles*, 271, § 5.03.

63.   American Law Institute, *Principles*, 350, § 5.08.

64.   American Law Institute, *Principles*, 357, § 5.09.

65.   American Law Institute, *Principles*, 280, § 5.05, and 317, § 5.06.

66.   American Law Institute, *Principles*, 406, § 5.17.

67.   Weitzman, *Divorce Revolution,* 184.

68.   Weitzman, *Divorce Revolution,* 387.

69.   Weitzman, *Divorce Revolution,* 112.

70.   Weitzman, *Divorce Revolution,* 390.

71.   Weitzman, *Divorce Revolution,* 396.

72.   Weitzman, *Divorce Revolution,* 400.

73.   Joan M. Krauskopf, "Recompense for Financing Spouse's Education: Legal Protection for the Marital Investor in Human Capital," *Kansas Law Review* 28 (Spring 1980): 379–417. She recognized that funds provided by a spouse tend to replace loans, 385; but then she argued that an equity interest had been created, 401.

74.   Krauskopf, "Recompense," 384–86, discusses the funds used to finance the education.

75.   Mary Ann Glendon, *Abortion and Divorce in Western Law* (Cambridge, MA: Harvard University Press, 1987), 82.

76.   Glendon, *Abortion*, 92.

77.   Glendon, "Family Law Reform," 1558.

78.   Glendon, "Family Law Reform," 1559.

79.   Glendon, "Family Law Reform," 1565; and Lenore J. Weitzman, *The Divorce Contract* (New York: Macmillan, 1981).

80.   Douglas W. Allen, "An Inquiry into the State's Role in Marriage," *Journal of Economic Behavior and Organization* 13 (1990): 171–91.

81.   A discussion of problems associated with the inappropriate definition of property is contained in Allen M. Parkman, "Human Capital as Property in Divorce Settlements," *Arkansas Law Review* 40, no. 3 (1987): 439–67.

82.   See Willard H. Da Silva, "Property Subject to Equitable Distribution," in John P. McCahey and Barbara E. Adelman, *Valuation & Distribution of Martial Property*, 4 (New York: Matthew-Bender, 1984).

83. American Law Institute, *Principles*, 90.

84. American Law Institute, *Principles,* 90.

85. Allen M. Parkman, "Bringing Consistency to the Financial Arrangements at Divorce," *Kentucky Law Journal* 87, no. 1 (1998–99): 51–93.

86. The standard work on earnings profiles and, therefore, on human capital is Gary S. Becker, *Human Capital,* 3d ed. (Chicago: University of Chicago Press, 1993).

87. It has been suggested that rather than incorporating human capital into the traditional notions of property, some of the situations discussed here should be treated as "exceptions" to the equal treatment of the spouses. See Weitzman, *Divorce Revolution,* 104–05. The incorporation of human capital into property is more systematic, however, and would permit equal treatment of the spouses.

88. Allen M. Parkman, "Human Capital as Property in Celebrity Divorces," *Family Law Quarterly* 29, no. 1 (Spring 1995): 141–69.

89. The court cited a 1980 law that stated that marriage is an economic partnership and that included medical licenses and law degrees as marital property. The court held that special skills that generate substantial income should not be distinguished from degrees or licenses. *USA Today,* July 3, 1991, 1D.

90. It is not common for the courts to hold that a spouse has wasted potential income during marriage. Mark Gastineau, a defensive end for the New York Jets football team, was required to pay his wife $100,000 for prematurely retiring from professional football to spend time with actress Brigitte Nielsen, however. *USA Today,* July 3, 1991, 11C.

91. One hundred dollars that I will receive a year from now is worth less than that amount to me at the present time. If the current rate of interest is 10 percent, I can borrow $91 now with the understanding that I will owe the bank $100 in a year. I will be able to pay off the loan with $100, when it arrives. The $100 a year from now has been discounted to its value now, which is $91. The same procedure can be used for a series of payments.

92. The standard formula for valuing an infinite income stream is $V = I/(r - g)$, where V is the value, I is the initial annual income, r is the required rate of return on the investment, and g is the anticipated growth rate of the annual income. In this example, $V = \$25,000/(0.5 - 0) = \$50,000$.

93. The determination of the career path of an individual who has limited his or her participation in the labor force is not easy. More people start out intending to become medical doctors than end up graduating from medical school. The courts have to be realistic in determining the career that a homemaker would have pursued.

94. John DeWitt Gregory, Peter N. Swisher, and Sheryl L. Scheible-Wolf, *Understanding Family Law* (New York: Matthew-Bender, 1993), 346.

95. If one spouse fraudulently induced the other spouse into incurring this loss, then the full amount of the loss should be levied on the defrauding spouse. For example, a husband might ask his wife to give up a high-paying, but unique, job. The husband has been offered a high-paying job in a new location that would benefit the entire family. The wife's employment prospects are much poorer in that location, however. The husband might assure the wife that the marriage is stable, but if he takes actions that contradict that situ-

ation, such as having an affair, it would seem reasonable that he should be assessed the full amount of his wife's loss if there is a divorce.

96.   The $10,000 lost during the current year has a discounted value of $10,000. The loss in the second year is $9,000. Because it will occur in the future, it has a discounted value of $8,182. The calculation can be made with the lost earnings in each of the future years. The sum of the discounted values will be $42,410.

97.   Knowing that they were going to be absent from the labor force for certain periods, women traditionally went into careers that tended to be less sensitive to absences from the labor force. These careers entailed general skills supported by certification. Teaching and nursing are obvious examples.

98.   Allen M. Parkman, "An Investment Approach to Valuing Spousal Support of Education," in *Valuing Professional Practices and License,* 3d ed., ed. Ronald L. Brown (Gaithersburg, NY: Aspen, 1998), 32-1–32-25.

99.   See Severin Borenstein and Paul N. Courant, "How to Carve a Medical Degree: Human Capital Assets in Divorce Settlements," *American Economic Review* 79, no. 5 (December 1989): 992–1009.

100.   Margaret F. Brinig and June Carbone, "The Reliance Interest in Marriage and Divorce," *Tulane Law Review* 62, no. 5 (May 1988): 893.

101.   Weitzman, "Economics of Divorce," 1221.

102.   Weitzman, *Divorce Revolution,* 143.

103.   Posner, *Economic Analysis,* 148.

104.   American Law Institute, *Principles,* 259, § 5.02.

105.   American Law Institute, *Principles,* 257, § 5.01(1).

106.   American Law Institute, *Principles,* 280, § 5.05. Compensation, without any evidence of the type of sacrifice covered by § 5.06, has caused some commentators to call for the abolition of this section. J. Thomas Oldham, "ALI Principles of Family Dissolution: Some Comments," *Illinois Law Review,* (1997): 816–31.

107.   American Law Institute, *Principles,* 317, § 5.06.

108.   American Law Institute, *Principles,* 380, § 5.12.

109.   American Law Institute, *Principles,* 383, § 5.15.

110.   American Law Institute, *Principles,* 394, § 5.16.

111.   American Law Institute, *Principles,* 350, § 5.08.

112.   American Law Institute, *Principles,* 357, § 5.09.

113.   Compensation based on the parties' disparate financial capacity is determined by applying a marriage-duration factor to "the difference between the incomes the spouses are expected to have after dissolution," American Law Institute, *Principles,* 272, § 5.05(3), whereas compensation for primary caretaker's residual loss in earning capacity is determined by applying a "child care durational factor to the difference between the incomes that spouses are expected to have after dissolution." American Law Institute, *Principles,* 318, § 5.06(4). Another concern is based on most divorces being initiated by the lower income spouse with the result that the person who initiated the divorce is rewarded with

an income transfer from the spouse who wanted the marriage to continue. See Sanford L. Braver, Marnie Whitley, and Christine Ng, "Who Divorced Whom? Methodological and Theoretical Issues," *Journal of Divorce and Remarriage* 20 (1993): 1–19. Still, a sharing of postdissolution income is popular among many academics. For example, see Jana Singer, "Divorce Reform and Gender Justice," *North Carolina Law Review* 67 (1989): 1103–21; Sally F. Goldfarb, "Marital Partnership and the Case for Permanent Alimony," *Journal of Family Law* 27 (1988–89): 351–72; and Cynthia Starnes, "Divorce and the Displaced Homemaker," *University of Chicago Law Review* 60 (Winter 1993): 67–139.

114.   American Law Institute, *Principles*, 335, § 5.06, Reporter's Notes, Comment a.

115.   American Law Institute, *Principles,* 325, § 5.06, Reporter's Notes, Comment d.

116.   The current child support guidelines are based on the financial cost incurred by parents to raise a child. See Andrea H. Beller and John W. Graham, *Small Change: The Economics of Child Support* (New Haven, CT: Yale University Press, 1993).

117.   See Allen M. Parkman, "The Government's Role in the Support of Children," *BYU Journal of Public Law* 11, no. 1 (1995): 55–74. It has been argued that by reducing the cost of having children outside of marriage, AFDC has contributed to the increase in the number of children born to unwed mothers. See Charles A. Murray, *Losing Ground: American Social Policy, 1950–1980* (New York: Basic Books, 1984).

118.   Glendon argued that the two issues should be combined. Glendon, "Family Law Reform," 1565.

119.   Fuchs, *How We Live*, 152. The remarriage rate for women has fallen dramatically over recent decades. U.S. Bureau of the Census, *Statistical Abstract of the United States, 1998* (Washington, DC: U.S. Government Printing Office, 1998), Table 161, 113.

120.   Fuchs, *How We Live*, 151.

121.   Lloyd Cohen, "Marriage, Divorce, and Quasi Rents; or 'I Gave Him the Best Years of My Life,'" *Journal of Legal Studies* 16 (1987): 287.

122.   Cohen, "Marriage," 293.

123.   See John Mordechai Gottman, "Psychology and the Study of Marital Processes," *Annual Review of Psychology* 49 (1998): 169–97.

124.   In 46 percent of marriages in 1988, at least one of the spouses had already been married before. Census, *Statistical Abstract 1998*, Table 157, 111.

125.   There has been a sharp decline in the remarriage rate since the late 1960s, which is reflected in the huge increase in the number of divorced women. Between 1965–69 and 1980–84, the percentage of women who had remarried within five years of a divorce fell from 73 percent to 45 percent. Census, *Statistical Abstract 1998*, Table 161, 113.

126.   Wallerstein and Kelly noted that children recognize when their parents do not have a happy marriage, but an overwhelming majority of the children that they interviewed preferred the unhappy marriage to the divorce. See Judith S. Wallerstein and Joan Berlin Kelly, *Surviving the Breakup* (New York: Basic Books, 1980), 10.

127.   Paul Amato and Alan Booth found that between 1980 and 1992 only a minority of divorces that they reviewed involved high-conflict marriages. Paul R. Amato and Alan Booth, *A Generation at Risk* (Cambridge, MA: Harvard University Press, 1997), 220.

128. Amato and Booth, *Generation*, 17.

129. E. Mavis Hetherington and W. Glenn Clingempeel, "Coping with Marital Transitions," *Monographs of the Society for Research in Child Development*, 57, nos. 2 and 3 (1992).

130. Sara McLanahan and Gary Sandefur, *Growing Up with a Single Parent* (Cambridge, MA: Harvard University Press, 1994), 1.

131. Parkman, "Bringing."

132. Allen M. Parkman, "Reform of the Divorce Provisions of the Marriage Contract," *The BYU Journal of Public Law* 8, no. 1 (1993): 91–106.

133. Posner, *Economic Analysis*, 89–138.

134. Posner, *Economic Analysis*, 230. Contract law can be viewed as filling in the gaps in a contract. Economists assume that the parties would have chosen rules that maximize their joint net benefits, which effectively establishes efficiency as their goal. See A. Mitchell Polinsky, *An Introduction to Law and Economics* (Boston: Little, Brown, 1989), 27.

135. Janet K. Smith and Richard L. Smith, "Contract Law, Mutual Mistake, and Incentives to Produce and Disclose Information," *Journal of Legal Studies* 19, no. 2 (June 1990): 467–88.

136. For example, the courts have held that liquidated damages that exceed the expected damages due to a breach create for at least one party a disincentive to perform under a contract. The result would be inefficient. Therefore, the courts review liquidated damage provisions in a contract to make sure that they are reasonable. *Lake River Corporation v. Carborundum Company*, 769 Fed.2d 1284 (1985).

137. This outcome is based on the Coase Theorem, which was presented in Ronald H. Coase, "The Problem of Social Cost," *Journal of Law and Economics* 3 (1960): 3–44.

138. William Bishop, "The Choice of Remedy for Breach of Contract," *Journal of Legal Studies* 14 (June 1985): 299.

139. Posner, *Economic Analysis,* 130.

140. Posner, *Economic Analysis,* 117–19. In other legal systems, such as Germany's, specific performance is the general remedy to a breach of a contract. See Bishop, "Remedy for Breach," 299–320.

141. For a thorough discussion of the efficiency-enhancing characteristics of contract law, see Posner, *Economic Analysis,* 89–138.

142. Stephen Sugarman has objected to treating marriage as a contract. He argued that no-fault is like a contract-at-will in which there is no place for the concept of a breach and resulting damages. See Stephen D. Sugarman, "Dividing Financial Interests on Divorce," in *Divorce Reform at the Crossroads*, ed. Stephen D. Sugarman and Herma Hill Kay (New Haven, CT: Yale University Press, 1990), 139. We do not talk about "fault," however, when a party unilaterally breaches a commercial contract and subjects itself to damages. The parties anticipated performance, but they recognized that each party had a right to breach the contract, subject to the requirement of compensation. That is the more appropriate analogy.

143. Krause, *Family Law,* 41.

144. Some scholars have described the marriage contract as a relational contract that relies on social and relational norms to promote cooperation and to enforce intramarital promises. Legal enforcement is limited to policing massive defections from the cooperative norms and to resolving economic and parental claims on termination of the marriage. See Elizabeth S. Scott and Robert E. Scott, "Marriage as Relational Contract," *Virginia Law Review* 84 (October 1998): 1225–1334.

145. Gregory, Swisher, and Scheible-Wolf, *Understanding Family Law*, 12.

146. Parkman, *Consistency*, 63.

147. The decision for the wife to sacrifice her human capital for the benefit of the family can be viewed as resulting in an implied contract of indemnification for which compensation is appropriate if the marriage is dissolved. The divorce laws do not provide for this remedy in any systematic way.

148. Marriage is the result of a search process during which the parties weigh the benefits and the costs of additional search. See Gary S. Becker, *A Treatise on the Family* (Cambridge, MA: Harvard University Press, 1991), 328.

149. See Gary S. Becker and Kevin M. Murphy, "The Family and the State," *Journal of Law and Economics* 31, no. 1 (1988): 1–18. Generally, children prefer an unhappy marriage to a divorce. Also see Judith S. Wallerstein and Sandra Blakelee, *Second Chances* (New York: Ticknor & Fields, 1990), 11.

150. Traditionally, the American family has been viewed as the cornerstone of our society, with the result that the state legislatures and courts have been reluctant to intervene in family affairs. See, for example, *Maynard v. Hill*, 125 U.S. 190, 205 (1888). Still, if a legislature wanted to intervene, its powers were viewed as broad until 1965. In *Griswold v. Connecticut*, 381 U.S. 479 (1965), the Supreme Court held that the Connecticut statute forbidding the use of contraceptives was unconstitutional as applied to married couples. Some authors have described marriage as a long-term relational contract in which the parties contemplate a long-term commitment to pursue shared goals without providing specific standards for how those goals are to be reached. The terms for dissolving the relationship are important in establishing the incentives for cooperation. See Scott and Scott, "Marriage," 1225.

151. *Williams v. North Carolina*, 317 U.S. 287, 289 (1942). Of course, the state's adoption of no-fault divorce laws can be interpreted as the state's reversing their paternalistic position on marriage, thereby acknowledging the right of couples to have a greater control over their own affairs. See Theodore F. Haas, "The Rationality and Enforceability of Contractual Restrictions on Divorce," *North Carolina Law Review* 66 (June 1988): 910.

152. Because the state controls the grounds for divorce, people who do not like the legally prescribed ease of and arrangements at divorce have been forced to turn to premarital agreements. These agreements traditionally were difficult to enforce, but that situation has improved in the states that have passed the Uniform Premarital Agreement Act, 9B U.L.A. 369 (1987). See Brian Bix, "Bargaining in the Shadow of Love: The Enforcement of Premarital Agreements and How We Think about Marriage," *William and Mary Law Review* 40 (October 1998): 145–207. Still, premarital agreements are not attractive for most couples because they do not have a clear idea of the range of potential future events and of the conditions that they want to attach to these events. Also see Gregory S.

Alexander, "The New Marriage Contract and the Limits of Private Ordering," *Indiana Law Journal* 73 (Spring 1998): 507.

153.   This topic is discussed in more detail in Parkman, "Consistency," 56.

154.   Ira M. Ellman, "The Theory of Alimony," *California Law Review* 77, no. 1 (1989) 1–81; Homer H. Clark, *The Law of Domestic Relations in the United States, 2d ed.* (St. Paul, MN: West, 1988), 620; Krause, *Family Law*, 404; and American Law Institute, *Principles*, 5.

155.   For example, the wedding vows in West Virginia include the statement for both the bride and the groom, "to have and to hold, from this day forward, for better, for worse, for richer, for poorer, in sickness and in health, to love and to cherish, as long as life shall last, and thereto I pledge thee my faith." W. Va. Code § 48-1-12b (1998).

156.   It was commonly recognized prior to the shift from fault to no-fault grounds for divorce that there was a conflict between the divorce law on the books, which declared marriage indissoluble except for marital fault, and the law in practice, which tolerated divorce by mutual consent. See Herma Hill Kay, "An Appraisal of California's No-Fault Divorce Law," *California Law Review* 75 (1987): 297.

157.   See Bradford, "The Counter-Revolution"; Ira Mark Ellman, "The Place of Fault in a Modern Divorce Law," *Arizona State Law Journal* 28 (Fall 1996): 773–836; and Ira Mark Ellman and Sharon Lohr, "Marriage as Contract, Opportunistic Violence, and Other Bad Arguments for Fault Divorce," *University of Illinois Law Review* (1997): 719–72.

158.   Under no-fault divorce, many divorces occur when there has only been a minor discord between the spouses. See Amato and Booth, *Generation*, 220.

159.   Glendon, "Family Law Reform," 1558.

160.   Bishop, "Remedy for Breach,"300.

161.   Wallerstein and Kelly, *Surviving*, 17.

162.   When the opportunities available to men and women were very different, then there were substantial gains from specialization that made most adults better off married. As employment opportunities have improved for women and as labor-saving devices have become more common in the home, some men and women have found that they have less to gain from marriage. The reduced gains from marriage are particularly apparent for a couple that does not want children.

163.   Some critics of reform have suggested that the elevation of the criterion for divorce based on children degrades couples who have either not had or are not capable of having children. David M. Wagner, "Divorce Reform: New Directions," *Current* (February 1998): 7.

164.   Eighty-four percent of family lawyers in an American Bar Association's survey opposed rescinding no-fault divorce. See ABA Press Release (October 18, 1996).

165.   See Max Rheinstein, *Marriage Stability, Divorce, and the Law* (Chicago: University of Chicago Press, 1972), 247.

166.   201 U.S. 562 (1905).

167.   *Williams v. North Carolina*, 317 U.S. 287 (1942).

168.   *Williams v. North Carolina*, 317 U.S. 287, 299 (1942).

169. *Williams v. North Carolina*, 325 U.S. 226 (1945).

170. *Williams v. North Carolina*, 325 U.S. 226, 230 (1945).

171. *Williams v. North Carolina*, 325 U.S. 226, 239 (1945).

172. 207 F.2d 667 (3d Cir. 1953), vacated as moot, 347 U.S. 610 (1954) (per curiam). Also see, Rhonda Wasserman, "Divorce and Domicile: Time to Sever the Knot," *William and Mary Law Review* 39 (October 1997): 1–63.

173. U.S. Constitution, Article V.

174. 207 F.2d 667, 677 (3d Cir. 1953).

175. 207 F.2d 667, 677 (3d Cir. 1953).

176. *Cooper v. Cooper*, 217 N.W.2d 584 (Iowa, 1974).

177. Gregory, Swisher, and Scheible-Wolf, *Understanding Family Law*, 193.

178. The Alaskan legislature, for example, removed the residency requirement for divorce in 1975; so their divorce statute contains no residency requirement for a divorce uncomplicated by alimony, property division, or child custody. *Perito v. Perito*, 756 P.2d 895 (1988).

179. The U.S. Supreme Court could reconcile interstate judgments law in divorce cases to conform to the law in other contexts, which would permit states to reject the status exception, the domicile rule, and its choice-of-law corollary. See Wasserman, "Divorce," 56. Alternatively, uniform legislation could be enacted, or Congress could enact a federal statute requiring states to recognize the divorce degrees of other states. Wasserman, "Divorce," 57.

180. See *Restatement (Second) of Conflicts of Law* §§ 186–188 (1971).

181. Although their agreement could call for damages as remedy for a breach, it is argued later that the more appropriate remedy for breach of a marital contract should be specific performance.

182. A bill was introduced into the State of Washington legislature that would have permitted couples the option to sign a prenuptial contract excluding no-fault divorce. Common among the opponents of any change in the no-fault divorce laws has been concern for the people who make a mistake when they marry. For example, the minority leader of the Washington legislature, who was a family lawyer, argued that this bill might induce many couples to sign prenuptial contracts that they would later regret. Kenneth Cole, "Bills Would Make Divorce Harder," *Detroit News*, February 13, 1996, 1.

183. Because marriage was not treated as a contract, the only contracts were severely restricted pre- and postmarital agreements between the spouses. The states had preempted the grounds for divorce, so grounds were not a legitimate subject for these contracts. Other issues have gradually been recognized as appropriate for premarital contract under certain conditions. Initially, these contracts addressed property at death and, later, property at divorce. More recently, they have been expanded to consider alimony. See Clark, *Domestic Relations*, 1–20.

184. *Restatement (Second) of Conflict of Laws*, §187 (1971).

185. *Restatement (Second) of Conflict of Laws*, §187(2)(a).

186. *Restatement (Second) of Conflict of Laws*, §187(2)(b).

187. See Haas, "Rationality," 910.

188. Bix, "Bargaining"; Allison A. Marston, "Planning for Love: The Politics of Prenuptial Agreements," *Stanford Law Review* 49 (April 1997): 887–916; and Jana Singer, "The Privatization of Family Law," *Wisconsin Law Review* 1992 (September/October 1992): 1443–1567.

189. 233 So. 2d 381 (Fla. 1970).

190. See Haas, "Rationality," 907; and Bix, "Bargaining," 152, n. 20.

191. 233 So. 2d 381, 384 (Fla. 1970).

192. 233 So. 2d 381, 387 (Fla. 1970).

193. 233 So. 2d 381, 394 (Fla. 1970).

194. *Uniform Premarital Agreement Act*(UPAA), 9B U.L.A. 369 (1987).

195. As of September 1999, twenty-six jurisdictions had adopted the UPAA. The jurisdictions are listed in the 1999 Supplement to the UPAA.

196. UPAA, § 6(a)(1).

197. UPAA, § 6(c).

198. 238 Conn. 839; 679 A.2d 937 (1996).

199. 238 Conn. 839, 845; 679 A.2d 937, 941 (1996).

200. Comment e to § 187 of the *Restatement* provides,

> Prime objectives of contract law are to protect the justified expectations of the parties and to make it possible for them to foretell with accuracy what will be their rights and liabilities under the contract. These objectives may best be attained in multistate transactions by letting the parties choose the law to govern the validity of the contract and the rights created thereby. In this way, certainty and predictability of result are most likely to be secured. Giving parties this power of choice is also consistent with the fact that, in contrast to other areas of the law, persons are free within broad limits to determine the nature of their contractual obligations.

201. Danielle Crittenden made a suggestion that is only attractive if a woman feels very comfortable in her relationship. She argued that a woman would be wise to marry early, putting off a career until her children have grown, because the pool of attractive men is larger when women are younger and a mother is more capable of the demands of child care at that age. See Danielle Crittenden, *What Our Mothers Didn't Tell Us* (New York: Simon & Schuster, 1999).

202. Many people who work long hours may command high salaries, but that doesn't mean they're happy: 45 to 50 percent of workers "and 80 percent of those working more than 50 hours per week" said that they would prefer to work fewer hours, and more than 25 percent said they would take a pay cut to make it happen. See Jerry A. Jacobs and Kathleen Gerson, "Who Are the Overworked Americans?" *Review of Social Economy* 56, no. 4 (1998): 442–59.

References

Abell, Peter. *Rational Choice Theory*. Aldershot, UK: Elgar, 1991.

Akerloff, George A., Janet L. Yellen, and Michael L. Katz. "An Analysis of Out-of-Wedlock Childbearing in the United States." *Quarterly Journal of Economics* 111, no. 2 (May 1996): 277–317.

Alexander, Gregory S. "The New Marriage Contract and the Limits of Private Ordering." *Indiana Law Journal* 73 (Spring 1998): 503–10.

Allen, Douglas W. "An Inquiry into the State's Role in Marriage." *Journal of Economic Behavior and Organization* 13 (1990): 171–91.

———. "Marriage and Divorce: Comment." *American Economic Review* 82, no. 3 (June 1992): 679–85.

Amato, Paul R. "Implications of Research Findings on Children in Stepfamilies." In *Stepfamilies: Who Benefits? Who Does Not?* ed. Alan Booth and J. Dunn, 81–87. Hillsdale, NJ: Lawrence Erlbaum, 1994.

———. "The Post-divorce Society: How Divorce Is Shaping the Family and Other Forms of Social Organization." In *The Post- divorce Family: Children, Parenting, and Society*, ed. Ross Thompson. Thousand Oaks, CA: Sage, 1999: 161–90.

Amato, Paul R., and Alan Booth. *A Generation at Risk*. Cambridge, MA: Harvard University Press, 1997.

Amato, Paul R., and Stacy Rogers. "Do Attitudes toward Divorce Affect Marital Quality?" *Journal of Family Issues* 20, no. 1 (January 1999): 69–87.

American Law Institute. *Principles of the Law of Family Dissolution: Analysis and Recommendations, Proposed Final Draft*, Part 1. Philadelphia, PA: American Law Institute, 1997.

Arendell, Terry. *Mothers and Divorce*. Berkeley: University of California Press, 1986.

Arnold, Roger. "Marriage, Divorce, and Property Rights: A Natural Rights Framework." In *The American Family and the State,* ed. Joseph R. Peden and Fred R. Glahe, 195–227. San Francisco: Pacific Research Institute for Public Policy, 1986.

Bahr, Steven J. "Marital Dissolution Laws: Impact of Recent Changes for Women." *Journal of Family Issues* 4 (1983): 455–66.

Baker, Lynn A. "Promulgating the Marriage Contract." *Journal of Law Reform* 23 (1990): 217–64.

Baker, Lynn A., and Robert E. Emery. "When Every Relationship Is above Average: Perceptions and Expectations of Divorce at the Time of Marriage." *Law and Human Behavior* 17 (1993): 439–50.

Bayer, A. E. "Marriage Plans and Educational Aspirations." *American Journal of Sociology* 75 (1969): 239–44.

Becker, Gary S. "A Theory of the Allocation of Time." *Economic Journal* 75 (1965): 493–517.

———. *The Economic Approach to Human Behavior.* Chicago: University of Chicago Press, 1976.

———."Family." In *The New Palgrave: Social Economics,* ed. John Eatwell, Murray Milgate, and Peter Newman, 64–76. New York: Norton, 1989.

———. *A Treatise on the Family.* Enl. ed. Cambridge, MA: Harvard University Press, 1991.

———. *Human Capital.* 3d ed. Chicago: University of Chicago Press, 1993.

Becker, Gary S., Elizabeth M. Landes, and Robert Michael. "An Analysis of Marital Instability." *Journal of Political Economy* 85 (1977): 1141–87.

Becker, Gary S., and Kevin M. Murphy. "The Family and the State." *Journal of Law and Economics* 31, no. 1. (1988): 1–18.

Beller, Andrea H., and John W. Graham. *Small Change: The Economics of Child Support.* New Haven, CT: Yale University Press, 1993.

Belsky, Jay. "Parental and Nonparental Child Care and Children's Socioemotional Development: A Decade in Review." in *Contemporary Families: Looking Forward, Looking Back*, ed. Alan Booth, 122–40. Minneapolis, MN: National Council on Family Relations, 1991.

Belsky, Jay, and David Eggebeen. "Early and Extensive Material Employment and Young Children's Socioemotional Development: Children of the National Longitudinal Survey on Youth." *Journal of Marriage and the Family* 53, no. 4 (November 1991): 1083–98.

Ben-Porath, Yoram. "Economics and the Family—Match or Mismatch? A Review of Becker's *A Treatise on the Family.*" *Journal of Economic Literature* 20 (1982): 52–64.

Bennett, William J., John J. DiIulio, Jr., and John P. Walters. *Body Count.* New York: Simon & Schuster, 1996.

Bianchi, Suzanne M., and Daphne Spain. *American Women in Transition*. New York: Russell Sage Foundation, 1986.

Billington, Ray Allen. *American's Frontier Heritage*. Albuquerque, NM: University of New Mexico Press, 1974.

Bishop, William. "The Choice of Remedy for Breach of Contract." *Journal of Legal Studies* 14 (June 1985): 299-320.

Bix, Brian. "Bargaining in the Shadow of Love: The Enforcement of Premarital Agreements and How We Think about Marriage." *William and Mary Law Review* 40 (October 1998): 145–207.

Black, Duncan. *The Theory of Committees and Elections*. Cambridge, UK: Cambridge University Press, 1958.

Blakemore, Arthur E., and Stuart A. Low. "Sex Differences in Occupational Selection: The Case of College Majors." *Review of Economics and Statistics* 66 (1984): 157–63.

Blau, Francine D. "Trends in the Well-Being of American Women, 1970–95," *Journal of Economic Literature* 36, no. 1 (March 1998): 112–65.

Blau, Francine D., and Marianne A. Ferber. *The Economics of Women, Men, and Work*. 2d ed. Englewood Cliffs, NJ: Prentice-Hall, 1992.

Blau, Peter M. *Exchange and Power in Social Life*. New York: John Wiley & Sons, 1964.

Blumberg, Grace Ganz. "New Models of Marriage and Divorce." In *Contemporary Marriage*, ed. Kingsley Davis, 349–72. New York: Russell Sage Foundation, 1985.

———. "Marital Property Treatment of Pensions, Disability Pay, Workers' Compensation, and Other Wage Substitutes: An Insurance, or Replacement, Analysis." *UCLA Law Review* 33 (1986): 1250–1308.

Borenstein, Severin, and Paul N. Courant. "How to Carve a Medical Degree: Human Capital Assets in Divorce Settlements." *American Economic Review* 79 (1989): 992-1009.

Boskin, Michael J., and Dale W. Jorgenson. "Implications of Overstating Inflation for Indexing Government Programs and Understanding Economic Progress." *American Economic Review* 87, no. 2 (May 1997): 89–93.

Bouton, Katherine. "Women and Divorce." *New York,* October 8, 1984, 34–41.

Boyer, Helen. "Equitable Interest in Enhanced Earning Capacity: The Treatment of a Professional Degree at Dissolution." *Washington Law Review* 60 (1985): 431–59.

Bradford, Laura. "The Counterrevolution: A Critique of Recent Proposals to Reform No-Fault Divorce Laws." Stanford Law Review 49, (February 1997): 607–36.

Braver, Sanford L. *Divorced Dads*. New York: Putnam, 1998.

Braver, Sanford L., Marnie Whitley, and Christine Ng. "Who Divorces Whom? Methodological and Theoretical Issues." *Journal of Divorce and Remarriage* 20, nos. 1 and 2 (1993): 1–19.

Brinig, Margaret F. "The Law and Economics of Covenant Marriage." *Gender Issues* 16, nos. 1 and 2 (Winter-Spring 1998): 4–33.

Brinig, Margaret F., and Douglas W. Allen. "These Boots Are Made for Walking: Why Wives File for Divorce." Paper presented at the meeting of the Canadian Law and Economics Association, Toronto, Ontario, September 27–28, 1998.

Brinig, Margaret F., and Frank H. Buckley. "Joint Custody: Bonding and Monitoring Theories." *Indiana Law Journal* 73 (Spring 1998): 393–423.

Brinig, Margaret F., and F. H. Buckley. "No-Fault Laws and At-Fault People." *International Review of Law and Economics* 18 (1998): 325–40.

Brinig, Margaret F., and June Carbone. "The Reliance Interest in Marriage and Divorce." *Tulane Law Review* 62 (1988): 855–905.

Brinig, Margaret F., and Steven M. Crafton. "Marriage and Opportunism." *Journal of Legal Studies* 23 (June 1994): 869–94.

Brody, Stuart A. "California's Divorce Reform: Its Sociological Implications." *Pacific Law Journal* 1 (1970): 223–32.

Brown, Murray. "Optimal Marriage Contracts." *Journal of Human Resources* 27, no. 3 (Summer 1992): 534–50.

Bruch, Carol S. "The Definition and Division of Marital Property in California: Towards Parity and Simplicity." *Hastings Law Journal* 33 (1982): 769–869.

———. "Developing Standards for Child Support Payments: A Critique of Current Practice." *UC-Davis Law Review* 16 (1982): 49–64.

———. "Of Work, Family Wealth, and Equality." *Family Law Quarterly* 17 (1983): 99–108.

Bumpass, Larry L. "What's Happening to the Family? Interactions between Demographic and Institutional Change." *Demography* 27, no. 4 (November 1990): 483–98.

Carbone, June. "Economics, Feminism, and the Reinvention of Alimony: A Reply to Ira Ellman." *Vanderbilt Law Review* 43 (1990): 1463–1501.

Carbone, June, and Margaret F. Brinig. "Rethinking Marriage: Feminist Ideology, Economic Change, and Divorce Reform." *Tulane Law Review* 65 (1991): 953–1010.

Carr, Deborah. "The Fulfillment of Career Dreams at Midlife: Does It Matter for Women's Mental Health?" *Journal of Health and Social Behavior* 38, no. 4 (December 1997): 331–44.

Casper, Lynne M. "My Daddy Takes Care of Me! Fathers as Care Providers." *Current Population Reports,* P70-59, 1–9. Washington, DC: U.S. Bureau of the Census, 1997.

Chandler, Jon Andrew. "A Property Theory of Future Earning Potential in Dissolution Proceedings." *Washington Law Review* 56 (1981): 277–88.

Chase, Marilyn. "Single Trouble: The No-Fault Divorce Has a Fault of Its Own, Many Women Learn." *Wall Street Journal,* January 21, 1985, 1.

Cherlin, Andrew J. *Marriage, Divorce, Remarriage,* rev. ed. Cambridge, MA: Harvard University Press, 1992.

Chira, Susan. *A Mother's Place.* New York: HarperCollins, 1998.

Clark, Homer H., Jr. *The Law of Domestic Relations in the United States.* 2d ed. St. Paul, MN: West, 1988.

Clarke, Sally C. "Advance Report of Final Marriage Statistics, 1989 and 1990." National Center for Health Statistics, *Monthly Vital Statistics Report* 43, no. 12 (July 14, 1995), Table 6, ii.

Coase, Ronald H. "The Problem of Social Cost." *Journal of Law and Economics* 3 (1960): 3–44.

Cohen, Harriet N., and Patricia Hennessey. "Valuation of Property in Marital Dissolutions." *Family Law Quarterly* 23 (1989): 339–81.

Cohen, Lloyd. "Marriage, Divorce, and Quasi Rents; or 'I Gave Him the Best Years of My Life.'" *Journal of Legal Studies* 16, no. 2 (1987): 267–304.

Coleman, James S. *Foundations of Social Theory.* Cambridge, MA: Belknap Press, 1990.

Coombs, E. Raedene. "The Human Capital Concept as a Basis for Property Settlement at Divorce: Theory and Implementation." *Journal of Divorce* 2 (Summer 1979): 329–55.

Coontz, Stephanie. *The Way We Really Are.* New York: BasicBooks, 1997.

Cooter, Robert, and Mevin Aron Eisenberg. "Damages for Breach of Contract." *California Law Review* 73 (1985): 1432–81.

Cox, W. Michael. "What's Happening to Americans' Income." *The Southwest Economy*, no. 2 (1995): 3–6.

Crittenden, Danielle. *What Our Mothers Didn't Tell Us.* New York: Simon & Schuster, 1999.

Daniel, Kermit. "The Marriage Premium." In *The New Economics of Human Behavior*, ed. Mariano Tommasi and Kathryn Ierulli, 113–25. Cambridge, UK: Cambridge University Press, 1994.

Davis, Kingsley, ed. *Contemporary Marriage: Comparative Perspectives on a Changing Institution.* New York: Russell Sage Foundation, 1985.

Dennerstein, Lorraine. "Mental Health, Work, and Gender." *International Journal of Health Services* 25, no. 3 (1995): 503–09.

DeWitt, Paula Mergenbagen. "Breaking Up Is Hard to Do." *American Demographics* 14, no. 10 (October 1992): 52–59.

Dixon, Ruth B., and Lenore J. Weitzman. "When Husbands File for Divorce." *Journal of Marriage and the Family* 44 (1982): 103–15.

Duncan, Greg J., and Saul D. Hoffman. "A Reconsideration of the Economic Consequences of Divorce." *Demography* 22 (1985): 485–97.

Egge, Karl A., and Robert L. Bunting. "Divorce Settlements: How to Divide Human Capital Assets." *Trial* (August 1985): 27–29.

Eisler, Riane Tennenhaus. *Dissolution, No-Fault Divorce, Marriage, and the Future of Women.* New York: McGraw-Hill, 1977.

Ellman, Ira M. "The Theory of Alimony." *California Law Review* 77, no. 1 (1989): 1–81.

———. "The Place of Fault in a Modern Divorce Law." *Arizona State Law Journal* 28 (Fall 1996): 773–836.

Ellman, Ira M., and Sharon Lohr. "Marriage as Contract, Opportunistic Violence, and Other Bad Arguments for Fault Divorce." *University of Illinois Law Review* (1997): 719–72.

Ellman, Ira M., and Stephen D. Sugarman. "Spousal Emotional Abuse as a Tort?" *Maryland Law Review* 55 (1996): 1277, n.24.

Elrod, Linda D., and Robert G. Spector. "A Review of the Year in Family Law: A Search for Definitions and Policy." *Family Law Quarterly* 31, no. 4 (Winter 1998): 613–65.

England, Paula, and George Farkas. *Households, Employment, and Gender.* New York: Aldine De Gruyter, 1986.

Espensade, Thomas J. "The Economic Consequences of Divorce." *Journal of Marriage and the Family* 41 (1979): 615–25.

Ferber, Marianne A., and William Sander. "Of Women, Men, and Divorce: Not by Economics Alone." *Review of Social Economics* 47 (1989): 15–24.

Fineman, Martha L. "Illusive Equality: On Weitzman's *Divorce Revolution.*" In "Review Symposium on Weitzman's *Divorce Revolution,*" ed. Howard S. Erlanger, *American Bar Foundation Research Journal* 1986 (1986): 781–90.

Foote, Caleb, Robert Levy, and Frank E. Sander. *Cases and Materials on Family Law.* 2d ed. Boston: Little, Brown, 1976.

Freed, Doris J., and Timothy B. Walker. "Grounds for Divorce in the American Jurisdictions." *Family Law Quarterly* 6 (1972): 178–212.

———. "Family Law in the Fifty States: An Overview." *Family Law Quarterly* 18 (1985): 369–471.

———. "Family Law in the Fifty States: An Overview." *Family Law Quarterly* 22 (1989): 367–521.

———. "Family Law in the Fifty States: An Overview." *Family Law Quarterly* 23 (1990): 495–608.

Freiden, Alan. "The United States Marriage Market." *Journal of Political Economy* 82, Pt. 2 (1974): s34–s53.

Frey, Bruno S., and Reiner Eichenberger. "Marriage Paradoxes." *Rationality & Society* 8, no. 2 (May 1996): 187–206.

Friedberg, Leora. "Did Unilateral Divorce Raise Divorce Rates? Evidence from Panel Data." *American Economic Review* 88, no. 3 (June 1998): 608–27.

Friedman, Lawrence M. *A History of American Law.* New York: Simon & Schuster, 1973.

———. "Rights of Passage: Divorce Law in Historical Perspective." *Oregon Law Review* 63 (1984): 649–69.

Friedman, Daniel. "The Efficient Breach Fallacy." *Journal of Legal Studies* 18 (1989): 1–24.

Fuchs, Victor R. *How We Live.* Cambridge, MA: Harvard University Press, 1983.

———. "Sex Differences in Economic Well-Being." *Science* 232, April 25, 1986, 459–64.

————. *Women's Quest for Economic Equality.* Cambridge, MA: Harvard University Press, 1988.

Fulop, Marcel. "A Brief Survey of the Literature on the Economic Analysis of Marriage and Divorce." *American Economist* (1980): 12–18.

Gallagher, Maggie. *The Abolition of Marriage.* Washington, DC: Regnery Publishing, 1996.

Glendon, Mary Ann. *The New Family and the New Property.* Toronto: Butterworths, 1981.

————. "Family Law Reform in the 1980s." *Louisiana Law Review* 44 (1984): 1553–73.

————. *Abortion and Divorce in Western Law.* Cambridge, MA: Harvard University Press, 1987.

————. *The Transformation of Family Law.* Chicago: University of Chicago Press, 1989.

Glenn, Norval D. "Values, Attitudes, and the State of American Marriages." In *Promises to Keep,* ed. David Popenoe, Jean Bethke Elshtain, and David Blankenhorn, 15–34. Lanham, MD: Rowman & Littlefield, 1996.

Glick, Paul C., and Graham B. Spanier. "Married and Unmarried Cohabitation in the United States." *Journal of Marriage and the Family* 42 (1980): 19–30.

Glick, Paul C., Graham B. Spanier, and Arthur J. Norton. "Perspectives on the Recent Upturn in Divorce and Remarriage." *Demography* 10 (1973): 301–14.

Goddard, John Leslie. "The Proposal for Divorce upon Petition and without Fault." *Journal of the State Bar of California* 43 (1968): 90–102.

Golden, Lawrence J. *Equitable Distribution of Property.* Colorado Springs, CO: Shepard's/McGraw-Hill, 1983.

Goldfarb, Sally F. "Marital Partnership and the Case for Permanent Alimony." *Journal of Family Law* 27 (1988–99): 351–72.

Goldin, Claudia. "Life-Cycle Labor Force Participation of Married Women: Historical Evidence and Implications." *Journal of Labor Economics* 7 (1989): 20–47.

————. *Understanding the Gender Gap.* Oxford, UK: Oxford University Press, 1990.

————. "Career and Family: College Women Look to the Past." In *Gender and Family Issues in the Workplace,* ed. Francine D. Blau and Ronald G. Ehrenberg, 20–58. New York: Russell Sage Foundation, 1997.

Goldscheider, Frances K., and Linda J. Waite. *New Families, No Families?: Transformation of the American Home.* Berkeley, CA: University of California Press, 1991.

Goode, William J. *After Divorce.* Glencoe, IL: Free Press, 1956.

Gordon, Robert M. "The Limits of Limits on Divorce." *Yale Law Journal* 107 (1998): 1435–65.

Gorman, Elizabeth H. "Bringing Home the Bacon: Marital Allocation of Income-Earning Responsibilities, Job Shifts, and Men's Wages." *Journal of Marriage & the Family* 61, no. 1 (February 1999): 110–22.

Gormley, William T., Jr. *Everybody's Children: Child Care as a Public Problem.* Washington, DC: The Brookings Institution, 1995.

Gottlieb, Beatrice. *The Family in the Western World from the Black Death to the Industrial Age.* New York: Oxford University Press, 1993.

Gottman, John Mordechai. "Psychology and the Study of Marital Processes." *Annual Review of Psychology* 49 (1998): 169–97.

Gove, Walter. "Sex, Marital Status, and Mortality." *American Journal of Sociology* 79, no. 1 (July 1973): 45–68.

Gray, Jeffrey S. "The Fall in Men's Return to Marriage: Declining Productivity Effects or Changing Selection?" *Journal of Human Resources* 32, no. 2 (Summer 1997): 481–504.

————. "Divorce-Law Changes, Household Bargaining, and Married Women's Labor Supply." *American Economic Review* 88, no. 3 (June 1998): 628–42.

Gregory, John Dewitt, Peter N. Swisher, and Sheryl L. Scheible-Wolf. *Understanding Family Law.* New York: Matthew Bender, 1993.

Grossbard-Shechtman, Shoshana A., and Shoshana Neuman. "Women's Labor Supply and Marital Choice." *Journal of Political Economy* 96 (1988): 294–302.

Gunning, J. Patrick. "Marriage Law and Human Capital Investment: A Comment." *Southern Economic Journal* 51 (1984): 594–97.

Gunter, B. G., and Doyle Johnson. "Divorce Filing as Role Behavior: Effect of No-Fault Law on Divorce Filing Patterns." *Journal of Marriage and the Family* 40 (1978): 571–74.

Haas, Theodore F. "The Rationality and Enforceability of Contractual Restrictions on Divorce." *North Carolina Law Review* 66, (June 1988): 879–930.

Halem, Lynne Carol. *Divorce Reform.* New York: Free Press, 1980.

Hannan, Michael T. "Families, Markets, and Social Structures: An Essay on Becker's *A Treatise on the Family.*" *Journal of Economic Literature* 20 (1982): 65–72.

Haurin, Donald R. "Women's Labor Market Reactions to Family Disruptions." *Review of Economics and Statistics* 71 (1989): 54–61.

Hauserman, Nancy R. "Homemakers and Divorce: Problems of the Invisible Occupation." *Family Law Quarterly* 17 (1983): 41–63.

Hayes, James A. "California Divorce Reform: Parting Is Sweeter Sorrow." *American Bar Association Journal* 56 (1970): 660–63.

Hecker, Daniel E. "Earnings of College Graduates: Women Compared with Men." *Monthly Labor Review* 121, no. 3 (March 1998): 62–71.

Helburn, Suzanne W. *Cost, Quality, and Child Outcomes in Child Care Centers: Technical Report.* Denver, CO: Department of Economics, Center for Research in Economic and Social Policy, University of Colorado, 1995.

Hersch, Joni. "The Impact of Nonmarket Work on Market Wages." *American Economic Review* 81 (1991): 157–60.

Hetherington, E. Mavis, and W. Glenn Clingempeel. "Coping with Marital Transitions." *Monographs of the Society for Research in Child Development,* 57, nos. 2 and 3 (1992).

Hewlett, Sylvia Ann. *A Lesser Life: The Myth of Women's Liberation in America.* New York: William Morrow, 1986.

Hochshild, Arlie Russell. *The Time Bind: When Work Becomes Home and Home Becomes Work.* New York: Metropolitan Books, 1997.

Hoffman, Saul D., and Greg J. Duncan. "What Are the Economic Consequences of Divorce?" *Demography* 25 (1988): 641–45.

Homans, George C. *Social Behavior: Its Elementary Forms.* New York: Harcourt, Brace, Jovanovich, & World, 1961.

Hulten, Charles R. "Quality Change in the CPI." *Federal Reserve of St. Louis Review* (May-June 1997): 87–100.

Jacob, Herbert. "Faulting No-Fault." In "Review Symposium on Weitzman's *Divorce Revolution*," ed. Howard S. Erlanger, *American Bar Foundation Research Journal* 1986 (1986): 773–80.

———. *Silent Revolution: The Transformation of Divorce Law in the United States.* Chicago: University of Chicago Press, 1988.

———. "Another Look at No-Fault Divorce and the Post-Divorce Finances of Women." *Law and Society Review* 23 (1989): 95–115.

Jacobs, Jerry A., and Kathleen Gerson. "Who Are the Overworked Americans?" *Review of Social Economy* 56, no. 4 (1998): 442–59.

Jacobsen, Joyce P., and Laurence M. Levin. "Effects of Intermittent Labor Force Attachment on Women's Earnings." *Monthly Labor Review* 118, no. 9 (September 1995): 14–19.

Johnson, Ronald, and Allen M. Parkman. "Premerger Notification and the Incentive to Merge and Litigate." *Journal of Law, Economics and Organization* 7, no. 1 (1991): 145–62.

Johnson, William R., and Jonathan Skinner. "Labor Supply and Marital Separation." *American Economic Review* 76 (1986): 455–69.

———. "Accounting for Changes in the Labor Supply of Recently Divorced Women." *Journal of Human Resources* 23 (1988): 417–36.

Juhn, Chinhui, and Kevin M. Murphy. "Wage Inequality and Family Labor Supply." *Journal of Labor Economics* 15, no. 1 (1997): 72–97.

Karoly, Lynn A., Peter W. Greenwood, Susan S. Everingham, Jill Hoube, M. Rebecca Kilburn, C. Peter Rydell, Matthew Sanders, and James Chiesa. *Investing in Our Children: What We Know and Don't Know about the Costs and Benefits of Early Childhood Interventions.* Santa Monica, CA: Rand, 1998.

Kay, Herma Hill. "A Family Court: The California Proposal." *California Law Review* 56 (1968): 1205–48.

———. "An Appraisal of California's No-Fault Divorce Law." *California Law Review* 75 (1987): 291–319.

———. "Equality and Difference: A Perspective on No-Fault Divorce and Its Aftermath." *University of Cincinnati Law Review* 56 (1987): 1–90.

Kiker, B. F. "Divorce Litigation: Valuing the Spouse's Contribution to the Marriage." *Trial* (December 1980), 48–50.

Kimenyi, Mwangi S., and John Mukum Mbaku. "Female Headship, Feminization of Poverty and Welfare." *Southern Economic Journal* 62, no. 1 (July 1995): 44–52.

King, Allan G. "Human Capital and the Risk of Divorce: An Asset in Search of a Property Right." *Southern Economic Journal* 49 (1982): 536–41.

———. "Divorce Settlements: The Value of Human Capital." *Trial* (August 1982), 48–51.

Kisker, Ellen, and Rebecca Maynard. "Quality, Cost and Parental Choice of Child Care." In *The Economics of Child Care*, ed. David M. Blau, 127–43. New York: Russell Sage Foundation, 1991.

Klein, Benjamin, Robert G. Crawford, and Armen A. Alchian. "Vertical Integration, Appropriable Rents, and the Competitive Contracting Process." *Journal of Law and Economics* 21 (1978): 297–326.

Krause, Harry D. *Family Law*. 3d ed. St. Paul, MN: West, 1995.

Krauskopf, Joan M. "A Theory for 'Just' Division of Marital Property in Missouri." *Missouri Law Review* 41 (1976): 165–78.

———. "Marital Property at Marriage Dissolution." *Missouri Law Review* 43 (1978): 157–98.

———. "Recompense for Financing Spouse's Education: Legal Protection for the Marital Investor in Human Capital." *Kansas Law Review* 28 (1980): 379–417.

———. "Theories of Property Division/Spousal Support: Searching for Solutions to the Mystery." *Family Law Quarterly* 23 (Summer 1989): 253–78.

Kressel, Kenneth. *The Process of Divorce*. New York: Basic Books, 1985.

Krom, Howard. "California's Divorce Law Reform: An Historical Analysis." *Pacific Law Journal* 1(1970): 156–81.

Kronman, Anthony T. "Specific Performance." *University of Chicago Law Review* 45 (1978): 351–82.

Laine, Charles R. "Distribution of Jointly Owned Private Goods by the Demand-Revealing Process: Applications to Divorce Settlements and Estate Administration." *Public Choice* 47 (1985): 437–57.

Landes, Elizabeth. "Economics of Alimony." *Journal of Legal Studies* 7 (1978): 35–63.

Lazear, Edward P., and Robert T. Michael. *Allocation of Income within the Household*. Chicago: University of Chicago Press, 1988.

Leigh, J. Paul. "Divorce as a Risky Prospect." *Applied Economics* 17 (1985): 309–20.

Levy, Robert. *Uniform Marriage and Divorce Legislation: A Preliminary Analysis*. Chicago: American Bar Association, 1969.

Lichter, Daniel T., and Janice A. Costanzo. "How Do Demographic Changes Affect Labor Force Participation of Women?" *Monthly Labor Review* (November 1987): 23-25.

Lillard, Lee A., and Linda J. Waite. "Determinants of Divorce." *Social Security Bulletin* 53 (February 1990): 29–31.

Litwak, Eugene, and Peter Messeri. "Organizational Theory, Social Supports, and Mortality Rates: A Theoretical Convergence." *American Sociological Review* 54, no. 1 (February 1989): 49–66.

Lommerud, Kjell Erik. "Marital Division of Labor with Risk of Divorce: The Role of 'Voice' Enforcement of Contracts." *Journal of Labor Economics* 7 (1989): 113–27.

London, Kathryn A. "Cohabitation, Marriage, Marital Dissolution, and Remarriage: United States, 1988." U.S. Department of Health and Human Services, Advanced Data No. 194, January 4, 1991.

Lundberg, Shelly, and Robert A. Pollak. "Bargaining and Distribution in Marriage." *Journal of Economic Perspectives* 10, no. 4 (Fall 1996): 139–58.

———. "Do Husbands and Wives Pool Their Resources? Evidence from the United Kingdom Child Benefit." *Journal of Human Resources* 32, no. 3 (Summer 1997): 463–480.

Maccoby, Eleanor E., and Robert H. Mnookin. *Dividing the Child.* Cambridge, MA: Harvard University Press, 1992.

Manser, Marilyn, and Murray Brown. "Marriage and Household Decision Making: A Bargaining Analysis." *International Economic Review* 21, no. 1 (February 1980): 31–44.

McElroy, Marjorie B., and Mary Jean Horney. "Nash Bargained Household Decisions." *International Economic Review* 22, no. 2 (June 1981): 333–49.

McLanahan, Sara, and Gary Sandefur. *Growing Up with a Single Parent.* Cambridge, MA: Harvard University Press, 1994.

Melli, Marygold S. "Constructing a Social Problem: The Post-Divorce Plight of Women and Children." In "Review Symposium on Weitzman's *Divorce Revolution,*" ed. Howard S. Erlanger, *American Bar Foundation Research Journal* (1986): 759–72.

Michael, Robert T. "The Rise in Divorce Rates, 1960–1974: Age-Specific Components." *Demography* 15 (1978): 345–47.

———. "Consequences of the Rise in Female Labor Force Participation Rates: Questions and Probes." *Journal of Labor Economics* 3 (1985): s117–s146.

———. "Why Did the U.S. Divorce Rate Double within a Decade?" In *Research in Population Economics,* ed. T. Paul Schultz, 367–400. Greenwich, CT: JAI Press, 1988.

Mincer, Jacob, and Haim Ofek. "Interrupted Work Careers: Depreciation and Restoration of Human Capital." *Journal of Human Resources* 17 (1982): 1–24.

Mincer, Jacob, and Solomon Polachek. "Family Investments in Human Capital: Earnings of Women." *Journal of Political Economy* 82, Pt. 2 (1974): s76–s108.

———. "Women's Earnings Reexamined." *Journal of Human Resources* 8 (1978): 118–34.

Mnookin, Robert H., and Lewis Kornhauser. "Bargaining in the Shadow of the Law: The Case of Divorce." *Yale Law Journal* 88 (1979): 950–97.

Mott, Frank L., and Sylvia F. Moore. "The Causes and Consequences of Marital Breakdown." In *Women, Work, and Family,* ed. Frank L. Mott, 113–36. Lexington, MA: Lexington Books, 1978.

Mueller, Dennis C. *Public Choice II.* Cambridge, UK: Cambridge University Press, 1989.

Murray, Charles A. *Losing Ground: American Social Policy, 1950–1980.* New York: Basic Books, 1984.

Nock, Steven L. "A Comparison of Marriages and Cohabiting Relationships." *Journal of Family Issues* 16, no. 1 (January 1995): 53–76.

———. "The Consequences of Premarital Fatherhood." *American Sociological Review* 63 (April 1998): 250–63.

Nock, Steven L., James D. Wright, and Laura Sanchez, "America's Divorce Problem." *Society* 36, no. 4 (May-June 1999): 43–52.

Nye, F. Ivan. "Choice, Exchange, and the Family." in *Contemporary Theories about the Family.* Vol. 2, ed. Wesley R. Burr, Reuben Hill, F. Ivan Nye, and Ira L. Reiss. New York: Free Press, 1979.

O'Connell, Mary E. "Alimony after No-Fault: A Practice in Search of a Theory." *New England Law Review* 23 (1988): 437–513.

O'Neill, June. "Women and Wages." *American Enterprise* 1 (November-December 1990): 25–33.

Oldham, J. Thomas. "ALI Principles of Family Dissolution: Some Comments." *Illinois Law Review* (1997): 816–31.

———. *Divorce, Separation and the Distribution of Property.* New York: Law Journal Seminars-Press, 1997.

Parkman, Allen M. "The Treatment of Professional Goodwill in Divorce Proceedings." *Family Law Quarterly* 18 (1984): 213–24.

———. "The Economic Approach to Valuing a Sacrificed Career in Divorce Proceedings." *Journal of the American Academy of Matrimonial Lawyers* 2 (1986): 45–56.

———. "Human Capital as Property in Divorce Settlements." *Arkansas Law Review* 40 (1987): 439–67.

———. "Dividing Human Capital with an Eye to Future Earnings." *Family Advocate* 12 (1989): 34–37.

———. "Unilateral Divorce and the Labor Force Participation Rate of Married Women, Revisited." *American Economic Review* 82 (1992): 671–78.

———. "Reform of the Divorce Provisions of the Marriage Contract." *BYU Journal of Public Law* 8, no. 1 (1993): 91–106.

———. "Human Capital as Property in Celebrity Divorces." *Family Law Quarterly* 29, no. 1 (Spring 1995): 141–69.

———."The Government's Role in the Support of Children." *BYU Journal of Public Law* 11, no. 1 (1995): 55–74.

———. "The Deterioration in the Family: A Law and Economics Perspective." In *The Individual, the Family and Social Good: Personal Fulfillment in Times of Change,* ed. Gary Melton, 21–52. Lincoln, NE: University of Nebraska Press, 1995.

———. "Why Are Married Women Working So Hard?" *International Review of Law and Economics* 18, no. 1 (Winter 1998): 41–49.

———. "A Systematic Approach to Valuing the Goodwill of Professional Practices." In *Valuing Professional Practices and License.* 3d ed., ed. Ronald L. Brown, 6-1–6-18. Gaithersburg, NY: Aspen Law & Business, 1998.

———. "An Investment Approach to Valuing Spousal Support of Education." In *Valuing Professional Practices and License,* 3d ed., ed. Ronald L. Brown, 32-1–32-26. Gaithersburg, NY: Aspen Law & Business, 1998.

———. "Valuing and Allocating Celebrity Status at Divorce." In *Valuing Professional Practices and License,* 3d ed., ed. Ronald L. Brown, 42-1–42-32. Gaithersburg, NY: Aspen Law & Business, 1998.

———. "Bringing Consistency to the Financial Arrangements at Divorce." *Kentucky Law Review* 87, no. 1 (1998–99): 51–93.

Peters, H. Elizabeth. "Marriage and Divorce: Informational Constraints and Private Contracting." *American Economic Review* 76 (1986): 437–54.

Peters, Joan K. *When Mothers Work.* Reading, MA: Addison-Wesley, 1997.

Peterson, Richard R. "A Re-Evaluation of the Economic Consequences of Divorce." *American Sociological Review* 61 (June 1995): 528–36.

Polinsky, A. Mitchell. *An Introduction to Law and Economics.* 2d ed. Boston: Little, Brown, 1989.

Pollak, Robert A. "A Transaction Cost Approach to Families and Households." *Journal of Economic Literature* 23 (1985): 581–608.

Popenoe, David. *Life without Father.* New York: Martin Kessler Books, 1996.

Popenoe, David, Jean Bethke Elshtain, and David Blankenhorn, eds. *Promises to Keep: Decline and Renewal of Marriage in America.* Lanham, MD: Rowman & Littlefield, 1996.

Posner, Richard. *The Economic Analysis of Law.* 4th ed. Boston: Little, Brown, 1992.

Preston, Samuel H., and John McDonald. "The Incidence of Divorce within Cohorts of American Marriage Contracted since the Civil War." *Demography* 16 (February 1979): 1–25.

Price, Sharon J., and Patrick C. McKenry. *Divorce.* Newbury Park, CA: Sage, 1988.

Reppy, William A., Jr. "Major Events in the Evolution of American Community Property Law and Their Import to Equitable Distribution States." *Family Law Quarterly* 23 (1989): 163–92.

Reppy, Susan W. "The End of Innocence: Elimination of Fault in California Divorce Law." *UCLA Law Review* 17 (1970): 1306–32.

Reynolds, Suzanne. "The Relationship of Property Division and Alimony: The Division of Property to Address Need." *Fordham Law Review* 56, no. 5 (April 1988): 827–916.

Rheinstein, Max. *Marriage, Stability, Divorce and the Law.* Chicago: University of Chicago Press, 1972.

Riley, Glenda. *Divorce: An American Tradition.* Oxford, UK: Oxford University Press, 1991.

Ross, Heather L., and Isabel V. Sawhill. *Time of Transition: The Growth of Families Headed by Women.* Washington, DC: Urban Institute, 1975.

Rowthorn, Robert. "Marriage and Trust: Some Lessons from Economics." *Cambridge Journal of Economics* 23 (September 1999): 661–91.

Samuelson, Paul A., and William D. Nordhaus. *Economics.* 15th ed. New York: McGraw-Hill, 1995.

Sandell, Steven H., and David Shapiro. "An Exchange: The Theory of Human Capital and the Earnings of Women." *Journal of Human Resources* 8 (1978): 103–17.

Sander, William. "Women, Work, and Divorce." *American Economic Review* 75 (1985): 519–23.

Schneider, Carl E., and Margaret F. Brinig. *An Invitation to Family Law.* St. Paul, MN: West, 1996.

Schoen, Robert, Harry N. Greenblatt, and Robert B. Mielke. "California's Experience with Non-Adversary Divorce." *Demography* 12 (1975): 223–44.

Schoen, Robert, and Verne E. Nelson."Marriage, Divorce, and Mortality." *Demography* 11 (1974): 267–90.

Schoen, Robert, William Urton, Karen Woodrow, and John Baj. "Marriage and Divorce in Twentieth-Century American Cohorts." *Demography* 22 (1985): 101–14.

Schwartz, Alan. "The Case for Specific Performance." *Yale Law Journal* 89 (1979): 271–306.

Schwartz, Leonard Charles. "Divorce and Earning Ability." *Detroit College of Law Review* (1982): 69–80.

Scott, Elizabeth. "Rational Decision Making about Marriage and Divorce." *Virginia Law Review* 76 (1990): 9–94.

Scott, Elizabeth, and Robert E. Scott. "Marriage as Relational Contract." *Virginia Law Review* 84 (October 1998), 1225–1334.

Singer, Jana. "Divorce Reform and Gender Justice." *North Carolina Law Review* 67 (1989): 1103–21.

———. "The Privatization of Family Law." *Wisconsin Law Review* (September-October 1992): 1443–1567.

Smith, James P., and Michael P. Ward. "Time-Series Growth in the Female Labor Force." *Journal of Labor Economics* 3, no. 1 (January 1985 Supplement): s59–s90.

Smith, Janet K., and Richard L. Smith. "Contract Law, Mutual Mistake, and Incentives to Produce and Disclose Information." *Journal of Legal Studies* 19, no. 2 (June 1990): 467–88.

Sonenstein, Freya L. "The Child Care Preferences of Parents with Young Children." In *Parental Leave and Child Care: Setting a Research and Policy Agenda*, ed. Janet Hyde and Marilyn Essex, 337–50. Philadelphia, PA: Temple University Press, 1991.

South, Scott J., and Kim M. Lloyd. "Spousal Alternatives and Marital Dissolution." *American Sociological Review* 60, no. 1 (February 1995): 21–35.

Spaht, Katherine Shaw. "Propter Honoris Prestum: For the Sake of the Children: Recapturing the Meaning of Marriage." *Notre Dame Law Review* 73 (May 1998): 1547–79.

Spanier, Graham B. "Cohabitation in the 1980s: Recent Changes in the United States." In *Contemporary Marriage,* ed. Kingsley Davis, 91–112. New York: Russell Sage Foundation, 1985.

Starnes, Cynthia. "Divorce and the Displaced Homemaker." *University of Chicago Law Review* 60 (Winter 1993): 67–139.

Suen, Wing, and Hon-Kwong Lui. "A Direct Test of the Efficient Marriage Market Hypothesis." *Economic Inquiry* 37, no. 1 (January 1999): 29–46.

Sugarman, Stephen D. "Dividing Financial Interests on Divorce." In *Divorce Reform at the Crossroads*, ed. Stephen D. Sugarman and Herma Hill Kay, 130–65. New Haven, CT: Yale University Press, 1990.

Sugarman, Stephen D., and Herma Hill Kay, eds. *Divorce Reform at the Crossroads.* New Haven, CT: Yale University Press, 1990.

Swan, George Steven. "The Political Economy of American Family Policy, 1945–85." *Population and Development Review* 12 (1986): 739–58.

Sweet, James A., and Ruy Teixeira. "Breaking Tradition: Schooling, Marriage, Work, and Childrearing in the Lives of Young Women, 1960–1980." Center for Demography and Ecology, University of Wisconsin-Madison, CDE Working Paper 84-13, 1984.

Thibaut, John W., and Harold H. Kelly. *The Social Psychology of Groups.* New York: John Wiley & Sons, 1959.

Thompson, Linda, and Alexis J. Walker. "Gender in Families: Women and Men in Marriage, Work, and Parenthood." In *Contemporary Families: Looking Forward, Looking Back*, ed. Alan Booth, 76–102. Minneapolis, MN: National Council on Family Relations, 1991.

Tiger, Lionel. *The Decline of Males.* New York: Golden Books, 1999.

U.S. Bureau of the Census. *Statistical Abstract of the United States, 1998.* Washington, DC: Government Printing Office, 1998.

Wadlington, Walter. "Divorce without Fault without Perjury," *Virginia Law Review* 52 (1966): 32–87.

U.S. National Center for Health Statistics. *Births, Marriages, Divorces and Deaths: Provisional Data for November 1998.* National Vital Statistics Reports 47, no. 17 (March 16, 1999).

Waite, Linda J. "Does Marriage Matter?" *Demography* 32, no. 4 (November 1995): 483–507.

Walker, Timothy B. "Beyond Fault: An Examination of Patterns of Behavior in Response to Present Divorce Laws." *Journal of Family Law* 10 (1971): 267–99.

Wallerstein, Judith S., and Sandra Blakelee. *Second Chances.* New York: Ticknor & Fields, 1990.

Wallerstein, Judith S., and Joan Berlin Kelly, *Surviving the Breakup.* New York: Basic Books, 1980.

Wardle, Lynn D. "No-Fault Divorce and the Divorce Conundrum." *Brigham Young University Law Review* 1991, no. 1 (1991): 79–142.

Wasserman, Rhonda. "Divorce and Domicile: Time to Sever the Knot." *William and Mary Law Review* 39 (October 1997): 1–63.

Weiss, Yoram, and Robert J. Willis. "Children as Collective Goods and Divorce Settlements." *Journal of Labor Economics* 3 (1985): 268–92.

———. "Transfers among Divorced Couples: Evidence and Interpretation." *Journal of Labor Economics* 11, no. 4 (October 1993): 629–79.

Weitzman, Lenore J. *The Divorce Contract.* New York: Macmillan, 1981.

———. "The Economics of Divorce: Social and Economic Consequences of Property, Alimony and Child Support Awards." *UCLA Law Review* 28 (1981): 1181–1268.

———. *The Divorce Revolution.* New York: Free Press, 1985.

———. "The Divorce Law Revolution and the Transformation of Legal Marriage" in *Contemporary Marriage.* ed. Kingsley Davis, 301–48 New York: Russell Sage Foundation, 1985.

———. "Bringing the Law Back." In "Review Symposium on Weitzman's *Divorce Revolution,*" ed. Howard S. Erlanger, 791–97. *American Bar Foundation Research Journal* (1986).

———."The Economic Consequences of Divorce Are Still Unequal: Comment on Peterson." *American Sociological Review* 61 (June 1996): 537–40.

Welch, Charles E., III, and Sharon Price-Bonham. "A Decade of No-Fault Divorce Revisited: California, Georgia, and Washington." *Journal of Marriage and the Family* 45 (1983): 411–18.

Wheeler, Michael. *No-Fault Divorce.* Boston: Beacon, 1974.

———. *Divided Children.* New York: Norton, 1980.

Whelan, Christine B. "No Honeymoon for Covenant Marriage." *Wall Street Journal,* August 17, 1998, A12.

Williamson, Oliver E. *Markets and Hierarchies: Analysis and Antitrust Implications.* New York: Free Press, 1975.

Winkler, Anne E. "Earnings of Husbands and Wives in Dual-Earner Families." *Monthly Labor Review* 121, no. 4 (April 1998): 42–48.

Wright, Gerald C., and Dorothy M. Stetson. "The Impact of No-Fault Divorce Law Reform on Divorce in American States." *Journal of Marriage and the Family* 40 (1978): 575–80.

Zalokar, Nadja. "Male-Female Differences in Occupational Choice and the Demand for General and Occupation-Specific Human Capital." *Economic Inquiry* 26 (1988): 59–74.

Zelder, Martin. "Inefficient Dissolutions as a Consequence of Public Goods: The Case of No-Fault Divorce." *Journal of Legal Studies* 22, no. 2 (June 1993): 503–20.

Zinsmeister, Karl. "Longstanding Warnings from Experts." *The American Enterprise* 9, no. 3 (May-June 1998): 34–35.

Index

abandonment, 156. *See also* desertion
abuse, 156, 190, 191–92
academic degrees, 161. *See also* education
adultery, 1, 22, 23, 156
advantage, comparative, 38
ALI. *See* American Law Institute
alimony, 107, 172–74; amount of, 2; California law, 75; fault in, 7; functions, 173; human capital and, 172; limitation by agreement, 121; prohibited, 52; rationale for, 60; replacement of, 158; under UMDA, 157
Allen, Douglas, 99, 110
Alton v. Alton, 193
altruism, 126
Amato, Paul, 129, 130
American Law Institute (ALI), 161, 166, 195
annulment, 22, 183
assets, 7–8, 53, 54, 159; career, 132, 162; financial/economic treatment of, 166; intangible, 160. *See also* human capital; property
attorneys. *See* lawyers
awards: courts' influence on, 104; in fault divorce, 101–2; limited, 104; permanent, 102

bargaining, noncooperative, 45–46
bargaining power, 1, 13n4, 28, 73, 83; no-fault's reduction of, 6, 58, 96, 100, 105
Becker, Gary, 36, 50, 60, 99
Blau, Francine, 120
Booth, Alan, 129, 130
Braver, Sanford, 108, 109
breach of contract, 180; damages for, 180–82; efficient, 180–81
Brinig, Margaret, 99, 110
Brody, Stuart, 76
Brown, Edmund G., 73, 79
Bruch, Carol, 104
Buckley, Frank, 99
businesses, valuation of, 159, 164. *See also* goodwill

California law, 1, 5, 24, 71, 152; change to no-fault, 72–77; effects of, 101–2; men's self-interest in, 79–82; re property division, 158
Calvin, John, 23
career assets, 162–63
careers: conflict with children, 197; dual, 128, 147n138; limiting, 47, 115, 198. *See also* employment; work
caregiver, primary, 2, 14n5

229

About the Author

Allen M. Parkman is the Regents' Professor of Management at the University of New Mexico. He has a Ph.D. in economics from UCLA and a law degree from the University of New Mexico. His articles on the family have appeared in numerous journals, including the *American Economic Review*, the *International Review of Law and Economics,* the *Family Law Quarterly*, and the *ABA Journal*. During 1981–82, he was a Senior Staff Economist on the President's Council of Economic Advisers.